First World War
and Army of Occupation
War Diary
France, Belgium and Germany

3 DIVISION
Divisional Troops
'A' Squadron 15 Hussars,
'C' Squadron North Irish Horse,
Divisional Cyclist Company,
23 Brigade Royal Field Artillery
and 30 Brigade Royal Field Artillery
4 August 1914 - 29 January 1916

WO95/1399

The Naval & Military Press Ltd
www.nmarchive.com
Published in association with The National Archives

Published by

The Naval & Military Press Ltd

Unit 10 Ridgewood Industrial Park,

Uckfield, East Sussex,

TN22 5QE England

Tel: +44 (0) 1825 749494

www.naval-military-press.com

www.nmarchive.com

This diary has been reprinted in facsimile from the original. Any imperfections are inevitably reproduced and the quality may fall short of modern type and cartographic standards.

© **Crown Copyright**
Images reproduced by permission of The National Archives, London, England, 2015.

Contents

Document type	Place/Title	Date From	Date To
Heading	3rd Division A Sqdr 15th Hussars Aug 1914-Mar 1915 To 1 Cav Div 9 Bde		
Heading	3rd Div. Cavalry (A. Sqn. 15th Hussars) Aug-Dec 21st 1914		
Heading	War Diary Div Cavalry 3rd Division. (A Squadron 15th Hussars) Volume I 16-31-8-14		
War Diary	Long-Moor	16/08/1914	22/08/1914
War Diary	Hyon	23/08/1914	23/08/1914
War Diary	Mons	23/08/1914	23/08/1914
War Diary	Frameries	24/08/1914	31/08/1914
Heading	A. Squadron 15th Hussars 3rd Division. Vol II 1.9-2.10.14		
War Diary	Vauciennes	01/09/1914	01/09/1914
War Diary	Villers-St-Genest	02/09/1914	02/09/1914
War Diary	Monthyon	03/09/1914	03/09/1914
War Diary	La Haute Maison	04/09/1914	04/09/1914
War Diary	Chartres	05/09/1914	06/09/1914
War Diary	Farmouties	07/09/1914	07/09/1914
War Diary	Coulommiers	08/09/1914	08/09/1914
War Diary	Bussorres	09/09/1914	09/09/1914
War Diary	Bentry	10/09/1914	10/09/1914
War Diary	Dammard	11/09/1914	11/09/1914
War Diary	Grand Rozey	12/09/1914	12/09/1914
War Diary	Braine	13/09/1914	13/09/1914
War Diary	Chassemy	14/09/1914	18/09/1914
War Diary	Braine	19/09/1914	28/09/1914
Heading	A. Squadron. 15th Hussars. (Div Cavy. 3rd Division) Vol III 1-31.10.14		
War Diary	Braine (Chateau Belleme)	01/10/1914	02/10/1914
War Diary	Arcy	03/10/1914	03/10/1914
War Diary	Crepy	04/10/1914	04/10/1914
War Diary	Roberval	05/10/1914	05/10/1914
War Diary	Abbeville	06/10/1914	08/10/1914
War Diary	Reignauxville	09/10/1914	09/10/1914
War Diary	Pressy Les Pernes	10/10/1914	11/10/1914
War Diary	Busnes	12/10/1914	12/10/1914
War Diary	Fosse	13/10/1914	16/10/1914
War Diary	A of Rue Bacquerot	17/10/1914	17/10/1914
War Diary	Aubers	18/10/1914	22/10/1914
War Diary	A of Rue Bacquerot	23/10/1914	23/10/1914
War Diary	Bour Deville	24/10/1914	31/10/1914
Miscellaneous	Divnl Cavalry "A" Sqdn. 15th Hussars		
Heading	A. Squadron. 15th Hussars (Div Cao 3rd Division) Vol IV 1-30.11.14		
War Diary	Meteren	01/11/1914	01/11/1914
War Diary	Locre	02/11/1914	07/11/1914
War Diary	Halte in E of Ypres	08/11/1914	08/11/1914
War Diary	In Trenches	09/11/1914	09/11/1914
War Diary	Halte (Ypres)	10/11/1914	11/11/1914
War Diary	In Trenches	11/11/1914	13/11/1914

War Diary	Halte	14/11/1914	14/11/1914
War Diary	Halte (Ypres)	15/11/1914	18/11/1914
War Diary	In Trenches	19/11/1914	20/11/1914
War Diary	Ypres	21/11/1914	21/11/1914
War Diary	Westoutre	24/11/1914	24/11/1914
War Diary	Berthen	25/11/1914	25/11/1914
War Diary	Mont Noir	27/11/1914	30/11/1914
Heading	A. Squadron 15th Hussars. (3rd Div Cavalry) Vol V 1-21.12.14		
War Diary	La Manche (as Mont Noir)	01/12/1914	21/12/1914
Heading	3rd Div Cavalry A Sqn. 15th Hussars War Diary Jan-Mar 1915		
Heading	A. Squadron. 15th Hussars Div Cav 3rd Division. Vol VI 1-31.1.15		
War Diary	Billets Lamance		
Heading	3rd Division A. Squad 15th Hussars. Vol VII 1-28.2.15		
War Diary		01/02/1915	28/02/1915
Heading	A Squadron 15th Hussars (3rd Div Cavy.) Vol VIII 1-31-3-15		
Miscellaneous	At the Field La Manche st Jans Chappell	00/00/1915	00/00/1915
Heading	3rd Division Divl. Troops. "C" Sqdn. Nth Irish Horse. Oct 1915-Jan-June 1916 To 10 Corps		
Heading	3rd Div Cavalry. C Sqn. The N. Irish Horse War Diary Oct-Dec, 1915		
Heading	3rd Division e. Sqn. Nth Irish Horse Oct 1915 Vol I		
Miscellaneous	Adjutant G. Office Base	01/12/1915	01/12/1915
Miscellaneous	O C "e" Sqn. Nth Irish Hussars.		
War Diary	3rd Division	01/10/1915	01/10/1915
War Diary	Sanctuary Wood	02/10/1915	02/10/1915
War Diary	3rd Division	03/10/1915	05/10/1915
War Diary	Sanctuary Wood	06/10/1915	06/10/1915
War Diary	3rd Division	07/10/1915	10/10/1915
War Diary	Sanctuary Wood	11/10/1915	11/10/1915
War Diary	3rd Division	12/10/1915	15/10/1915
War Diary	Sanctuary Wood	16/11/1915	16/11/1915
War Diary	3rd Division	01/10/1915	01/10/1915
War Diary	Sanctuary Wood	21/10/1915	21/10/1915
War Diary	3rd Division	22/10/1915	31/10/1915
Heading	3rd Division O.C. "E" Sqn. Nth Irish Horse Nov 1915 Vol II		
War Diary	3rd Division	01/11/1915	30/11/1915
Heading	3rd Div "E" Sqn. Nth Irish Horse Dec Vol III		
War Diary	3rd Division	01/12/1915	31/12/1915
Heading	3rd Div "E" Sqn. Nth. Irish Hse Jan Vol V		
War Diary	3rd Division	01/01/1916	31/01/1916
War Diary	III Div	01/02/1916	29/02/1916
Heading	C Sqd N Irish Horse Vol VII		
War Diary	3rd Division	01/03/1916	28/03/1916
Heading	C Sqd N.I. Horse Vol VII		
War Diary	3rd Division	29/03/1916	11/04/1916
War Diary	2nd. Cav. Division	12/04/1916	26/04/1916
War Diary	3rd. Division.	27/04/1916	10/05/1916
War Diary	49th Div.	11/05/1916	30/06/1916
Heading	3rd Division Divl. Troops. 3rd Divl. Cyclist Coy. Jan-May 1916		
War Diary		01/01/1916	05/01/1916

War Diary	Unit 3rd Divisional Cyclist Coy A.C.C.	06/01/1916	05/02/1916
War Diary	Sht. 27 (1/40000) 31.B.4.7	06/02/1916	06/02/1916
War Diary	Sht 27 A.S.E. 1/2000 R.33 D.3.2	07/02/1916	10/03/1916
War Diary	Sh 27-1/40,000 I. 30. A. 5.0	11/03/1916	11/03/1916
War Diary	Sht 27 1/4000 R.10.A 3.5	12/03/1916	18/03/1916
War Diary	Sht 28 1/40000 I.33 A.	19/03/1916	22/03/1916
War Diary	Sht 28 1/40000 I.33 A	23/03/1916	09/04/1916
War Diary	Sheet 27 1/40,000 I. 30. C. 3.9	10/04/1916	27/04/1916
War Diary	Sheet 28 1/40,000 M. 16. C.2.9.	28/04/1916	27/05/1916
War Diary	(R. 25.c. 8.8. Sheet 27 1/40,000)	28/05/1916	31/05/1916
Miscellaneous	3rd Divisional Cyclist Coy. A.C.C.	12/11/1915	12/11/1915
Miscellaneous	The Officer Commanding, 3rd Divisional Cyclist Company.	29/10/1915	29/10/1915
Heading	3rd Division Divl Artillery 23rd Brigade R.F.A. Aug-Dec 1914		
Heading	3rd Divisional Artillery. 23rd Brigade R.F.A. August 1914 To 5/9/14		
War Diary	Bulford Camp	04/08/1914	22/08/1914
War Diary	Cuesmes	23/08/1914	27/08/1914
War Diary	Flechin	27/08/1914	05/09/1914
Miscellaneous	Extracts From Private Artillery Diaries 3rd Division, 2nd Corps.		
Heading	3rd Divisional Artillery. 23rd Brigade R.F.A. September 1914		
War Diary		01/09/1914	05/09/1914
War Diary	Liverdy	06/09/1914	16/09/1914
War Diary	Braine	17/09/1914	07/10/1914
Heading	3rd Divisional Artillery 23rd Brigade R.F.A. October 1914		
War Diary		01/10/1914	25/10/1914
Miscellaneous	Extracts From Battery Diaries to br inserted under Bde Heading	10/10/1914	31/10/1914
War Diary		26/10/1914	31/10/1914
War Diary	23rd Bde R.F.A.	14/10/1914	01/11/1914
Heading	3rd Divisional Artillery. 23rd Brigade R.F.A. November 1914		
War Diary		01/11/1914	02/12/1914
Heading	3rd Divisional Artillery. 23rd Brigade R.F.A. December 1914		
Heading	Copied from diary for November 1914 23rd November to 2nd December 1914 Positions occupied as on 20th.		
War Diary		03/12/1914	31/12/1914
Heading	3rd Division Divl Artillery 23rd Brigade R.F.A. 107th, 108th & 109th Batteries Aug-Oct 1914		
Heading	3rd Divisional Artillery 23rd Brigade R.F.A. 107th Battery R.F.A. August 1914		
War Diary	Bulford Camp	05/08/1914	17/08/1914
War Diary	Southampton	18/08/1914	18/08/1914
War Diary	Havre	19/08/1914	21/08/1914
War Diary	Aulnois	21/08/1914	21/08/1914
War Diary	Longueville	22/08/1914	22/08/1914
War Diary	Cuesmes	23/08/1914	24/08/1914
War Diary	Bermeries	25/08/1914	26/08/1914
War Diary	Hargicourt	27/08/1914	27/08/1914
War Diary	Vermand	28/08/1914	28/08/1914
War Diary	Ham	28/08/1914	28/08/1914

War Diary	Noyon	29/08/1914	29/08/1914
War Diary	Morsains	30/08/1914	30/08/1914
War Diary	Montois	31/08/1914	31/08/1914
Heading	3rd Divisional Artillery. 23rd Brigade R.F.A. 107th Battery R.F.A. 28th August-30th September 1914		
War Diary	Vauciennes	01/09/1914	01/09/1914
War Diary	Bouillancie	02/09/1914	02/09/1914
War Diary	Penchard	03/09/1914	03/09/1914
War Diary	Haute Maison	04/09/1914	04/09/1914
War Diary	Liverdy	05/09/1914	06/09/1914
War Diary	Lumigny	07/09/1914	07/09/1914
War Diary	Chateau Le Buisson	08/09/1914	08/09/1914
War Diary	Les Feucheres	09/09/1914	09/09/1914
War Diary	Ventelet	10/09/1914	10/09/1914
War Diary	Dammard	11/09/1914	11/09/1914
War Diary	Go Rozoy	12/09/1914	12/09/1914
War Diary	Brenelle	13/09/1914	16/09/1914
War Diary	Braine	17/09/1914	18/09/1914
War Diary	Brenelle	19/09/1914	23/09/1914
War Diary	Braine	24/09/1914	25/09/1914
War Diary	Brenelle	26/09/1914	26/09/1914
War Diary	Position on Chasseny Brenelle Road	27/09/1914	27/09/1914
War Diary	Position S of Chasseny Brenelle Road	28/09/1914	30/09/1914
Heading	3rd Divisional Artillery. 23rd Brigade R.F.A. 107th Battery R.F.A. October 1914		
War Diary	Position South of Brenelle Chassen Road	01/10/1914	02/10/1914
War Diary	Cramaille	03/10/1914	03/10/1914
War Diary	Troesme	04/10/1914	04/10/1914
War Diary	Crepy	05/10/1914	05/10/1914
War Diary	Roberval	06/10/1914	06/10/1914
War Diary	Pont St Maxence	06/10/1914	06/10/1914
War Diary	Longueil St Marie	06/10/1914	06/10/1914
War Diary	Noyelle	07/10/1914	07/10/1914
War Diary	Buigny St Mallou	07/10/1914	08/10/1914
War Diary	Bonneval Farm Buigny St. Maclou	09/10/1914	09/10/1914
War Diary	Tollent	09/10/1914	09/10/1914
War Diary	Tangry	10/10/1914	11/10/1914
War Diary	Haute Rieux	12/10/1914	12/10/1914
War Diary	Robecq	13/10/1914	13/10/1914
War Diary	Les Lobes	14/10/1914	15/10/1914
War Diary	La Pilaterie	16/10/1914	16/10/1914
War Diary	Croix Rouge	17/10/1914	17/10/1914
War Diary	Ht. Pommereau	18/10/1914	21/10/1914
War Diary	La Pietre	22/10/1914	22/10/1914
War Diary	Rue Du Bacquerot	23/10/1914	23/10/1914
War Diary	Pont Du Hem	24/10/1914	30/10/1914
War Diary	Croix Barbee	31/10/1914	31/10/1914
Heading	3rd Divisional Artillery. 23rd Brigade R.F.A. 108th Battery R.F.A. August 1914		
Heading	War Diary of 108th Battery R.F.A. 23rd R.F.A. Bde. III Div. from mobilization to 31.8.14 Volume I		
War Diary		05/08/1914	31/08/1914
Heading	3rd Divisional Artillery. 23rd Brigade R.F.A. 108th Battery R.F.A. September 1914		
War Diary		01/09/1914	31/10/1914

Heading	3rd Divisional Artillery. 23rd Brigade R.F.A. 109th Battery R.F.A. August 1914		
War Diary	Bulford Camp	05/08/1914	18/08/1914
War Diary	Southampton	18/08/1914	18/08/1914
War Diary	Hovre	19/08/1914	20/08/1914
War Diary	Landrecies	21/08/1914	21/08/1914
War Diary	La Longueville	22/08/1914	22/08/1914
War Diary	Cuesmes	23/08/1914	24/08/1914
War Diary	Frameries	24/08/1914	25/08/1914
War Diary	Troisville	26/08/1914	27/08/1914
War Diary	Vermont	28/08/1914	28/08/1914
War Diary	Noyon	29/08/1914	29/08/1914
War Diary	Morsains	30/08/1914	30/08/1914
War Diary	Berny Riviere	31/08/1914	31/08/1914
Heading	3rd Divisional Artillery. 23rd Brigade R.F.A. 109th Battery R.F.A. September 1914		
War Diary	Vauciennes	01/09/1914	01/09/1914
War Diary	Bouillancy	02/09/1914	02/09/1914
War Diary	Penchard	03/09/1914	03/09/1914
War Diary	Laloge Dartus	04/09/1914	05/09/1914
War Diary	Liverdy	06/09/1914	06/09/1914
War Diary	Lumigny	07/09/1914	07/09/1914
War Diary	Le Buisson	08/09/1914	09/09/1914
War Diary	Bezu	10/09/1914	10/09/1914
War Diary	Dammard	11/09/1914	11/09/1914
War Diary	Rozoy	12/09/1914	12/09/1914
War Diary	Brenelle	13/09/1914	16/09/1914
War Diary	Braine	17/09/1914	18/09/1914
War Diary	Brenelle	19/09/1914	23/09/1914
War Diary	Braine	24/09/1914	25/09/1914
War Diary	Brenelle	26/09/1914	30/09/1914
Heading	3rd Divisional Artillery. 23rd Brigade R.F.A. 109th Battery R.F.A. October 1914		
War Diary	Brenelle	01/10/1914	02/10/1914
War Diary	Cremaille	03/10/1914	03/10/1914
War Diary	Troesnes	04/10/1914	05/10/1914
War Diary	Roberval	06/10/1914	07/10/1914
War Diary	Bonneval	08/10/1914	09/10/1914
War Diary	Tangry	10/10/1914	11/10/1914
War Diary	Lecleme	12/10/1914	12/10/1914
War Diary	Lacon	13/10/1914	16/10/1914
War Diary	Rouge Croix	17/10/1914	17/10/1914
War Diary	Aubers	18/10/1914	22/10/1914
War Diary	Rouge Croix	23/10/1914	23/10/1914
War Diary	Pont Du Hem	24/10/1914	24/10/1914
War Diary	Vieille Chapelle	25/10/1914	30/10/1914
War Diary	La Couture	31/10/1914	31/10/1914
Heading	3rd Div. R.F.A. 23rd Brigade. Jan-Dec, 1915		
Heading	3rd Division 23rd Brigade R.F.A. Vol V 1.1.-28.2.15		
War Diary		01/01/1915	28/01/1915
Heading	3rd Division 23rd Bde R F A Vol VI 1-31.3.15		
War Diary		01/03/1915	31/03/1915
Heading	3rd Division 23rd Bde. R.F.A. Vol VII 1-30.4.15		
War Diary	Brigade In Action Near Dickebush	01/04/1915	30/04/1915
Heading	3rd Division 23rd Bde R.F.A. Vol VIII 6-31.5.15		
War Diary		06/05/1915	31/05/1915

Heading	3rd Division. 23rd Bde R.F.A. Vol IX 1-30.6.15		
War Diary	23rd Bn In Actiion SE Of Ypres With H.Q. On Zillebeke Lala	01/06/1915	30/06/1915
Heading	3rd Division. 23rd Bde. R.F.A. Vol X 1-31-9-15		
War Diary		01/07/1915	31/07/1915
Heading	3rd Division 23rd Bde. R F A Vol XI August 15		
War Diary	B in position 1/2 Mile S E of Ypres B? H Q At Kruistraat	01/08/1915	31/08/1915
Heading	3rd Division War Diary of 23rd Brigade R F. a. from September 1sr to September 30th 1915 Vol XII		
War Diary	Brigade in position 1/2 mile S.E of Ypres Bde H Q At Kruistraat	01/09/1915	30/09/1915
Heading	3rd Division War Diary of 23rd Brigade R.F.A. from October to October 31st Vol XIII		
War Diary	Brigade in position 1/2 mile S.E of Ypres. Bde HQ-Kruisstraat	01/10/1915	31/10/1915
Heading	3rd Division War Diary of 23rd Brigade R.F.A. From. November 1st To November 30th 1915		
War Diary	Brigade in rest 1 mile S. E of Eteenvoorde	01/11/1915	30/11/1915
Heading	23 Bde. R.F.A. Dis Vol XV		
War Diary		01/12/1915	31/12/1915
Map	Neuve Eglise		
Map	Belgium		
Miscellaneous	Belgium		
Miscellaneous	Transparent Drawing Overlay On Map Sheet 2 (Position Located on map) (Box 1399)		
Diagram etc	Tracing		
Miscellaneous	Transparent Drawing Overlay On Map Sheet 1 (Position Located On Map) [Box 1399		
Diagram etc			
Heading	3rd Division Divl. Artillery 23rd Brigade R.F.A. Jan-Dec 1916 Became Army Brigade June 1917 2 Army		
Heading	3rd Divisional Artillery. 23rd Brigade. R.F.A. January 1916		
War Diary		01/01/1916	31/01/1916
Heading	3rd Divisional Artillery. 23rd Brigade R.F.A. February 1916		
War Diary		02/02/1916	29/02/1916
Heading	3rd Divisional Artillery. 23rd Brigade R.F.A. March 1916		
War Diary		01/03/1916	31/03/1916
Heading	3rd Divisional Artillery. 23rd Brigade R.F.A. April 1916		
War Diary		01/04/1916	30/04/1916
Heading	3rd Divisional Artillery. 23rd Brigade R.F.A. May 1916		
War Diary		01/05/1916	31/05/1916
Heading	3rd Divisional Artillery. 23rd Brigade R.F.A. June 1916		
Miscellaneous	I D.A.G. IIIrd. Echelon		
War Diary		01/06/1916	30/06/1916
Heading	3rd Divisional Artillery. 23rd Brigade R.F.A. July 1916		
War Diary	Acquin	01/07/1916	31/07/1916
Heading	3rd Divisional Artillery 23rd Brigade Royal Field Artillery August 1916		
Miscellaneous	To B.M. 3rd D.A.		
War Diary		01/08/1916	31/08/1916

Heading	3rd Divisional Artillery. 23rd Brigade R.F.A. September 1916		
Miscellaneous	To Brigade Major 3rd DA	01/10/1916	01/10/1916
War Diary		01/09/1916	30/09/1916
Heading	3rd Divisional Artillery. 23rd Brigade R.F.A. October 1916		
Miscellaneous	To Bde. Major 3rd D. A	02/11/1916	02/11/1916
War Diary		01/10/1916	31/10/1916
Heading	3rd Divisional Artillery. 23rd Brigade R.F.A. November 1916		
Miscellaneous	To Brigade Major 3rd DA	01/12/1916	01/12/1916
War Diary	Brigade H. Qrs. at. Colincamps	01/11/1916	30/11/1916
Heading	3rd Divisional Artillery. 23rd Brigade R.F.A. December 1916		
Miscellaneous	To Brigade Major 3rd D.A.	01/01/1917	01/01/1917
War Diary		01/12/1916	27/12/1916
Heading	3rd Division Divl Artillery 30th Brigade R.F.A. Aug-Dec 1914		
Heading	3rd Divisional Artillery. 30th Brigade R.F.A. August 1914		
Heading	War Diary 30th Brigade R.F.A. 3rd Division Vol. I. 4-31.8.14 Lean A.G.G.		
War Diary	Bulford	04/08/1914	10/08/1914
War Diary	Amesburry	18/08/1914	18/08/1914
War Diary	Southampton	18/08/1914	19/08/1914
War Diary	Harvre	19/08/1914	20/08/1914
War Diary	Rouen	20/08/1914	22/08/1914
War Diary	Valenciennes	23/08/1914	23/08/1914
War Diary	Bavay	23/08/1914	24/08/1914
War Diary	Ciply	24/08/1914	24/08/1914
War Diary	Bermeris	24/08/1914	25/08/1914
War Diary	Solesmes	25/08/1914	25/08/1914
War Diary	Viesly	25/08/1914	25/08/1914
War Diary	Caudray	25/08/1914	26/08/1914
War Diary	Estrees	27/08/1914	27/08/1914
War Diary	Villeret	27/08/1914	27/08/1914
War Diary	Vermand	27/08/1914	27/08/1914
War Diary	Ham	28/08/1914	28/08/1914
War Diary	Tarlefesse	28/08/1914	28/08/1914
War Diary	Noyon	29/08/1914	29/08/1914
War Diary	Cuts	30/08/1914	30/08/1914
War Diary	Vassens	30/08/1914	30/08/1914
War Diary	Drcamp	30/08/1914	31/08/1914
War Diary	Coyolles	31/08/1914	31/08/1914
Heading	3rd Divisional Artillery. 30th Brigade R.F.A. September 1914		
War Diary	Coyolles	01/09/1914	01/09/1914
War Diary	Bouillancy	02/09/1914	02/09/1914
War Diary	Penchard	02/09/1914	03/09/1914
War Diary	Villemareuil	03/09/1914	03/09/1914
War Diary	Haute Maison	04/09/1914	04/09/1914
War Diary	Montanon Fm	04/09/1914	04/09/1914
War Diary	Liverdy	05/09/1914	06/09/1914
War Diary	In S of Keufmoutiers	06/09/1914	06/09/1914
War Diary	La Houssaye	06/09/1914	06/09/1914
War Diary	Hautefeuil	07/09/1914	07/09/1914

War Diary	Faremoutiers	07/09/1914	07/09/1914
War Diary	St. Pierre	08/09/1914	08/09/1914
War Diary	Nr. Rebais	08/09/1914	08/09/1914
War Diary	Bussieres	09/09/1914	09/09/1914
War Diary	Nanteuil	09/09/1914	09/09/1914
War Diary	Bezu	10/09/1914	10/09/1914
War Diary	Dammard	10/09/1914	11/09/1914
War Diary	Grand Rozoy	12/09/1914	12/09/1914
War Diary	Braine	13/09/1914	13/09/1914
War Diary	Nr Chassemy	13/09/1914	13/09/1914
War Diary	La Grange Farm	14/09/1914	14/09/1914
War Diary	Chateau Bois Morin	14/09/1914	14/09/1914
War Diary	Larue Den Haut	14/09/1914	14/09/1914
War Diary	Chateau & La Rue Den Haut	15/09/1914	16/09/1914
War Diary	Chateau	17/09/1914	17/09/1914
War Diary	Quarry near La Rue D'En Haut	18/09/1914	18/09/1914
War Diary	Chateau	19/09/1914	19/09/1914
War Diary	Quarry	19/09/1914	19/09/1914
War Diary	Quarry near La Rue D'En Haut	20/09/1914	27/09/1914
War Diary	Vailly	28/09/1914	28/09/1914
War Diary	Quarry	28/09/1914	30/09/1914
Heading	3rd Divisional Artillery. 30th Brigade R.F.A. October 1914		
War Diary	La Rue D'Enhaut	01/10/1914	02/10/1914
War Diary	Cuiry Housse	03/10/1914	03/10/1914
War Diary	Noroy	04/10/1914	04/10/1914
War Diary	Coyolles	04/10/1914	05/10/1914
War Diary	Labreviere	06/10/1914	06/10/1914
War Diary	Abbeville	06/10/1914	09/10/1914
War Diary	La Broye	09/10/1914	09/10/1914
War Diary	Tangry	10/10/1914	11/10/1914
War Diary	Gonnehem	12/10/1914	12/10/1914
War Diary	Pont D'Hinges	12/10/1914	12/10/1914
War Diary	Croix Marmeuse	12/10/1914	12/10/1914
War Diary	Le Cornet Malo	13/10/1914	13/10/1914
War Diary	Croix Marmeuse	13/10/1914	13/10/1914
War Diary	Vieille Chapelle	13/10/1914	13/10/1914
War Diary	Zelobes	14/10/1914	16/10/1914
War Diary	Lacouture	17/10/1914	17/10/1914
War Diary	Neuve Chapelle	18/10/1914	18/10/1914
War Diary	Bas Pommereau	18/10/1914	22/10/1914
War Diary	Croix Barbee	23/10/1914	01/11/1914
Heading	3rd Divisional Artillery. 30th Brigade R.F.A. November 1914		
War Diary	Croix Barbee	01/11/1914	15/11/1914
War Diary	Bout Deville	16/11/1914	16/11/1914
War Diary	Vieux Berquin	16/11/1914	17/11/1914
War Diary	Croix Poperinghe	18/11/1914	23/11/1914
War Diary	Laclytte	24/11/1914	30/11/1914
Heading	3rd Divisional Artillery. 30th Brigade R.F.A. December 1914		
War Diary	La Clytte	01/12/1914	31/12/1914
Heading	3rd Div R.F.A. 30th Brigade Jan-Dec, 1917		
Heading	3rd Division. 30th Bde. R.F.A. Vol IV 1-31.1.15		
War Diary	La Clytte	01/01/1915	06/01/1915
War Diary	Kemmel	07/01/1915	31/01/1915

Type	Location	Start	End
Heading	3rd Division 30th Bde R.F.A. Vol V 1.2-31.3.15		
War Diary	Kemmel	01/02/1915	31/03/1915
Heading	3rd Division. 30th Brigade R.F.A. Vol VI 1-30.4.15		
War Diary	Kemmel	01/04/1915	19/04/1915
War Diary	Laclytte	20/04/1915	30/04/1915
Heading	3rd Division. 30th Bde. R.F.A. Vol VII 1-31.5.15		
War Diary	La Clytte	01/05/1915	30/05/1915
War Diary	Dickebusch	31/05/1915	31/05/1915
War Diary	La Clytte	30/05/1915	30/05/1915
War Diary	Dickebusch	31/05/1915	31/05/1915
Heading	3rd Division. 30th Bde R.F.A. Vol 1-30.6.15		
War Diary	Dickebusch	01/06/1915	24/06/1915
War Diary	Busseboom	25/06/1915	26/06/1915
War Diary	Dickebusch	22/06/1915	24/06/1915
War Diary	Busseboom	25/06/1915	26/06/1915
War Diary	Dickebusch	22/06/1915	24/06/1915
War Diary	Busseboom	25/06/1915	28/06/1915
War Diary	Kruisstrat	29/06/1915	30/06/1915
Heading	3rd Division. 30th Bde R.F.A. Vol X August 15		
War Diary	Dickebusch	01/08/1915	03/08/1915
War Diary	S. of Poperinghe	04/08/1915	14/08/1915
War Diary	Dickebusch	15/08/1915	24/08/1915
War Diary	Ypres	25/08/1915	31/08/1915
Heading	3rd Division 30th Bde R.F.A. Vol XI Sept. 15		
War Diary	Ypres	01/09/1915	30/09/1915
Heading	3rd Division 30th Bde R.F.A. Oct 15 Vol XII		
War Diary	Ypres	01/10/1915	26/10/1915
War Diary	Steenvoorde	27/10/1915	31/10/1915
Heading	3rd Division 30th Bde. R.F.A. Nov Vol XIII		
War Diary	Steenvoorde	01/11/1915	30/11/1915
Heading	30th Bde. R.F.A. Dec Vol XIV		
War Diary	Reninghelst	01/12/1915	31/12/1915
Heading	3rd Divisional Artillery. 30th Brigade R.F.A. January 1916		
War Diary	Reninghelst	01/01/1916	29/01/1916
Heading	3rd Divisional Artillery. 30th Brigade R.F.A. No diary for:- February 1916 March 1916 April 1916 May 1916		

3rd Division

"A" Sqdn 15th Hussars
Aug 1914 — Mar 1915

TO 1 CAV DIV 9 BDE

Index

SUBJECT.

No.	Contents.	Date.
	3RD DIV. CAVALRY. (A. SQN, 15TH HUSSARS) AUG - DEC. 21st 1914	

M.O1.

O.T/3

121/966

WAR DIARY.
Div.al Cavalry 3rd Division.
(A Squadron 15th Hussars)

Volume I   16 – 31.8.14.

Army Form C. 2118.

WAR DIARY
or
INTELLIGENCE SUMMARY.
of "A" Squadron
15th Hussars - Sir hd Tr Kfo
3rd Division

(Erase heading not required.)

Instructions regarding War Diaries and Intelligence Summaries are contained in F. S. Regs., Part II. and the Staff Manual respectively. Title pages will be prepared in manuscript.

Hour, Date, Place	Summary of Events and Information	Remarks and references to Appendices
LONGMOOR 9.30 a.m. Aug 16th 1914	Entrained at BORDON - Arrives Southampton where Squadron embarks.	
17.8.14	Sailed at 4.30 A.M. - Arrives LE HAVRE 4 p.m. ROUEN 12 midnight	
18.8.14	Disentrained at 7 A.M. - Camped at BRUYÈRES.	
19.8.14	Capt R.P. Wells joined the Squadron from "C" - Left Camp at 8 p.m. entrained 11 p.m.	
20.8.14	Passed through St QUENTIN - Detrained at LANDRECIES 2 p.m. Marched to ALNOYE 8 miles, where squadron camped.	
21.8.14	1st 2nd & 4th Troops formed advanced guards to respecting Brigades - 3rd Troop attached to Div. Head Quarters - Camped at GOGNIES - 1st Troop with Lieut C.H.S. Whittle camped at BONNET.	
22.8.14	Squadron formed Adv. Gd. to 3rd Division - 1st Troop sent out at 4.30 a.m. to BINCHE - kept in touch with 5 Cav. Bde. 2nd Troop took up Advanced Post near HARMIGNIES station - 3rd Troop with G.O.C Div. went to MONS to observe German position - 1st & 2nd Troops camped that night at BONNET 3rd & 4th Troops at HYON.	

WAR DIARY or INTELLIGENCE SUMMARY

Army Form C. 2118.

of "A" Squadron
15th Hussars.

Hour, Date, Place	Summary of Events and Information	Remarks and references to Appendices
NYON 23-8-14 MONS	3rd & 4th Troops ordered to reconnoitre HAVRE and BRAY (BELGIUM) under Capt. Wells. 3rd Troop came in contact with enemy at HAVRE, and reported 1 Batt Art?, 1 Bde Cav + 1 Bn. Inf. in occupation - 4th Troop moved via BRAY to BINCHE linking up with the 1st Troop on the way. They were fired on by a Uhlan patrol, wounding Lieut Rogerson and subsequently were heavily shelled - our Artillery coming to the rescue. Capt Wells was left behind wounded, but was picked up by an ambulance. They were ordered to proceed to MONS to relieve the Moores on the Infantry. 2nd Troop were ordered to a rear guard action until 8 p.m. when they were ordered to escort a Battery out of action, which had been almost surrounded and brought it to NOUVELLES, where the Troop camped. Captain O.B. Walker went off that evening on a Special Mission and has not been seen since -	S.E. of MONS

The Major(?) Burck and his Corporal were both killed previously - |
| FRAMERIES 24.8.14 | The Squadron concentrated at 2 a.m. and proceeded to BLAREGNIES, where they received orders to reconnoitre BLAUGIES reported held by Germans - The 2nd Troop under Lieut René Boughen reconnoitred up to ATHIS and reported to G.O.C. 5th Division, then retiring BAVAI. The 1st, 3rd & 4th Troops were sent Lieut Whittle hearing of Germans in OFFIGNIES went OFFIGNIES | |

Army Form C. 2118.

WAR DIARY
or
INTELLIGENCE SUMMARY.
(Erase heading not required.)

Instructions regarding War Diaries and Intelligence Summaries are contained in F. S. Regs, Part II. and the Staff Manual respectively. Title pages will be prepared in manuscript.

Hour, Date, Place	Summary of Events and Information	Remarks and references to Appendices
24-8-14 (Cont.)	to clear it, and fell into an ambush, and suffered severely - Lieutenants Whistle + Hoare and 34 men failed to return from this affair - the remnant of these troops camped the night at BERNERIES.	
25-8-14	The Squadron under 2/Lieut R. Boughton and S.S.M. Sexton 2nd in Command, formed rear guard to the 3rd Division as they retired to LE CATEAU.	
26.8.14	Squadron escorted baggage convoy to JONCOURT	
27.8.14	Continued to escort baggage convoy through VERMAND to HAM arriving 11.45 p.m.	
28.8.14	Rearguard to Division to PONTOISE	
29.8.14	Rest Day - 11 p.m. moved to join Division at CUTS. 2 miles away -	
30.8.14	Sent out 4 a.m. back to PONTOISE Bridge to report to Gen! McCracken. Squadron was to Rearguard in two columns as far as MONTOIS	
31.8.14	Rearguard again during march to VAUCIENNES.	

WO D.I./3

121/1638

A. Squadron 16th Hussars
     3rd Division.
Vol II   1.9. — 2.10.14.

Army Form C. 2118.

"A" Squadron
"K" Squadron
15th "The King's Hussars"

WAR DIARY
or
INTELLIGENCE SUMMARY.
(Erase heading not required.)

Instructions regarding War Diaries and Intelligence
Summaries are contained in F. S. Regs., Part II.
and the Staff Manual respectively. Title pages
will be prepared in manuscript.

Hour, Date, Place		Summary of Events and Information	Remarks and references to Appendices
VAUCIENNES	Sept 1st/14	Acted with 3rd Bde Rear-guard – Patrols out	
VILLERS–ST–GENEST	2/9/14	Same again	
MONTHYON	3.9.14	Same again	2 Machine joined Squadron
La VOULTERNAISON	4.9.14	Same again. Small action on flank with German patrols.	
CHARTRES	5.9.14	Advance this am – after night march – fired with German patrols about 2.30 P.M.	Lt Cornwall R.A. took over command of Squn.
CHARTRES	6.9.14	Formed part of Advanced Guard – Capt Hannam's troop with one sqdn such time Divl took German Squadron sent out to left flank to protect Division	
TARMOULES	7.9.14		
COULOMMIERS	8.9.14	Formed rear of R.R. Bde X – Cpl Aveling joined with 10 men – out of 36 sent out –	Capt A. Courage took Command St Lawrie 3rd Hussars attached
BUSSIERES	9.9.14	Quiet day. Still advancing.	
BENTRY	10.9.14	Advanced Guard to Division, who came into action.	
DAMMARD	11.9.14	More am – sent to the guns – no incident.	
GRAND ROZOY	12.9.14	Advance Guard to Division – no action	

WAR DIARY

INTELLIGENCE SUMMARY.

"A" Squadron 15th "The King's" Hussars

Army Form C. 2118.

Instructions regarding War Diaries and Intelligence Summaries are contained in F. S. Regs., Part II. and the Staff Manual respectively. Title pages will be prepared in manuscript.

(Erase heading not required.)

Hour, Date, Place		Summary of Events and Information	Remarks and references to Appendices
BRAIYE	13.9.14	Reconnoitred towards VAILLY. Found Germans in position in force. Sergt Barker and Pte Stringfellow killed. Ptes Spencer & Winterbottom wounded. Moved on to road to CHASSEMY.	
CHASSEMY	14.9.14	Patrols sent out across VAILLY Bridge. Artillery duel.	
"	15.9.14	Same again.	
"	16.9.14	Same again.	
"	17.9.14	Remained saddled up all night in expectation of attack. Stephens post near CONDÉ bridge.	
"	18.9.14	Moved into BRAIYE at 8 p.m.	
BRAINE	19.9.14 to	Refitted squadron – Cervices and trained. Received reinforcements. Sent out a few patrols.	Capt Burgham) Ridehalgh) 15th Hussars Pvt Mutting) joined J.A Lieut Atkinson 47 N.C.O's & men 53 horses
"	27.9.14	Regtl H-Q arrives from Rear. Machine Gun Section transferred to 3rd Cav Bde	Capt Nutting & Lieut Atkinson
"	28.9.14	Sent out to CHASSEMY to guard CONDÉ Bridge.	Capt Bradshaw Indian Army attached to squadron.

Army Form C. 2118.

"A" Squadron
15th "The Kings" Hussars

WAR DIARY
or
INTELLIGENCE SUMMARY.
(Erase heading not required.)

Instructions regarding War Diaries and Intelligence Summaries are contained in F. S. Regs., Part II. and the Staff Manual respectively. Title pages will be prepared in manuscript.

Hour, Date, Place	Summary of Events and Information	Remarks and references to Appendices
BRAINE 26.9.14.	2/Cpl Stanford and Bywater transferred to 1st Division.	
" 28.9.14	Moved Squadron up to CHATEAU BELLEME where they remained until 2.10.14.	

Maurice Cobb
15th Hussars

121/2265

A. Squadron. 15th Hussars.
(Div' Cavy: 3rd Division)

Vol III. 1-31.10.14

WAR DIARY
of "A" Squadron, 15th "The Kings" Hussars
INTELLIGENCE SUMMARY

October 1st – 9th

Army Form C. 2118.

Hour, Date, Place	Summary of Events and Information	Remarks and references to Appendices
Oct 1/10/14 BRAINE (CHATEAU BELLEVUE)	Nothing unusual occurred. Received preparatory orders to move 9 p.m.	D/B. Good Bayne every right D/B.
2.10.14 "	Squadron moved at 6 p.m. and marched to ARCY, arriving 9 p.m. Billeted for the night	D/B. Maxim gun section bivouacked elsewhere
3.10.14 ARCY	Marched at 12 midday to TROESNES arriving by troops between 3.30 and 4.20 p.m. Halted for tea and marched again at 5.20 p.m. to CREPY - arrived 10.0 p.m. Billeted at ST GERMAIN. Seized factory.	Distance 35 miles. D/B
4.10.14 CREPY	Marched at 5.30 p.m. to ROBERVAL arriving 9 p.m.	D/B.
5.10.14 ROBERVAL	Marched at 10 a.m. to REMEUX & entrain - there received orders to go on to COMPIEGNE, where we arrived 2 p.m. - Very bad entraining facilities - all trains up at 8.45 p.m. - Left at 9 p.m. Detrainment unknown.	Entraining took 4½ hours owing to no platforms available. D/B.
6.10.14 ABBEVILLE	Passed through AMIENS about 1 a.m. and arrived ÉTAPLES 10 a.m. Entrained here at 1 p.m. - travelled at 2 p.m. back to ABBEVILLE where we billeted at 10 p.m.	D/B. Distance 31 miles
7.10.14 ABBEVILLE	Rested horses and cleaned up	
8.10.14 ABBEVILLE	Marched at 11 p.m. upon 7th Inf Bde. marched at 10 a.m. thro' to REIGNEUXVILLE arriving 5.30 a.m.	
9.10.14 REIGNAUXVILLE	Rested all day, and marched again at 5.20 p.m. to PRESSY LES PERNES arriving 1 a.m.	Total distance in 24 hours was 48 miles. D/B.

Oct 10th – 13th

Army Form C. 2118.

WAR DIARY
"A" Squadron
or
INTELLIGENCE SUMMARY.
15th Hussars

(Erase heading not required.)

Hour, Date, Place	Summary of Events and Information	Remarks and references to Appendices
10.10.14 PRESSY LES PERNES	Rested horses & men – Found out Squadron	D.T.S.
11.10.14 " "	Marched at 6.30 a.m. – 1st Cavalry Corps Bivouacked at BUSNES. 1st troop held bridge over canal at night	D.T.S.
12.10.14 BUSNES	Reveille 4 a.m. Marched at 5.30 a.m. & reconnoitred towards LESTREM – Enemy holding village of FOSSE which was captured by Gordons that night – Squadron billetted near us.	1 squadron 19th Hussars, Bde Cav. y to 5th Bde joined us.
13.10.14 FOSSE	Reveille 4 a.m. 3rd troop under Capt Bald reconnoitred beyond FOSSE – Came in contact with enemy at 6 a.m at BOUR DEVILLE & killed Uhlan Officer – Gordons then came up, & 3rd troop rejoined Squadron acting on left flank. At 10 a.m. 1st troop under Capt Bradshaw was sent out to clear up the situation on other left flank. At 10.30 a.m. Capt Bradshaw with remainder of Squadron and machine gun section went up to support left of Gordons, but was not required, & as the Squadron then withdrew (which arrived in support). The Infantry, about 3 p.m. a shell burst amongst the men & horses, wounding 5 men & four horses. About 16 horses of Capt Bradshaw's troop returned by at intervals and the men in charge of them a while later, they state horses had been fired on, the horses stampeded. Capt Bradshaw and 19 dismounted men were missing.	19th Hussars at LE MARAIS farm held in check – D.T.S.

WAR DIARY of "A" Squadron

INTELLIGENCE SUMMARY.
(Erase heading not required.)

Oct 14th – 19th.

15th "The Kings" Hussars —

Army Form C. 2118.

III

Instructions regarding War Diaries and Intelligence Summaries are contained in F. S. Regs, Part II. and the Staff Manual respectively. Title pages will be prepared in manuscript.

Hour, Date, Place		Summary of Events and Information	Remarks and references to Appendices
14.10.14 FOSSE	5.30 a.m.	Capt Bradshaw this morn still in possession of BOUR DEVILLE. Fighting continues at daylight. Village taken by 5th & 7th Dragoons leaving the bay. Squadron billeted at CHATEAU.	Gen¹ Hubert Hamilton killed by shrapnel bullet near LACOUTURE – FOSSE Road. DJS
15.10.14 FOSSE		Heavy engagement all along the line. Squadron advanced to BOUR DEVILLE but had to withdraw slightly owing to shelling. One man – horse hit. Capt Bradshaw rejoined rgts west about 400 yds reported dying (stab) wear an Uhlan archer. W of BOUR DEVILLE – Capt Ritchie when reconnoitred ave'd buried them in the orchard. No signs of remaining 5 men.	Gen¹ Colin Mackenzie in command of 3rd Div. DJS
16.10.14 FOSSE		Squadron advances to PONT DU HEM and on to FAUQUISSART. 3d Troop in advance patrol fired on from factory near AUBERS – one man there wounded. Rgt. advanced to position near to AUBERS – Billeted at A & Rue BACQUEROT.	DJS
17.10.14 A at Rue BACQUEROT		AUBERS evacuated during the night – Infantry advanced beyond and took HERLIES with bayonet – Billeted at AUBERS	DJS
18.10.14 AUBERS		Advance to HERLIES. Germans still holding trenches at far end. Squadron unable to advance further.	DJS
19.10.14 "		Squadron turned out at 2.45 p.m. with orders to support Royal Irish in attack on LE PILLY. Regts as far as LE PLOICH from where bivouacked and advanced to LE RIEZ. Squadron remained in support there, until	

W. Lyall Gr
15 Hussars

Oct 20th — 24th

III

Army Form C. 2118.

WAR DIARY
of "A" Squadron
INTELLIGENCE SUMMARY. 15th "The King's" Hussars —
(Erase heading not required.)

Instructions regarding War Diaries and Intelligence Summaries are contained in F. S. Regs., Part II. and the Staff Manual respectively. Title pages will be prepared in manuscript.

Hour, Date, Place	Summary of Events and Information	Remarks and references to Appendices
20.10.14 AUBERS.	MIDDLESEX Regt. — our machine guns on left flank of R.I. who took LE PILLY with the exception of a few houses into N.309. Our men wounded by stray bullet.	DTS.
21.10.14. "	Heavy fighting all day — Germans apparently reinforced, but held in check — French Cavy. Divs at FROMELLES.	DTS.
"	Squadron occupies trenches at LE PLOUCH farm all day. LE PILLY retaken by Germans — LE RIEZ heavily shelled — Royal Scots retires to in trenches at noon —	DTS.
22.10.14. "	French heavily shelled in FROMELLES. Place intenable — Division wanted slight retirement during night — Germans did the same — Our cyclists and machine Guns occupies trenches until 3 a.m.	DTS.
23.10.14. A of RUE BACQUEROT	Division occupies new position along RUE DU BOIS without incident. Squadron in Reserve all day — one horse wounded by enemy shrapnel shell.	DTS.
24.10.14. BOUR DEVILLE	Squadron in Reserve — Patrols out to keep up communication between brigades and General Indian Divisions. German attacked Gordons at night — Squadron called out about 10 p.m. to assist — returned to billets when all quiet about 2 a.m	Genl. Boran C.in.g 8th B.G. DTS. invalided — [signature] 15 Huss.

1. Oct 25th — 31st

IV

Army Form C. 2118.

WAR DIARY

of "A" Squadron

INTELLIGENCE SUMMARY. 15th "The King's" Hussars

(Erase heading not required.)

Hour, Date, Place	Summary of Events and Information	Remarks and references to Appendices
BOUR DEVILLE 25.10.14.	Germans holding line of RUE DU BOIS - Germans attacked 15th Sussex without success on the left, and lost heavily -	Genl Bowes in command of 8th Inf Bde. DJB.
" 26.10.14.	Heavy rain all last night - All quiet on our front.	DJB.
" 27.10.14.	7th Inf Bde attacked by Germans in force, and lost some trenches - an attempt to retake them failed - 2nd Cavy Bde arrives and billeted in RICHEBOURG ST VAAST - Gurkhas and Seaforth Highlanders also arrived.	DJB.
" 28.10.14.	Sharp fighting at intervals all day on our front - 2nd Cavy Bde associated in trenches with Manchester Reg't - 47th Sikhs assaulted NEUVE CHAPELLE successfully, but could not retain it.	DJB.
" 29.10.14.	Front of 3rd Divn quiet but heavy firing on our right & left at some distance during the night.	Genl Colin Mackenzie DSO invalided home -
" 30.10.14.	Very wet last night and again today - some artillery fire between 3 & 5 pm.	
" 31.10.14.	Reveillé 4 a.m. - Marched at 6 a.m. to METTEREN - Bde H.Q. 3rd Divn there. Remainder of Bde split up and sent to other Divisions. 8th Bde remained at FAUQUISSART - 9th Bde gone to support Cavalry Corps - 7th Bde resting at MORRIS - Guns with 8th Bde.	Genl King took over command of 3rd Division - DJB.

[signature]

32

Date	Officers			Other Ranks		
	Killed	Wounded	Missing	Killed	Wounded	Missing
13.10.14	Capt O.G Bradshaw			5	4	5 x 2nd Army
30.10.14					1	

Second Cavalry Brigade 15th Hussars

$\frac{121}{3871}$

A. Squadron. 15th Hussars. (Div Cav 3rd Division)

Vol IV. 1 — 30.11.14

Army Form C. 2118

WAR DIARY
of
"A" Squadron
15th "The King's" Hussars

INTELLIGENCE SUMMARY.
(Erase heading not required.)

Hour, Date, Place	Summary of Events and Information	Remarks and references to Appendices
1.11.14. MÉTÉREN	Received orders suddenly to march at 2 p.m. to LOCRE - situation apparently unsatisfactory but resulted in Tw evening.	DTS.
2.11.14. LOCRE	Squadron not employed today - French troops arriving in large numbers.	DTS.
3.11.14. "	French and 1st Cav Bde attacked MESSINES at 4 p.m. but failed.	DTS.
4.11.14. "	No unusual incident to record.	DTS.
5.11.14. "	Further attack on MESSINES - unsuccessful. 12 remounts arrived.	DTS.
6.11.14. "	Received orders to move - marched at 5 p.m. but had to return, as no space available for billeting.	DTS.
7.11.14. "	Marched at 6.30 a.m.) billeted near DICKEBUSHE. Had to move again at 5 p.m. to HALTE 1 mile E. of YPRES, latter place in flames in many places.	DTS.
8.11.14. HALTE 1m E. of YPRES	Turned out at 4 a.m. and marched up to trenches in support of Bedford Regt. 1 mile S.E. of HOOGE. Squadron in Reserve trenches all day. Two local attacks between 6 and 7 p.m. Squadron lined road all night with fixed bayonets. Cyclists in trenches with us. Remainder of night quiet.	
9.11.14. IN TRENCHES	Considerable shelling during daytime. Heavy attack about 5 p.m. (Capt Bold wounded left arm - Squadron relieved at 7.30 p.m. returned to HALTE.	Capt Bold wounded left arm. [signature] 15/11/14

Nov 10th - 14th

WAR DIARY
of "A" Squadron.
INTELLIGENCE SUMMARY.
15th "The King's" Hussars
(Erase heading not required.)

Army Form C. 2118
II

Instructions regarding War Diaries and Intelligence Summaries are contained in F.S. Regs., Part II. and the Staff Manual respectively. Title pages will be prepared in manuscript.

Hour, Date, Place	Summary of Events and Information	Remarks and references to Appendices
10.11.14. HALTE (YPRES)	Sent for our horses to DICKEBUSHE. Machine Gun Section and 1 troop ordered out to support point of 9th Bde at 8 p.m. under Lieut. Osborne.	DTB.
11.11.14. IN TRENCHES 5 a.m.	1st Troop split up + sent to form communicating posts to various Divs and Bde H.Q.s. — Received orders for remainder of Squadron (2 troops) to move up at once to 9th Bde H.Q.	DTB. Lieut. Osborne + gun section missing
10.30 a.m.		
3 p.m.	Two men from Machine Gun section returned to billets + reported loss of both guns and Lieut Osborne with his section – then trench was seized by the Prussian Guard – 1st troop under Sergt Clarke was ordered for an hour until the line reformed and Reserves came up – 2nd and 3rd troop went into Reserve trenches in haas Château – having received orders to attack two farms + a wood the evening – moved up to support trenches at 4 a.m. at various times.	DTB. Pte Bowman killed.
	Very stormy night with heavy thunderstorms – Squadron in open and very exposed trenches – no satisfactory news of Osborne – Corp.l Rigby under eyelid killed by shrapnell.	DTB Corpl Rigby killed
12.11.14	Very wet day – Squadron still in trenches – our fire which started at 5 p.m. had not returned at midnight.	DTB
13.11.14		
14.11.14 HALTE 4 a.m.	Squadron returned to billets – got orders to be ready for an attack in the evening – eventually only the cyclists were sent. Attack was successful and started south of Hooge Road Château of Château.	DTB

Abercroft
15/3/15

Nov 15th – 20th.

III

Army Form C. 2118

WAR DIARY
of "A" Squadron
INTELLIGENCE SUMMARY. 15th "The King's" Hussars

(Erase heading not required.)

Instructions regarding War Diaries and Intelligence Summaries are contained in F. S. Regs., Part II. and the Staff Manual respectively. Title pages will be prepared in manuscript.

Hour, Date, Place		Summary of Events and Information	Remarks and references to Appendices
15.11.14. HALTE (YPRES)	1.30 p.m.	The usual daily alarm. Squadron turned out in haste and proceeded to near HOOGE, and were then sent back. Very wet & cold.	DTB.
16.11.14		Nothing to report. Lively cannonade by French – weather very wet & cold.	DTB.
17.11.14	1 p.m.	Quiet fine during the morning. at 1 p.m. received order to move up at once, and reinforce 9th Brigade – took no part in actual operations – returned to billets at 8 p.m.	DTB.
18.11.14.		Beautiful weather but no alarm – nothing to report.	
19.11.14. IN TRENCHES	10 a.m.	Frost last night. Received orders to take over part of firing line trenches from 5th Fusiliers that evening.	DTB.
	5 p.m.	left billets in a snowstorm and got shelled on the HOOGE Road going up. Only 1 man with footover trenches without accident – freezing very hard & bitterly cold. Snipers very active.	
20.11.14	"	Enemy very quiet all day in their trenches, only occasional sniping – very cold. H.Q. Dug-outs badly shelled with "Crumps" – 2 19th Hussars orderlies killed & 2 wounded. 1 troop of Hussars on our left blown out of trenches by minenwerfer bombs – outburst of rapid fire from our trenches which soon subsided.	DTB.
	5 p.m.	Relieved by French at 10.30 p.m. – Reached billets midnight – still freezing.	

Alan Pagett
15th Hussars

Nov. 21st – 30th 1912

WAR DIARY
of
INTELLIGENCE SUMMARY.
(Erase heading not required.)

"A" Squadron.
15th (Service) Hussars.

Army Form C. 2118   IV

Instructions regarding War Diaries and Intelligence Summaries are contained in F. S. Regs., Part II. and the Staff Manual respectively. Title pages will be prepared in manuscript.

Hour, Date, Place			Summary of Events and Information	Remarks and references to Appendices
21.11.14	YPRES.	6.15 A.M	Squadron paraded and withdrew from YPRES Salient without mishap almost unopposed from front – marched via YPRES – ELVERDINGHE to HEKSKEN near WESTOUTRE, where in billeted a period of rest, and remained till morning of 24-11-12	23.11.12 Capt Bowney and Lieut Broughton proceeded to England on 7 days leave. D.T.B
26.11.14	WESTOUTRE	9.30 a.m	Squadron paraded and marched via MONT NOIR to find billets near BERTHEN – Roads in very bad state –	D.T.B.
26.11.14	BERTHEN	2 p.m	Showed evening light – Squadron moved again and took up billets ½ mile from Bn H.Q at MONT NOIR.	D.T.B.
27.11.14	MONT NOIR		Capt Rawlins the D.C.M medal and presented by Gen' Haldane at WESTOUTRE. Received orders for resumption of activity –	Capt Potter D.C.M. medal.
28.11.14	"	7.0 a.m	Commenced sending patrols sent to H.Qs of 3rd & 5th Div's also B2nd Div's at KEMMEL and DRANOUTRE – Liaison Officer with French B2nd Div's at DICKEBUSHE – Cyclists patrolling telephone wires –	Capt Rawlins & 90 Hotspurs reconnoitres German Trenches D.T.B
29.11.14.	"		Same work again – Nothing to report.	D.T.B.
30.11.14	"		As quiet along British front – patrols as usual nothing to report –	D.T.B.

Mowry Col
15 Hussars

121/3776

A. Squadron 15th Hertford.
(3rd Div.l Cavalry)

Vol V. 1 — 21.12.14

Army Form C. 2118.

WAR DIARY
of
INTELLIGENCE SUMMARY.

"A" Squadron
1/5" "The King's" Hussars

(Erase heading not required.)

Instructions regarding War Diaries and Intelligence
Summaries are contained in F. S. Regs, Part II.
and the Staff Manual respectively. Title pages
will be prepared in manuscript.

Hour, Date, Place	Summary of Events and Information	Remarks and references to Appendices
LA MANCHE 1.12.14 (near MONT NOIR)	Patrols established at all Brigades & Division Headquarters, and Liaison officer daily on duty with French Division on our left —	Daily patrols —
6	Remainder employed in building stables for horses —	Liaison officer on duty with French 32nd Division daily —
13.12.14		
14.12.14	3rd Division made heavy attack on WYTSCHAETE Ridge — bombardment commenced at 7 a.m, and Infantry attacked at 7.45 a.m and managed to gain a little ground. Another very heavy bombardment from 3.30 to 4.45 p.m, but Infantry advanced no further —	
15.12.14	Police patrol of 1 troop posted on WESTOUTRE — SCHERPENBERG Road to control traffic	
17.12.14	French Brigade on our left attempted to attack HOLLANDSESCHUR Farm, but failed —	
19.12.14	Bombardment of German Trenches from 3 to 3.30 p.m and again at 7 p.m. Gelisle ordered to act as Bomb Throwers to his Division —	28.12.14. Capt. E.E. Leslie arrived for duty with Squadron [illegible] officer 15 Division
21.12.14		

No.	Contents.	Date.
	3RD DIV. — CAVALRY. A SQN, 15TH HUSSARS — WAR DIARY, JAN – MAR, 1915	

121/4195

A. Squadron. 15th Hussars.

O.C. Cav. 3rd Division.

Vol VI. 1 — 31. 1. 15.

Army Form C. 2118.

WAR DIARY
or
INTELLIGENCE SUMMARY.
(Erase heading not required.)

Instructions regarding War Diaries and Intelligence Summaries are contained in F. S. Regs., Part II. and the Staff Manual respectively. Title pages will be prepared in manuscript.

Hour, Date, Place	Summary of Events and Information	Remarks and references to Appendices
Billet LA MANCE month of January	Traffic and Police Patrols.	Alonzo Taft Lt. R. 35th 15th Hussars

3rd Division

12/4634

A. Sqdn 15th Hussars

Vol VII 1 – 28.2.15

Army Form C. 2118.

WAR DIARY
INTELLIGENCE SUMMARY.
(Erase heading not required.)

A Sqdn. 15th Hussars

Instructions regarding War Diaries and Intelligence Summaries are contained in F. S. Regs., Part II. and the Staff Manual respectively. Title pages will be prepared in manuscript.

Hour, Date, Place	Summary of Events and Information	Remarks and references to Appendices
March month.		War Expenses. Remounts & Reinf. received and Intended for all ranks.
Feb 1st – 24th	Patrols on road. Supervision of Traffic.	
Feb 25th – 26th	Trenches.	
Feb 27th – 28th	Patrols on road. Supervision of Traffic.	
		Always Cpt. 15th Hussars

"A" Squadron 15th Hussars (8th Div¹ Cav.)

Vol VIII   1 — 31.3.15

Army Form C. 2118.

WAR DIARY
or
INTELLIGENCE SUMMARY.
(Erase heading not required.)

Instructions regarding War Diaries and Intelligence Summaries are contained in F. S. Regs., Part II. and the Staff Manual respectively. Title pages will be prepared in manuscript.

Hour, Date, Place	Summary of Events and Information	Remarks and references to Appendices
March 1915 In the Field. At the HQ LA MANCELLE LANG CAMP St JANS CAPPEL	Patrolling around in billeting area.	

Newhoft
A[?] 15th [?]

**3RD DIVISION
DIVL. TROOPS**

'C' SQDN.

NTH IRISH HORSE.
OCT 1915 —
JAN-JUNE 1916.

To 10 Corps

SUBJECT.

No.	Contents.	Date.
	3RD DIV. — CAVALRY. C. SQN, The N. IRISH HORSE — WAR DIARY, OCT–DEC, 1915	

121/7599

3rd Kurdon

"C. Sgr. Nii Inia Horea

Dec '15

Vol I

18/20

To
Adjutant G. Office
Base

From
O C C Squadron
Irish Horse

Reference attached.

Regret in Error   no dairies were kept for July August and September

Div M° Troop & Dr
1 " 12 " 15

[signature] Capt
Comm'd Sqn

O.C. "C" Sqn. Nth Irish Horse.

A.G.'s OFFICE AT THE BASE
CENTRAL REGISTRY
26 NOV 1915
C. R. No.

The Documents referred to in the War Diary Margin-forwarded under your memo _____ Oct. of the 15.11.15 have been received.

The diaries for July, Aug. + Sep. are awaited.

Captain,
D. A. A. G.
for D. A. G., 3rd Echelon.

Base,
25.11.15

Army Form C. 2118.

WAR DIARY
or
INTELLIGENCE SUMMARY.
(Erase heading not required.)

Instructions regarding War Diaries and Intelligence Summaries are contained in F. S. Regs., Part II. and the Staff Manual respectively. Title pages will be prepared in manuscript.

Hour, Date, Place			Summary of Events and Information	Remarks and references to Appendices
4.30 P.m.	1-10-15	3d Division	Routine duties as usual	Lt. Pon C/Lt
	2-10-15	Sanctuary Wood	A Party consisting of H.Q. & C.O.ymen. Under the Command of Lieut J. Grant was furnished for the purpose of constructing defence works	C.Q.m C/Lt
	3-10-15	3 Division	Routine duties as usual	Rt Pon C/Lt
	4-10-15	"	" " " "	R.O.Pon C/Lt
	5-10-15	"	" " " "	R.O.Pon C/Lt
	6-10-15	Sanctuary Wood	A Party consisting of H.Q. & C.O.ymen under the Command of Capt R.O. Rao was furnished for the Purpose of patrol & working party under Lieut J. Grant	Rt. Pon C/Lt
	7-10-15	3 Division	Routine duties as usual	R.O. Pon C/Lt
	8-10-15	"	" " " "	R.O.Pon C/Lt
	9-10-15	"	" " " "	R.D. Pon C/Lt
	10-10-15	"	" " " "	R.D.Pon C/Lt
4.15 P.m.	11-10-15	Sanctuary Wood	A Party consisting of H.Q. & C.O.ymen Under the Command of Lieut J. Grant was furnished for the Purpose of relieving working party under Capt R.O. Rao	R.O.Pon C/Lt
	12-10-15	3 Division	Routine duties as usual	Rt Pon C/Lt
	13-10-15	"	" " " "	R.O.Pon C/Lt
	14-10-15	"	" " " "	R.O.Pon C/Lt
	15-10-15	"	" " " "	R.O.Pon C/Lt
4.15 P.m.	16-11-15	Sanctuary Wood	A Party consisting of H.Q. & C.O.ymen Under the Command of Capt R.O. Rao was furnished for the purpose of relieving working party under Lieut J. Grant	R.O.Pon C/Lt
	17-11-15	3 Division	Routine duties as usual	R.O.Pon C/Lt

Army Form C. 2118.

WAR DIARY
or
INTELLIGENCE SUMMARY.
(Erase heading not required.)

Instructions regarding War Diaries and Intelligence Summaries are contained in F. S. Regs., Part II. and the Staff Manual respectively. Title pages will be prepared in manuscript.

Hour, Date, Place	Summary of Events and Information	Remarks and references to Appendices
18.10.15 1st Division	Routine duties as usual	R O Rm C/H
19.10.15 "	" "	R O Rm C/H
20.10.15 "	" "	R O Rm C/H
9.45 P.m 21.10.15 Sanctuary Wood	In course of the periodical survey which parties was in the heavy wood, wire was put in front of the following trenches NOTTINGHAM ROAD. ROBB STREET. DAWSON STREET End of B3. BODEN STREET. Junction B.4. R. B.3.S. B.2.S.A.R.R. WARINGTON AVENUE. Working party setting Aleured parader at 5.30 P.m.	R O Rm C/H
	Enl returned to public at 8.45 P.m. 2. Casualties	
5.30 P.m 22.10.15 1st Division	The Squadron Paraded at 5.30 and proceeded to relieve J.16. C.9.9. in the Summer of WINNEZEELE MAP 27.	R M P Rm C/H
2. P.m 23.10.15 8th Hussars	The Squadron Paraded & marched to new Billets J.23 D.9.7. J.23.C.1.9 Map 27. 8 environs of WINNEZEELE	R O Rm C/H
24.10.15 "	Routine duties as usual	R O Rm C/H
25.10.15 "	Routine duties as usual	R D Rm C/H
26.10.15 "	Routine duties as usual	R O Rm C/H
27.10.15 "	Routine duties as usual	R O Rm C/H
28.10.15 1st Division	Routine duties as usual	R O Rm C/H
29.10.15 8th Hussars	Routine duties as usual	R O Rm C/H
30.10.15 "	Routine duties as usual	R O Rm C/H
31.10.15 "	Routine duties as usual	R O Rm C/H

3rd Division

O.C. "C" Sqn. N.Z. Irish Horse

Nov 1915

vol II

21/7637

Army Form C. 2118.

WAR DIARY
or
INTELLIGENCE SUMMARY.
(Erase heading not required.)

Instructions regarding War Diaries and Intelligence Summaries are contained in F.S. Regs., Part II. and the Staff Manual respectively. Title pages will be prepared in manuscript.

	Hour, Date, Place	Summary of Events and Information	Remarks and references to Appendices
	1.11.15 3rd Denison	Routine duties as usual	RoR
	2.11.15 " "	Routine duties as usual	RoR
	3.11.15 " "	Routine duties as usual	RoR
	4.11.15 " "	Routine duties as usual	RoR
1 Bn.	5.11.15 3rd Denison	The squadron paraded at 1 P.m. and marched to new billets at HARTFORD 9.30.13. MAP 27	RoR
	6.11.15 3rd Denison	Routine duties as usual	RoR
	7.11.15 " "	Routine duties as usual	RoR
	8.11.15 " "	Routine duties as usual	12 R
	9.11.15 " "	Routine duties as usual	RoR
	10.11.15 " "	Routine duties as usual	RoR
	11.11.15 " "	Routine duties as usual	RoR
	12.11.15 " "	Routine duties as usual	RoR
	13.11.15 " "	Routine duties as usual	RoR
	14.11.15 " "	Routine duties as usual	RoR
	15.11.15 " "	Routine duties as usual	RoR
	16.11.15 " "	Routine duties as usual	RoR
10.45 pm	17.11.15 " "	The squadron paraded at 10.45 to be inspected with 8th Brigade by the G.O.C II Army. In the evening 21.3 Sqdn. & transport moved to new billets 9.30. D.9.6. owing to outbreak of foot & mouth disease.	99
	18.11.15 " "	Routine duties as usual	99

Army Form C. 2118.

WAR DIARY
or
INTELLIGENCE SUMMARY.

(Erase heading not required.)

Instructions regarding War Diaries and Intelligence Summaries are contained in F.S. Regs., Part II. and the Staff Manual respectively. Title pages will be prepared in manuscript.

Hour, Date, Place		Summary of Events and Information	Remarks and references to Appendices
	19-11-15	3rd Division	Routine duties as usual	J.G.
	20-11-15	"	" " " "	J.G.
	21-11-15	"	" " " "	J.G.
10 a.m.	22-11-15	3 Division	Whole Squadron paraded at 10 a.m. and marched to new Billets at Busseboom	J.G.
			T 10.A.3.Y. 1 N.C.O. & 12 men paraded at 8 a.m. & transferred to Camp Commandant 5th Corps & Ypres. To act as Mounted Town police	J.G.
	23-11-15		Routine duties as usual	J.G.
	24-11-15	"	" " " "	J.G.
8 a.m.	25-11-15	"	3 N.C.O. & 9 men paraded at 8.45 a.m. to report to A.P.M. 3 Division for road control	J.G.
12 noon	26-11-15	"	3 N.C.O. & 9 men reported today at 12 noon having finished their duties of road control	J.G.
	27-11-15	"	Routine as usual	J.G.
	28-11-15	"	" " "	J.G.
4.30 a.m.	29-11-15	"	A Party of 1 N.C.O. & 20 men paraded 4.30 and proceeded to Gouvencourt Ste. to load timber for 3rd Division and returned same day.	J.G.
	30-11-15	"	Routine duties as usual	J.G.

"C" Sqn. N&I Irish Horse

Dec.

Vol III

WAR DIARY or INTELLIGENCE SUMMARY.

(Erase heading not required.)

Army Form C. 2118.

"C" Squadron North Irish Horse
III Division

Instructions regarding War Diaries and Intelligence Summaries are contained in F.S. Regs., Part II. and the Staff Manual respectively. Title pages will be prepared in manuscript.

Hour, Date, Place	Summary of Events and Information	Remarks and references to Appendices
1.12.15 3rd Division	Routine duties as usual.	
2.12.15 "	do	
3.12.15 "	do	
4.12.15 "	do	
5.12.15 "	do	
6.12.15 "	do	
7.12.15 "	do	
8.12.15 "	do	
9.12.15 "	do	
10.12.15 "	do	
11.12.15 "	do	
12.12.15 "	N.C.O. & 10 men Proceeded to HAZEBROUCK to load brick for Division	
13.12.15 "	do	
14.12.15 "	do	
15.12.15 "	Horses were Malinged on this date as "C" Mis Squadron	
16.12.15 "	Routine duties as usual	
17.12.15 "	do	
18.12.15 "	do	
6.45 am 19.12.15 "	The Squadron moved by penny to move the front when ordered by the G.O.C. 3 Division.	
12 Noon 20.12.15 "	Being to Loadsman on our front & party NCO & 4 men under command of Major Harry paraded at 12 noon and proceeded to 76 Support H.Q. this point was in front of first trench B.2.9 at Square north of the Canal Bank 9.33 D.8.h. about 28.	
21.12.15 "	Routine duties as usual	
22.12.15 "	do	
23.12.15 "	do	
24.12.15 "	do	
25.12.15 "	do	
26.12.15 "	do	
27.12.15 "	do	
28.12.15 "	do	
29.12.15 "	do	
30.12.15 "	do	
31.12.15 "	do	

C/Sgt. M. Jainal Hoe

Jan

Vol VI

3rd Div

"C" Squadron
North Irish Horse
Divisional Cavalry
3rd Division

WAR DIARY
or
INTELLIGENCE SUMMARY.
(Erase heading not required.)

Army Form C. 2118

Instructions regarding War Diaries and Intelligence Summaries are contained in F. S. Regs., Part II. and the Staff Manual respectively. Title pages will be prepared in manuscript.

Hour, Date, Place	Summary of Events and Information	Remarks and references to Appendices
1·1·16 3rd Division	Routine duties as usual	
1.30 pm 2·1·16	A party of 2 officers & 60 men paraded at 1.30 pm for defence work on the Bluff (M. R. 28)	
3·1·16	3, 3+C.9.4 one casualty for horses, recently wounded.	
4·1·16	Routine duties as usual	
5·1·16	Routine duties as usual	
6·1·16	do	
7·1·16	do	
8·1·16	do	
9·1·16	do	
10·1·16	do	
11·1·16	do	
12·1·16	do	
13·1·16	do	
14·1·16	do	
15·1·16	do	
16·1·16	do	
17·1·16	do	
18·1·16	do	
19·1·16	do	
20·1·16	do	
21·1·16	do	
22·1·16	do	
23·1·16	do	
24·1·16	do	
25·1·16	do	
26·1·16	do	
27·1·16	do	
28·1·16	do	
29·1·16	do	
30·1·16	do	
31·1·16	do	

Major
Comm'd'g Squadron

February 1916

C. Squadron
North Irish Horse
III Division
Vol VI

WAR DIARY
INTELLIGENCE SUMMARY
Army Form C. 2118

Hour, Date, Place		Summary of Events and Information	Remarks and references to Appendices
1.2.16	III Div	Routine duties as usual	
2.2.16	"	do	
3.2.16	"	do	
4.2.16	"	do	
5.2.16	"	Sqdn paraded at 8AM and marched to billets at ANEKE remaining there for the night	map ref:-
6.2.16	"	Sqdn paraded at 9.15AM and proceeded to new billets at ST MARTIN in Div Rest Area	map ref:-
7.2.16	"	Routine duties as usual	
8.2.16	"	do	
9.2.16	"	do	
10.2.16	"	Sqdn paraded at 8.30am for the purpose of flagging boundary line of Div training area in Div Rest Area	
11.2.16	"	Flagging of Training Area was completed by Squadron	
12.2.16	"	Routine duties as usual	
13.2.16	"	Squadron Training	
14.2.16	"	do	
15.2.16	"	do	
16.2.16	"	do	
17.2.16	"	do	
18.2.16	"	do	
19.2.16	"	do	
20.2.16	"	do	
21.2.16	"	do	
22.2.16	"	do	
23.2.16	"	do	
24.2.16	"	do	
25.2.16	"	do	
26.2.16	"	do	
27.2.16	"	do	
28.2.16	"	do	
29.2.16	"	do	

Major
Commanding Squadron
3/16

3

C Sqt N Irish Horse

Vol VII

Army Form C. 2118.

WAR DIARY
—or—
INTELLIGENCE SUMMARY.
(Erase heading not required.)

"C" Squadron, North Irish Horse
Divisional Mounted Troops
3rd Division
B.E.F.

No. 1

MARCH 1916

Instructions regarding War Diaries and Intelligence Summaries are contained in F.S. Regs., Part II. and the Staff Manual respectively. Title pages will be prepared in manuscript.

Hour, Date, Place			Summary of Events and Information	Remarks and references to Appendices
	1.3.16	3rd Division At St.Martin R.33a.8.4	Routine duties and Squadron Training	J.J.G.
	2.3.16	Do. Do.	Do. (Map 24A)	J.J.G.
	3.3.16	Do. Do.	Do.	J.J.G.
	4.3.16	Do. Do.	Do.	J.J.G.
	5.3.16	Do. Do.	Do.	J.J.G.
	6.3.16	Do. Do.	Do.	J.J.G.
1.P.M.	7.3.16	Do. at Bayenghem	The squadron marched to new billets at Bayenghem – K.31a.	J.J.G.
	8.3.16	Do. Do.	Do. (Map 24A)	J.J.G.
	9.3.16	Do. Do.	Routine duties	J.J.G.
	10.3.16	Do. Do.	Do. One N.C.O. & 12 men proceeded to A.P.M. V Corps for traffic control post duty	J.J.G.
6.30 A.M.	11.3.16	Do. Do.	The Squadron marched from Bayenghem to new billets at Hartford I.30.b. (Map 24)	J.J.G.
9 A.M.	12.3.16	Do. at Hartford	The squadron marched to new billets at Boeschepe	J.J.G.
	13.3.16	Do. at Boeschepe R.10a.2.5 (Map 24)	Routine duties	J.J.G.
	14.3.16	Do. Do.	Do.	J.J.G.
	15.3.16	Do. Do.	Do.	J.J.G.
	16.3.16	Do. Do.	Do.	J.J.G.

Army Form C. 2118.

C. Sqdn. North Irish Horse
Divisional Mounted Troops
3rd Division BEF

WAR DIARY
~~INTELLIGENCE~~ SUMMARY.

(Erase heading not required.)

MARCH 1916

Instructions regarding War Diaries and Intelligence Summaries are contained in F. S. Regs., Part II. and the Staff Manual respectively. Title pages will be prepared in manuscript.

Hour, Date, Place			Summary of Events and Information	Remarks and references to Appendices
4.30 P.M.	17.3.16	3rd Division at BOESCHEPE	a party of 45 N.C.Os & men under the command of Major Holt, waring [proceeded] to VOORMEZEELE (I 36 D Map 28) to dig Cable Trenches for 76 Brigade 3rd Division. This party returned at 3.30 a.m.	J.G.
	18.3.16	do	Routine duties	J.G.
3.45 P.M.	19.3.16	do	do. a party of 40 N.C.Os & men under the Command of Capt. J Grant proceeded to 76th Bde H Q (I 20 C 6.2 Map 28) on a working party, returning at 3.30 A.M.	J.G.
5.30 P.M.	20.3.16	do	do. a party of 40 NCOs & men under the Command of Major Waring proceeded to VOORMEZEELE on a working party, returning at 4 AM	J.G.
5.15 P.M.	21.3.16	do	do. 40 NCOs & men proceeded to VOORMEZEELE on a working party, returning at 4.30 AM under the Command of Capt R.A.B. Henry	J.G.
5.30 P.M.	22.3.16	do	do. 40 NCOs & men under the Command of Capt Grant proceeded to VOORMEZEELE on a working party, returning at 3.45 A.M.	J.G.
	23.3.16	do	Routine duties	J.G.
	24.3.16	do	do	J.G.
	25.3.16	do	do	J.G.
9. P.M.	26.3.16	do	do Nos 1,2,3 Troops under the Command of Major Waring proceeded to DICKEBUSCHE (H.33. B Map 26) for the purpose of act to prisoners	J.G.
	27.3.16	do	do	J.G.
	28.3.16	do	This party was retained to clear communication trenches and batteries :- THE MOUND - ⊙ B.C. 10.9 Map 28	J.G.

G. Whitmore, Major
Comdg Sqdn N.I.H.

C/Sqd N.I. Horse
—————
Vol VIII

Army Form C. 2118

No 3

WAR DIARY
or
INTELLIGENCE SUMMARY.
(Erase heading not required.)

Instructions regarding War Diaries and Intelligence Summaries are contained in F.S. Regs., Part II. and the Staff Manual respectively. Title pages will be prepared in manuscript.

Hour, Date, Place		Summary of Events and Information	Remarks and references to Appendices
29.3.16	3rd Division	The party used at DICKEBUSCHE for the purpose of clearing trenches - O.b.C 10.9 may 28	Sg.
30.3.16	do	do	Sg.
31.3.16	do	do	

(9 29 6) W 4141—463 100,000 9/14 H W V Forms/C. 2118/10

Army Form C. 2118.

"C" Squadron NORTH IRISH HORSE
Divisional Mounted Troops 3rd Division

WAR DIARY
or
INTELLIGENCE SUMMARY.
(Erase heading not required.)

APRIL 1916

Hour, Date, Place		Summary of Events and Information	Remarks and references to Appendices
3rd Division	1.4.16	Routine duties.	J.G.
	2.4.16	do	J.G.
	3.4.16	do	J.G.
	4.4.16	do	J.G.
	5.4.16	do	J.G.
	6.4.16	do	J.G.
	7.4.16	do	J.G.
	8.4.16	do	J.G.
	9.4.16	do	J.G.
	10.4.16	The Squadron marched to new billets at HARTIFORD. I 30 b (sheet 24)	J.G.
	11.4.16	Routine duties	J.G.
2nd Cav. Division	12.4.16	The Squadron marched to new billets at ARQUINES for the purpose of training with 2nd Cavalry Division	J.G.
	13.4.16 to 26.4.16	Training with 2nd Cavalry Division	J.G.
3rd Division	27.4.16	The Squadron marched to billets at HARTIFORD.	J.G.
	28.4.16	The Squadron marched to new billets at WESTOUTRE (M.14 Central) (sheet 28)	J.G.
	29.4.16	One Officer and 12 men took over observation duties at KEMMEL (N.21 Central) from Yorkshire Hussars. No 4 Troop (Cpt. Whitaker) (increased) to 2nd Div HQ. at BAILLEUL S.14 (sheet 28)	J.G.
	30.4.16	to relieve Div HQ. Troop. Routine duties.	J.G.

W. Kerr Capt
for Major
Commdg Sqdn

1.5.16.

Army Form C. 2118.

WAR DIARY
or
INTELLIGENCE SUMMARY.

(Erase heading not required.)

"C" Squadron North Irish Horse

MAY 1916

Hour, Date, Place		Summary of Events and Information	Remarks and references to Appendices
1.5.16	WESTOUTRE 3rd Division	Capt. R.A.B. HENRY and 16 O.R. attached to V Corps H.Q. for duty.	#MR
2.5.16	"	Lieut. T.H.M. LEADER and working party proceeded to KEMMEL for the purpose of constructing defence works	#MR
3.5.16 to 7.5.16	"	Routine duties	
8.5.16	"	The Squadron marched out from WESTOUTRE at 6 A.M. and halted for the night at BUSNES	#MR
9.5.16	"	Marched out from BUSNES at 6 A.M. and rested for the night at HERLIN-LE-SEC	#MR
10.5.16	"	Left HERLIN-LE-SEC at 6 A.M. and marched 15 km and halted at VAL-DE-MAISON. Attached to 49th (West Riding Division)	#MR
11.5.16 to 13.5.16	49th Div.	The Squadron to form part of X Corps Cavalry Regiment.	#MR
14.5.16	"	Routine duties at VAL-DE-MAISON.	
18.5.16	"	Capt. F.G. Wrichan, Lieut T.H.M. Leader & 15 NCOs & men attached to 153rd & 143rd Brigades R.F.A. for a tour of the observation posts of 36th Div. Artillery front.	#MR
19.5.16	"	Routine duties	
20.5.16	"	Capt. J. Grant & a working party proceeded to MARTINSART for duty in connection with 36th (Ulster) Division	#MR
21.5.16	"	Capt. R.A.B. HENRY & party & NCOs & men relieved Capt. F.G. Wrichan & party at 36th Div. observation posts.	#MR #MR
22.5.16 to 24.5.16	"	Routine duty; Capt. HENRY and party returned to camp from observation posts – 24.5.16.	#MR

Army Form C. 2118.

WAR DIARY
or
INTELLIGENCE SUMMARY.

(2) "C" Sqdn. North Irish Horse

May 1916

(Erase heading not required.)

Instructions regarding War Diaries and Intelligence Summaries are contained in F. S. Regs., Part II. and the Staff Manual respectively. Title pages will be prepared in manuscript.

Hour, Date, Place	Summary of Events and Information	Remarks and references to Appendices
25.5.16 4PM Div	Routine duties.	
26.5.16 "		
27.5.16 "	Capt F.S. Wrixon & 25 N.C.Os & men relieved Capt J Brand & party at MARTINSART.	
28.5.16 to 31.5.16	Routine duties.	

J H Meany Major
Commdg C Sqdn N.I.H.
1.6.16.

WAR DIARY
INTELLIGENCE SUMMARY

C'Sqdn NORTH IRISH HORSE

JUNE 1916

Hour, Date, Place	Summary of Events and Information	Remarks and references to Appendices
1.6.16	The Squadron marched from VAR-DE-MAISON at 6 AM & arrived 15 HEDAUVILLE (M 36 a - sheet 57D) (P 34 d. sheet 57D) for duty with 36th (ULSTER) Division. Billeted in HEDAUVILLE WOOD. Routine duties	XIII
2.6.16	"	XIII
3.6.16	Capt. E.S. UPRICHARD & party of 25 NCOs & men returned from working duties at MARTINSART (W 3 a sheet 57D) Routine duties at HEDAUVILLE.	XIII
4.6.16 to 6.6.16	The Squadron took part in 36th Division manoeuvres Routine duties. The Squadron found number of working parties for 36th Division in connection with defensive works and barbed wire cable.	XIII
9.6.16		XIII
10.6.16 to 15.6.16		XIII
16.6.16	Marched 15 kilos to FORCEVILLE. (P 21 central sheet 57D) Routine duties & working parties.	XIII
19.6.16 20.6.16 21.6.16		
22.6.16 to 30.6.16	Marched to Regt. HQ at TOUTENCOURT were there joined by 6th Inniskilling Dragoons (Lance Sqdn) and "B" Squadron North Irish Horse — Unit of X Corps Cavalry Regt. Routine duties	(U.I.C (sheet 57D) XIII

B.M. Neury Major
CmdgC.Sqdn N.I.H.
30.6.16

3RD DIVISION
DIVL. TROOPS

3RD DIVL. CYCLIST COY.
JAN - MAY 1916.

WAR DIARY
or
INTELLIGENCE SUMMARY.
(Erase heading not required.)

Army Form C. 2118.

January 1916

Unit: 3rd DIVISIONAL CYCLIST COY. A.O.

Hour, Date, Place	Summary of Events and Information	Remarks and references to Appendices
1	Ordinary Routine	2/1
2	"	3/1
3	"	4/1
4	"	5/1
5	"	6/1
6 SK728 I.31.c (10.000) 1 Officer & 25 Men proceeded to 46th Bde for wiring		7/1
7	Ordinary Routine	8/1
8	"	9/1
9	"	10/1
10	"	11/1
11	"	12/1
12	"	13/1
13	"	14/1
14	"	15/1
15	"	16/1
16	"	17/1
17	"	18/1
18	"	19/1
19	"	20/1
20	"	21/1
21	"	22/1
22 SK728 I.34.c (41,850) Ordinary Routine. R.S. 290 Lofts are assumed		23/1
23	Ordinary Routine	24/1
24	"	25/1
25	"	26/1
26	"	27/1
27	"	28/1
28	"	29/1
29	"	30/1
30	"	31/1
31	"	

O.C. 3rd DIVNL. CYCLIST COY. A.O.W.

WAR DIARY
or
INTELLIGENCE SUMMARY.

(Erase heading not required.)

Army Form C. 2118.

February 1916   3RD DIVISIONAL CYCLIST COY. A.C.C.

Instructions regarding War Diaries and Intelligence Summaries are contained in F. S. Regs., Part II. and the Staff Manual respectively. Title pages will be prepared in manuscript.

Place	Hour, Date,	Summary of Events and Information	Remarks and references to Appendices
	1	Ordinary Routine	
	2	"	
	3	"	
	4	Working Party returned to billets in BOESCHEPE	
	5		
	6	I 3RD/47 Company marches to WEAMERS CAPPEL arriving at 2-30 P.M.	
	7	RELEASE OF THE RUSH Company marches to ST MARTIN AU LAERT arriving at 1-0 P.M.	
	8	Ordinary Routine	
	9	Platoon Parades	
	10	"	
	11	Lieut T.R. Burnett and 34 O.R. joined Coy. for further training	
	12	Ordinary Routine and inspections	
	13		
	14	Individual training commenced	
	15	"	
	16	"	
	17	"	
	18	"	
	19	End of Individual training. Inspections	
	20	Ordinary Routine	
	21	Platoon training commenced	
	22	"	
	23	"	
	24	"	
	25	"	
	26	End of Platoon training	
	27	Company training commenced	
	28	"	
	29	"	

E. McAine Capt
O.C. 3RD DIVNL CYCLIST COY. A.C.C.

WAR DIARY
or
INTELLIGENCE SUMMARY.

(Erase heading not required.)

March 1916 Army Form C. 2118.

Unit: 3RD DIVISIONAL CYCLIST COY. A.C.C.

Place	Hour, Date	Summary of Events and Information	Remarks and references to Appendices
	1	Company training	
	2	" "	
	3	" "	
	4	" "	
	5	" "	
	6	" "	
	7	Company marched to BAYINGHEM	
	8	Ordinary Routine	
	9	" "	
	10	Lieut T.R. Barnett & 26 O.R. left the Company for Cyclist Control duty.	
SHEET 7 – 60,000 I.30 A.S.O.	11	Company marched to HARDIFORT	
SHEET 27 R.10.A.15	12	Company marched to BOESCHEPE arriving 11-20 a.m.	
	13	Ordinary Routine	
	14	" "	
	15	" "	
	16	" "	
	17	" "	
	18	" "	
SHEET 27 I.34.C.	19	1 Officer and 34 OR proceeded to 9th Bde for wiring	
	20	Ordinary Routine	
	21	" "	
	22	" "	
SHEET 27 I.33.A	23	Working Party left Boesinghe at 8.30pm. One M. killed at YPRES [?] by 8th Brigade	
	24	Ordinary Routine	
	25	" "	
	26	" "	
	27	Working Party returned from YPRES to BOESCHEPE	
	28	Ordinary Routine	
	29	" "	
	30	" "	
	31	" "	

O.C. 3RD DIVNL. CYCLIST COY. A.C.C.

WAR DIARY
or
INTELLIGENCE SUMMARY.

(Erase heading not required.)

Army Form C. 2118.

April 1916.

3RD DIVISIONAL CYCLIST COY. A.C.C.

Hour, Date, Place	Summary of Events and Information	Remarks and references to Appendices
1		
2	Ordinary Routine	
3	"	
4	"	
5	"	
6	"	
7	"	Inspection
8	"	
9	"	
10 Sheet 27 2/500 I.30.C.3.9.	Company marched to IEFORT going for linner & training with 2 Inf. Div.	
11	Coy. Remained at HARDIFORT	
12	Company marched to ELMENTEL. Eight hour journey owing to bad weather	
13	Returns for officers at 3.0 P.M. by Gen. Haldrens comdg 3rd Inf. Divn.	
14	Regt. had to work with 2 other Divisional Mounted troops.	
15	Officers + NCO staff ride	
16	Ordinary Routine	
17	Outdoor Orderly Guards	
18	Advance Guard scheme	
19	In training. Owing to bad weather Lecture in afternoon.	
20	Rear Guard scheme. Lecture in afternoon	
21	Rear Guard scheme against another Divisional Mounted Troops.	
22	Outpost scheme	
23	Ordinary Routine	
24	Advance Guard scheme against another Divnl Mtd Troops.	
25	Flank Guard scheme	
26	Advance Guard scheme near LICQUES under Major NORTH comdg. M.M.G. 2	
27 Sheet 27 2/5000 I.30.C.3.9.	Marched to HARDIFORT. Halted for 2 hours at TATING H.M. Started 10.52 a.m. HE 4.10 p.m.	
28 Sheet 27 2/5000 M.16.C.3.9.	Marched to WESTOUT RE Started 9.55 a.m. arrived 1.30 P.M.	
29	Settled into billets. Likely to be here for some considerable time	
30		

Eugene Capt
O.C. 3RD DIVNL CYCLIST COY. A.C.C.

WAR DIARY or INTELLIGENCE SUMMARY.

Army Form C. 2118.

May 1916. 3rd Divl. Cyclist Company

Hour, Date, Place	Summary of Events and Information	Remarks and references to Appendices
1	Ordinary Routine.	
2		
3		
4	12 O.R.s rank attached to 76th Bde for wiring trenches	
5	Ordinary Routine	
6		
7		
8		
9		
10	1 man wounded with wiring party	
11	Working party returned. 9 Bicycles from 76th Bde at Stps.	
12		
13	O.R. proceeded to 76th Bde for attachment 2 new members of this party	
14	Ordinary Routine	
15		
16	1 Off. & 24 O.R. reported Company from 3rd Divn having attached to that Bde for duty	
17	Ordinary Routine	
18		
19	12 O.R. relieves wiring party with 76th Bde.	
20	Ordinary Routine.	
21		
22		
23	Working parade to fixed dKills for 76th Bde.	
24		
25		
26	Church Parade	
27		Ordinary Routine
28	R.A.&C.S.R. Log paraded at 12 Noon & marched to FLETRE	
29	(start 8.45 a.m.) Ordinary Routine	
30		
31	Coy paraded 10 A.M. marched to RACQUINGHEM arriving 12.25 P.M.

E Hughes. Capt.
O.C. 3RD DIVNL. CYCLIST COY. A.C.C.

3RD DIVISIONAL CYCLIST COY. A.C.C.

To,

The Officer i/c Army Cyclist Corps Records.
Hounslow.

With reference to the attached. The following is the information required as accurately as we can give it.

(i) This Company was formed on May 29th 1914. On August 4th the Company was dispersed & Officers & Men rejoined their units for Mobilization. On August 20th the Company, reinforced by 70 men from the Division, reformed at AULNOYE, in Northern France

(ii) Until December 1914, this Company was reinforced by men detached from their battalions in the 3rd Division. These men, as well as the original number, who also came from the different battalions of the Division, were transferred to the Army Cyclist Corps on January 12th 1915.

(iii) This Company was stationed at TIDWORTH from May 29th to August 4th 1914.

(iv) This Company was in action for the first time on August 22nd 1914. It took part in the Battles of MONS & LE CATEAU.

It did Rearguard work for the Division during the retreat, & Advance-Guard work during the Advance from CHATRES to the AISNE. It moved with the Division in September from the AISNE to FLANDERS.

It remained in the neighbourhood of NEUVE CHAPPELLE till the end of October when it moved with the Division to YPRES. It has been working on the line between HOOGE & KEMMEL ever since.

(v)

Nov 13th 1914 Lieut. E.S. Swaine (Northumberland Fusiliers) wounded EAST of HOOGE. Rejoined Coy Feb 13th 1914

Feb 12th 1915 Captain. A.C. Forster, (Royal Fusiliers) sent home sick. He rejoined his Regiment from Hounslow & has since been reported "Missing" (believed killed).

June 2nd 1915. Captain. G. Wolfe. (10th Bn Royal Scots) Missing, believed killed, at HOOGE.

June 6th 1915. Lieut. E.S. Swaine (Northumberland Fusiliers) Wounded at HOOGE. Rejoined Coy, October, 9th 1915

Sept 25th 1915 Lieut. H. Ibbitson. (Leicester Regt.) Wounded at HOOGE.

3

No 965 Pte Doherty. J. was awarded the Distinguished Conduct Medal for carrying Despatches under shell-fire on 15th Sept 1914. at VAILLY (AISNE.)

(VI) Drafts arrived on the following dates:-
Dec 8th 1914. 1 Officer + 24 Men. Name of Officer, Lieut C.H. Attfield (8th Essex Regiment)

Jan 26th 1915, 1 Officer 4 Men. Name of officer, Captain G. Wolfe. (10th Bn Royal Scots)

June 24th 1915. 20 Men. no officer.

In addition to the above, 21 Men joined the Company in small parties on various dates.

(VII) In the Field Almanac 1915 (Official Copy) it states that "First shot fired between German & British Forces took place at 12.40. p.m. August 23rd 1915.
This Company exchanged shots with German Cavalry before NOON on August 22nd 1915. One German Uhlan was wounded & his lance captured.

E Hwaine Captain
O.C. 3RD DIVNL. CYCLIST COY. A.C.C.

1 2 NOV 1915

The Officer Commanding,

3rd Divisional Cyclist Company.

To enable me to comply with para 1930 King's Regulations 1912, please forward the following information:-

(i) The Date of Formation of Company.

(ii) Any unusual means by which it was recruited or transfers received.

(iii) The Stations at which it was employed and the dates of its arrival at and departure from such Stations. 4th Aug. Reformed 20th

(iv) The Military operations in which it has been engaged, and its achievements.

(v) The names of all officers killed and wounded, and the name of any officer or soldier who has specially distinguished himself in action.

(vi) Drafts received and despatched, their strength, dates of their arrival and departure and the names of officers who accompany them. Drafts numerically weaker than an Officer Party should not be separately specified.

(vii) Any other matter which may be considered of historical importance.

HOUNSLOW. *[signature]* Major for Colonel
29-10-15   I/C Army Cyclist Corps Records Hounslow.

3RD DIVISION
DIVL ARTILLERY

23RD BRIGADE R.F.A.

AUG - DEC 1914

3rd Divisional Artillery.

23rd BRIGADE R. F. A.

AUGUST 1914. to 5/9/14

23 Bde
RFA
46-h-9-14

Army Form C. 2118.

WAR DIARY
or
INTELLIGENCE SUMMARY.

(Erase heading not required.)

Instructions regarding War Diaries and Intelligence Summaries are contained in F. S. Regs., Part II. and the Staff Manual respectively. Title pages will be prepared in manuscript.

Hour, Date, Place	Summary of Events and Information	Remarks and references to Appendices
5.15 A.M. 4 Aug 1914 Bulford Camp	Order to mobilize received	
5th Aug 1914	First day of mobilization	
14 to 17 Aug 1914	Mobilization reported complete	
18 Aug 1914	Entrained at Southampton on S.S. "Hare"	
19 Aug 1914	on steamships "SATURNIA" and "MINNEAPOLIS" Arrived at "HAVRE" and occupied a rest camp area BLEVILLE for 24 hours	
20 Aug 1914	Brigade entrained by night and reached ADLINOYE and LANDRICIES on night of 21st	
21st Aug 1914	Marched at 8 a.m. to LA LONGUEVILLE	
22nd Aug 1914	Bivouacking there for a few hours. Marched at 3.30 a.m. to area of 9th Infantry Brigade to the vicinity of CIESMES (somewhat Belgian frontier)	German cavalry reported advancing in strength on MONS from a few miles N.E.
Sunday 23rd Aug 1914 (CIESMES)	Took up position in the vicinity of Divisional reconnd. positions 23rd Brigade detailed to assist 9th Infantry Brigade in defence of Mons	

Army Form C. 2118.

WAR DIARY
or
INTELLIGENCE SUMMARY.
(Erase heading not required.)

Instructions regarding War Diaries and Intelligence Summaries are contained in F.S. Regs., Part II. and the Staff Manual respectively. Title pages will be prepared in manuscript.

Hour, Date, Place	Summary of Events and Information	Remarks and references to Appendices
Sunday 23rd Aug. 1914 2 p.m.	Two sections of 109 Battery placed in position in Mons arriving within rifle distance of Farmicourts. A section each 107 and 108 Battery entrenched at WERIEDS. The remaining 2 were held in reserve. Only a minor resistance offered by the infantry at this farm causing 2	
4.30 p.m.	all had retired on FRAMERIES by 4.30. Guns withdrawn to an entrenched position one mile N.E. of FRAMERIES. Here they came under the orders of 7th Infantry Brigade who were entrenched to west of locality.	
8.30 p.m.	Bivouacked in rear of position for the night. No casualties.	

Army Form C. 2118

WAR DIARY
or
INTELLIGENCE SUMMARY.
(Erase heading not required.)

Instructions regarding War Diaries and Intelligence Summaries are contained in F. S. Regs., Part II. and the Staff Manual respectively. Title pages will be prepared in manuscript.

Hour, Date, Place	Summary of Events and Information	Remarks and references to Appendices
3.45 a.m. 24 Aug 1914	ing Battery detailed to proceed to FRAMERIES to assist the 9th Infantry Brigade; only one section brought into action and fired continued against the German infantry and a battery. This section was under heavy rifle and artillery fire. Guns withdrawn without loss.	
9.30 a.m.	Casualties up to this night have not then by this white reconnoitring for another position. There were 6 killed by high explosive shell whilst wagon body. For his services on this day, 2nd Lieut. ... was for his services on this day, 2nd Lieut. ... was recommended to other units put on our rear Lopez D. Johnson the 8.3 Brigade the following morning.	

Army Form C. 2118.

WAR DIARY
or
INTELLIGENCE SUMMARY.
(Erase heading not required.)

Instructions regarding War Diaries and Intelligence Summaries are contained in F. S. Regs., Part II. and the Staff Manual respectively. Title pages will be prepared in manuscript.

Hour, Date, Place	Summary of Events and Information	Remarks and references to Appendices
24. August 1914 3.30 a.m.	107 and 108 Batteries occupied overnight positions.	
4.15 a.m.	Firing commenced	
4.30 a.m.	At first a section and afterwards all guns of 107 Battery were switched to the left and engaged German Infantry and C guns then moving N. of FRAMERIES against South Lancashire trenches (about which 107 was situated).	
9.30 a.m.	Under very heavy fire the just, the infantry having been sniped. 107 and 108 Batteries were withdrawn to a position 1½ m. to S.E. to cover retirement firing with effect on the advancing Germans.	Casualties 107 Batt. 2/Lt Wyatt K.W. and four men wounded. 108 Battery four men wounded.
	N.B. A section of the 108th assisted in covering the retirement of 107 & Battery, but previous to this had remained in observation and watched the severe attack of Infantry Brigade on BAVAIE.	
about 10.40 a.m.	M: EREBUS 107 and 108 Batteries withdrew and closed with 7th Infantry Brigade to BERMERIES bivouacked for the night	

(9 29 6) W 3352—1107 100,000 10/15 H W V Forms/C. 2118/10.

WAR DIARY or INTELLIGENCE SUMMARY.

Army Form C. 2118.

(Erase heading not required.)

Instructions regarding War Diaries and Intelligence Summaries are contained in F.S. Regs., Part II. and the Staff Manual respectively. Title pages will be prepared in manuscript.

Hour, Date, Place	Summary of Events and Information	Remarks and references to Appendices
Tuesday 25 Aug 1914 5.30 p.m.	Marched at 4 a.m. and at reached TROUVILLE. Positions reconnoitred, Batteries prepared for action.	
Wednesday 26 Aug 1914 3.30 a.m.	The Bde. Artillery in positions of readiness about 1200 yards S. of INCHY and 1000 yards W. of Troisville.	
4.30 a.m.	107 on right, 108 on centre and 109 on left. Positions overlooking INDE Copse. 107 had a section detached on the forward slopes on the right and 108 a similar section on the right. 108 section opened fire to support this fire and to compel the Germans to disclose of our available resistance on the forward slopes. 109 Battery and one section of 107 were detached to cover the first and only flank (the German Infantry who at that were advancing against the 7th Infantry Brigade from BETHENCOURT	
about 5.30 a.m.		

Army Form C. 2118.

WAR DIARY
or
INTELLIGENCE SUMMARY.
(Erase heading not required.)

Instructions regarding War Diaries and Intelligence Summaries are contained in F.S. Regs., Part II. and the Staff Manual respectively. Title pages will be prepared in manuscript.

Hour, Date, Place	Summary of Events and Information	Remarks and references to Appendices
21. August 1914 3.30 p.m.	A covering position was occupied close to the farm & village of BERTRY	
4. h.m.	Rdhead on BEAUREVOIR which was reached at	
5.30 a.m. on Thursday the Rec 27th Aug 14	107 and a section of 108 arriving the 9th Infantry Bigade as rearguard. At BEAUREVOIR 109 took on this duty which they continued to perform till 7 p.m. the same evening.	
9. a.m.	reached HARGICOURT	
11 a.m.	being passed by enemies Cavalry retired by JEANCOURT, FLECHIN → POEUILLY reaching VERMAND at 7.h.m	
FLECHIN ? 7. h.m.	arriving the remainder of the 3rd Division. N.B. Retirement carried out by 107, 108 and 119 Battys together with R.E. R.A.M.C. ammunition positions trans form up tat no firing.	
10. h.m	Trgn with 9th Infantry Brigade marched as rearguard to 3rd Division	

WAR DIARY
or
INTELLIGENCE SUMMARY.
(Erase heading not required.)

Army Form C. 2118.

Hour, Date, Place	Summary of Events and Information	Remarks and references to Appendices
1 p.m. 	Inclusive of 158 & 107 the Bailey Division section freed the difficult of front the Devonshire Infantry advancing were the slopes N. of WCHY against the 9 Infantry this not 107 shewed Willy now occupied by the enemy; during the morning our position was so [situated] to a fairly strong valley. The left the position of the [altair] was not found and no further steps [assumed] of they we were to break up	
About 3 p.m.	of the guns which were become very sweet. The 9th Division ordered to relieve as the fifth Division had given way on our right. All guns at once withdrawn except the sections of 107 and 108 in [touch] on four [and] slopes who were ordered to [keep] up the ammunition against WCHY when the German infantry were expected to be moving and case that estimate of our [with] [height]. They came then to quickly the guns and the [obstinacy] to [arches] with the infantry. This was nearly fully done. No casualties to detachments and the Infantry suffered very little loss.	

Army Form C. 2118.

WAR DIARY
or
INTELLIGENCE SUMMARY.
(Erase heading not required.)

Instructions regarding War Diaries and Intelligence Summaries are contained in F. S. Regs., Part II. and the Staff Manual respectively. Title pages will be prepared in manuscript.

Hour, Date, Place	Summary of Events and Information	Remarks and references to Appendices
5.30 a.m Friday 28 Aug 1914	reached HAM and overhid a position covering the retirement over the Canal but did not fire	
12 noon	Retired over the Canal reaching QUIROLES (two mile S of MOYAU) at 9 p.m.	
9 p.m.		
Saturday 29 August 1914 7.45 p.m	Marched by night to CUTS: arrived at	
1.30 a.m on Sunday 30 August 1st 5.30 p.m.	Continued the retirement reaching BERNY RIVIERES at	
Monday 31 August	Marched at 7.30 a.m reaching VARIENNES at 5.15 p.m.	
Tuesday 1st Sept. 1914	Marched to BOUILLANCY	
Wednesday 2 Sept 1914	Marched to PENCHARD	
Thursday 3 Sept 1914	Marched to LA LOGE ARTUS one mile S.W. of Forest du MANS	
Friday 4 Sept 1914 10.30 p.m	Marched by night and on Saturday 5th Sept 1914 at 7.15 a.m reached LIVERDY	

EXTRACTS FROM PRIVATE ARTILLERY DIARIES, 3RD DIVISION, 2ND CORPS.

108th Battery, 23rd Brigade R.F.A.

13th Sept.   The 108th Battery advanced to the heights overlooking the AISNE and one section was sent to the long spur above CHASSEMY PARK.

Target- Germans entrenching on CHIVRES plateau.

Our other batteries of the 23rd Brigade as far as I can remember were in action to the East of 108th Battery.

"J" Battery R.H.A., 5th Cavalry Brigade.

Night 12th/13th Sept.   Battery billetted at BRAISNE.

13th Sept.   Went out with 5th Cav. Bde. towards CHASSEMY to pursue the Germans across the AISNE, but stayed about the area between BRAISNE AND CHASSEMY all day with the Cav. Bde. and did nothing.
Billetted at BRAISNE for night.

14th Sept.   Went out again with the Cav. Bde. to cross the AISNE at VAILLY and continue the pursuit.
The Greys and I think one other Cavalry Regiment got across the bridge under fairly close range Artillery fire from North flank.(F.A.R.54)
"J" Battery was meant to cross but was stopped by Gen. Chetwode about 400 yards short of the bridge, as the village of VAILLY was full of Cavalry who could not get on as the Infantry attack was held up a short distance beyond VAILLY which was being shelled by the Germans.
The Battery then came into action near a chateau just East of the CHASSEMY-VAILLY road I think about ½ to 1 mile from VAILLY where we shot at a German battery or what we thought was a battery at about 5000 yards. The Cavalry galloped back across the VAILLY bridge in small parties to rendezvous in the woods South of CHASSEMY as pursuit on the front was obviously impossible.
In the afternoon the Battery was withdrawn through these woods, as the road was being heavily shelled(F.A.R. 18) over the ridge West of the AISNE, where it was caught by a 4.2" battery, past the Field Artillery positions and rejoined the 5th Cav. Bde. at CERSEUIL in the evening.

15th Sept.   "J" Battery and 5th Cav. Bde. remained in reserve at CERSEUIL.

16th Sept.   "J" Battery moved via FISMES to JUMIGNY to join the 4th Cav. Bde. on the CHEMIN DES DAMES on the right of the British Front, not a pleasant part of the line at all.

128th Battery, 30th (Howitzer) Brigade R.F.A.

13th Sept.   Moved from BRAINE to CHASSEMY CHATEAU.

14th Sept.   The Battery came into action some way North of CHASSEMY
CHATEAU in the park on the flat ground. The O.P. was about
100 yards behind the battery. The position was a semi-
covered one and the O.P. only saw the upper part of the
valley on the right bank of the river near VAILLY. I think
the 129th Battery was also in action in the Park.
   The Battery did not fire very much this day, but was
shelled at frequent intervals during the day.

15th Sept.   Less firing was done by both sides.
   During the day a position was reconnoitred behind the
ridge which ran down behind the battery position towards
CHASSEMY, and we moved there at dusk, digging in the next
morning. The horses were put into a sort of catacombs, and
the men were also withdrawn there at night.

130th Battery, 30th (Howitzer) Brigade R.F.A.
....

Sept.13th.   Marched out from BRAINE on CHASSEMY road. Shelled from
North-East. 40th Bde R.F.A. had some casualties. March
delayed.
   pm ? hr. One section into action on ridge 2000 yards East of
CHASSEMY watching VAILLY. No targets. Everything more or
less quiet except enemy shelling bridge. A second Section
brought into action exposed the position which was very
heavily shelled. One gun out of action, one wagon burnt,
10 casualties.

Sept.13th/14th Night.   Billets in BRENELLE.

Sept.14th.   Active early. Two Sections 1600 yards East of CHASSEMY
on plateau. One Section 1000 yards North-EAST overlooking
CONDE.
   Not sufficient information as to Infantry movements for
satisfactory support. Fired 2000 rds. Targets enemy
trenches and edges of woods on spurs North-East and North
West of VAILLY. Little movement seen except out of range.
Enemy shelling VAILLY continously especially the bridge
during withdrawal of 5th Cav. Bde.

NOTES.

1. On arrival at the AISNE the telephonic equipment of the
Batteries of R.A. 3rd Div. was in such a bad state that most
batteries had to take up open or, at best, screened positions.
Lines of orderlies were used to pass messages. F.O.O.
impossible but later (? about 18th Sept) enough wire was
raised to maintain one for 30th Bde R.F.A.

2. The steep sided valley with broad river bed and water
meadows made ranges very long from positions under cover. The
18 pdr. Bttys more cramped also for positions were almost
out of range (they had only Shrapnel) throwing a great
strain on ammunition supplies of 4.5" How. Btys.

3. To get closer one How. Bty. (the 128th) occupied a
position on the grounds of the "BOIS MORIN CHATEAU" but
was shelled out of it. Later a forward section was
maintained North of the AISNE but space very cramped and
positions very hard to find.

3. About Sept.15th the enemy cut down all the trees on the
Northern (CHEMIN DES DAMES) plateau that were shown on the
French maps as trig. points or bench marks.

O.O. 40th Brigade R.F.A.

Sept.13th. We marched with the 3rd Div: from BRAINE on VAILLY bridge, When the leading Bty.(49th) debouched from the woods near CHASSEMY and came in view of the heights North of the AISNE, the Boche started shelling with 4.2s pretty briskly. The 49th Bty: came into action on the front, North-West edge of the wood, and the remainder of the Bde: which had not debouched from the wood, reversed and went back. There was nothing to see to shoot at.

The 49th Bty. fired a little in the direction of Boche guns, but it was soon realised that no good was being done as even the approx: position of the Boche guns was unknown. Finally as the Boche fire was pretty intense the detachments were withdrawn.

At night the Bde: bivouacked behind the woods.

Sept.14th. We reached the pontoon bridge the Sappers had made at VAILLY about dawn and the whole Bde. crossed and waited in and about VAILLY for the Infantry to clear the high ground.

The ground North of VAILLY rose steeply at once and was thickly wooded, and no Bty. positions or O.Ps were possible, until we had a little ground to move in. I remember the situation was very vague and I dont think we were able to reconnoitre more than ½ mile or so North of the village. We hunted everywhere for targets and positions and though we were under intermittent rifle and gun fire it all seemed to come out of the blue.

Later on in the morning the Inf. Brigadier told the Colonel that the enemy were getting round our left and that we must clear out back across the river and try and find positions to support the Infantry from there.

By this time the pontoon VAILLY bridge was destroyed.

We sent out a reconnaissance party to go East along the AISNE to look for an intact bridge. One was eventually found at PONT 1 ARCY.

The Bde. moved to this along the road just North of the AISNE practically unmolested save a little M.G. fire from the heights. When we arrived at PONT 'ARCY all was quiet, but as the first battery started to cross salvoes of 4.2s started to fall. The whole Bde. crossed with the loss of about 20 men and 20 horses.

I think it was that night that the whole Bde. got into action North of BRENELLE and just in rear of the crest of the BRENELLE-CHASSEMY ridge.

42nd Brigade R.F.A.

Batteries were in action behind the PLATEAU between BRENELLE and BRAINE.

48th Heavy Battery R.G.A.

For some days the 48th Hy Bty. had been marching with the advanced-guard, in order that advantage might be taken of the long range of the 60 pdrs in the opportunities that were sometimes provided by the long columns of retreating enemy.

Sept.13th. On the 13th Sept. the Division was on the road from BRAINE to CONDE, and I do not think the 48th Battery had got as far as CHASSEMY, when orders were received to support the infantry.

Hitherto/.........

Hitherto the B.C. of the heavy Battery, with one subaltern and two or three men of the B.Cs staff accompanied the C.R.A. who marched with the advanced-guard and was always well in front of most of it. He was thus able to allot tasks to the H.B.B.C. in plenty of time for the latter to be able to make complete reconnaissance and to let his Battery come straight on to the selected position.

Orders were given by the G.O.C. of the Division, to the B.C. to turn his battery and go back through BRAINE, and select a position somewhere about BRENELLE to support the 8th Infantry Bde, who would attack from VAILLY, northwards.

13th Sept. The B.C. ordered the Bty. to march on BRENELLE. An O.P. was selected on the plateau, and a battery position behind the crest, just off the road. The O.P. was in the open, but concealed among the beet-roots, corn stalks, etc, and I consider it justified itself, as the view of the high ground North of VAILLY was good, including ROUGE MAISON FARM, and the woods containing the German machine guns. Also the long road was under observation, the road that runs East and West, South of COURTECON.

As regards the targets shelled, there is nothing of importance that can be set down.

The only possible course was to search for enemy batteries by any indication or probability of position, and to fire at any movement, of which there was quite an amount, because the enemy was not yet comfortably settled in his position. B.C. sent forward his O.O. with signallers to the North end of the plateau on which the O.P. was situated, in order to try and get communication with the 8th Infy. Bde. but he could not do so. A few aeroplane messages were received, I presume from Art. H.Q. but they could only roughly indicate one or two enemy gun positions.

14th Sept. On this day the 8th and 9th Infantry Bdes: were engaged on the slopes running up North of the AISNE and suffered severely from enemy attacks, especially from machine guns. On the 13th Sept. some progress had been made by the 8th Bde. The 48th Battery was in much the same difficulty as on the 13th Sept as regards information re enemy's artillery. I think there were some aeroplane messages received by orderly or telephone. The Battery was of course connected to the C.R.A.'s fighting H.Q. which was also up on the plateau, and the C.R.A. sent orderlies and visited the O.P. often. It may be remarked that the system of the Div.Arty. advanced H.Q's being up among the battery O.Ps was of the greatest possible advantage as regards quickness and co-ordination of fire. Communication with the infantry again was very difficult. I can hardly think that the B.C. could have kept communication with two infantry brigades, and probably the C.R.A's H.Q. is the only means of communication for a medium battery under such circumstances. However, a very sensible thing was done by the 9th Inf. Bde. whose Staff Captain came back, and showed B.C. of 48th Battery over the Director the parts where the enemy machine guns mostly were. It may be said that this was not the work for 60 Pdrs, but in such a situation it was necessary, and there was little counter-battery work to do. The battery shelled the woods where the machine guns were located and also machine guns at FOLEMPRISE FARM, where enemy could actually be seen, and where shelling appeared to be very effective. For all the latter part of the day's firing the 48th Battery was under fire from a German 5-9" battery (2nd Guard Foot Arty) that enfiladed it, or partly so. The men were alternately withdrawn from the guns and then brought back, according to the enemy's shelling, and our fire was kept up till nightfall. 9 men killed and 6 wounded. That night the guns were moved 500 yards back further behind the crest.

An important/.........

An important point to note is that four 60 pdrs, in action to cover the front of a division, have a terrible lot of targets to deal with: often the B.C. was shooting one section, and his subaltern the other. Sometimes all four guns were on different targets. The labour of continual switches was tremendous, and men from the R.F.A. columns, lent by the C.R.A. proved not strong enough to be of any assistance to the big gunners of 48th Battery. In future wars you will have much the same business, as the aeroplanes will be calling up the 60 pdrs batteries unceasingly, if, as so many of you assume, the weather will always be fit for flying.

The enemy was at ROUGE MAISON FARM and in the woods to the South of it. Sometimes we got a shot at enemy ammunition wagons on the move, or traffic on the long road I have spoken of- running East and West; at about 10,000 yds range we stopped the traffic. The battery also engaged enemy counter-attacks, which were plainly visible, with shrapnel.

15th Sept. The guns were now further back on the slope of the hill North of BRENELLE, and branches had been put over the guns to camouflage them from aeroplanes. Large natural caves were found now all over the country, and there was one in the middle of the gun position.

The 15th Sept. brought no appreciable development on the 3rd Division front. The field batteries of the Div:Arty: were all along behind the crest of the plateau North of BRENELLE, and some, I think, were pushed rather forward on the East part. The B.Cs of these batteries sat along a line of haystacks, not far in front of their batteries, like a lot of crows, on their O.Ps. In the midst was one of those sheds which consist of nothing but a roof and uprights, filled with hay. On top of the hay sat the C.R.A. and his staff. Communication was therefore very easy; except when the whole line of haystacks was shelled to blazes, as sometimes happened. I emphasize the extreme value of the Div:Art:O.P. in open warfare. It was a great loss in trench-warfare to have the C.R.A. behind, firmly convinced that all objectives had been obtained, and telephoning to that effect to battery O.Ps., which were firmly convinced that no objectives had been attained.

3rd Divisional Artillery.

23rd BRIGADE R.F.A.

SEPTEMBER 1914.

Army Form 2118.

WAR DIARY
or
INTELLIGENCE SUMMARY.
(Erase heading not required.)

Instructions regarding War Diaries and Intelligence Summaries are contained in F. S. Regs., Part II. and the Staff Manual respectively. Title pages will be prepared in manuscript.

Place	Date	Hour	Summary of Events and Information	Remarks and references to Appendices
	Tuesday 1st Sept 1914		Marched to BOUILLANCY	
	Wednesday 2nd Sept 1914		Marched to TENCHARD	
	Thursday 3rd Sept 1914		Marched to LA LOGE ARTUS / mile S.W. of Forest de MEAUX.	
	Friday 4th Sept 1914		Marched by night to on	
	Saturday 5th Sept 1914	7:15 am	reached LIVERDY.	

Army Form C.2118
23rd Bde RFA HQ

WAR DIARY
or
INTELLIGENCE SUMMARY.
(Erase heading not required.)

Instructions regarding War Diaries and Intelligence Summaries are contained in F.S. Regs., Part II. and the Staff Manual respectively. Title pages will be prepared in manuscript.

Hour, Date, Place	Summary of Events and Information	Remarks and references to Appendices
Sept 6th Sunday - LIVERDY	Information received that French Troops were about to take the offensive. Marched at 6.30 a.m. via LA HOUSSAYE TOULUMIGNY.	
Sept 7th Monday - BUISSON	Marched via COULOMMIER and camped at CHATEAU LE BUISSON	
Sept 8th Tuesday	Marched via CHAUFFRY & REBAIS. A.G. held up near GIBRALTAR. 108 Battery came into action to assist 5th Div on our left. 109 Battery and R.S. Fus pushed through A.G., taking up a position N of ORLY, and shelling retiring Germans - Camped at FEUCHÈRES —	
Sept 9th Wednesday -	9th Brigade and 22nd Bn A.G. to 3rd Div: 107 Battery came into action near N of MANTEUIL and silenced German Battery near BOIS DES ESSERTIS, which the Inhrs eventually captured - Bivouac 1/2 M. N of BEZU. 9th B.A. & 23rd B. A.G. - Marched via MARIGNY on far to NEUILLY. Bivouacked at DAMMARD.	
Sept 10th Thursday - Sept 11th Friday	Marched via NEUILLY to GRAND RUZOY	

WAR DIARY or INTELLIGENCE SUMMARY

Army Form C. 2118.

Hour, Date, Place	Summary of Events and Information	Remarks and references to Appendices
Sept 12th Saturday	Marched through MAAST & BRAINE – 9th 108 & 123rd Bde A.C. A section of 107 Battery assisted in clearing the woods north of BRAINE – Bivouac'd at BREVELLE –	
Sept 13th Sunday	23rd Bde in readiness about ½ an hour to cross 3rd Div crossing The AISNE – I Section 108 Bty came into action about 11 a.m. MET @ CHASSEMY. 107 Battery in action – Will further E covering the crossing of the river by the Royal Scots – Bivouac'd at BREVELLE	
Sept 14th Monday	In readiness ½ M N of BREVELLE – 108Bty in action at 11. on S of PEUPLIER – 109 Bty in action 11.30 – Lt 3 of their guns were in action – The position heavily shelled all day – Returns after dark to bivouac at BREVELLE –	
Sept 15th Tuesday	108Bty in their overnight position at 4.30 a.m. Battery on this ridge – 109 Bty in reserve all day –	
Sept 16th Wednesday	108 & 107 Batteries in their overnight positions at 4.30 a.m. 109 Bty in Reserve. A fairly quiet day. At 4 pm relieved by 23 Brigade – return to BRAINE	

Army Form C. 2118.

WAR DIARY
or
INTELLIGENCE SUMMARY.
(Erase heading not required.)

Instructions regarding War Diaries and Intelligence Summaries are contained in F. S. Regs., Part II. and the Staff Manual respectively. Title pages will be prepared in manuscript.

Hour, Date, Place	Summary of Events and Information	Remarks and references to Appendices
Sept 17th Thursday BRAMNE	In reserve.	
18th Friday	1 reserve relieved 40th Bty in action at 11:30 pm, and bivouacked at BRENELLE	
19th Saturday	107 in position at 4:30 am. 108 Bty in action at daybreak. 108 fired a lot at battery NE of FOREMPRISE farm. Heavy Shrapnel fire in late afternoon.	
20th Sunday	108 & 109 Bty in action at 5 am. Shelled enemy's trenches near ROUGEMAISON. About 4 pm 107 came into action. During the day the Brigade fired about 1000 R.S.	
21st Monday	Very quiet day, in the same position.	
22nd Tuesday	Very quiet day. Lt. Forsyth (109th) killed.	
23rd	Went into bivouac at BRAMNE.	
24th	In reserve at BRAMNE.	
25th	Moved to bivouac just S of BRENELLE.	

Army Form C. 2118.

WAR DIARY
or
INTELLIGENCE SUMMARY.
(Erase heading not required.)

Instructions regarding War Diaries and Intelligence Summaries are contained in F. S. Regs., Part II. and the Staff Manual respectively. Title pages will be prepared in manuscript.

Hour, Date, Place	Summary of Events and Information	Remarks and references to Appendices
Sept 26th	Occupied positions vacated by 40th Bn.	
27th	A very quiet day	
27th	A very quiet day in the same positions	
27th	" " " " "	
28th	" " " " "	
28th	" " " " "	
October 1st	" " " " "	
2nd	" " " " "	
2nd	A very misty day, evacuated the position at 6.45pm	
3rd	and marched to CANAILLE	
4th 5th	Marched at 6pm to TROESMES	
5th	" " " CREPY	
6th	" " " ROBERVAL	
7th	Brigade entrained at COMPIEGNE, LONGUEIL and LE MEUX. Brigade concentrated at BUIGNY	

3rd Divisional Artillery.

23rd BRIGADE R. F. A.

OCTOBER 1914.

Army Form C. 2118.

WAR DIARY
or
INTELLIGENCE SUMMARY.
(*Erase heading not required.*)

Instructions regarding War Diaries and Intelligence Summaries are contained in F. S. Regs., Part II. and the Staff Manual respectively. Title pages will be prepared in manuscript.

Place	Date	Hour	Summary of Events and Information	Remarks and references to Appendices
	1st October		A very quiet day in the same positions.	
	2nd "		A very misty day; evacuated the position at 6.45 pm and marched to CAMAILLE.	
	3rd "		Marched at 6 pm to TROESNES.	
	4th "		" " " " CREPY.	
	5th "		" " " " ROBERVAL.	
	6th "		Brigade entrained at COMPEIGNE, LONGUEIL and LEMEUX.	
	7th "		Brigade concentrated at BUIGNY.	

Army Form C. 2118.

WAR DIARY
or
INTELLIGENCE SUMMARY.
(Erase heading not required.)

Instructions regarding War Diaries and Intelligence Summaries are contained in F.S. Regs., Part II. and the Staff Manual respectively. Title pages will be prepared in manuscript.

Hour, Date, Place		Summary of Events and Information	Remarks and references to Appendices
Oct 8th		Rested at BUIGNY.	
Oct 9th	2 am	Brigade marches at 2.am in rear of 9th Inf Bde. to TOLLENT	
	8.30 am	Arrived at TOLLENT	
	5.30 pm	Marches with 57 Bty RFA and 9th FA	
" 10th	9.15 am	Arrived at TANGRY.	
" 11th	7.15 am	Marches with remainder 9th Bde Group to operate on the Canal nr BETHUNE	
	5.45 pm	Returned to Billet at ECLEME.	
" 12th	7. am	Marches in rear of 9th Bde towards VIEILLE CHAPELLE & FOSSE	
	1 pm	Billeted at LOEON	
" 13th		Brigade in Reserve.	
	7 pm	Bivouaced at LES LOBES.	
" 14th		Brigade in Reserve.	
" 15th	2. pm	Brigade in Reserve. Reconnoitred position	

Army Form C. 2118.

WAR DIARY
or
INTELLIGENCE SUMMARY.
(Erase heading not required.)

Instructions regarding War Diaries and Intelligence Summaries are contained in F.S. Regs., Part II. and the Staff Manual respectively. Title pages will be prepared in manuscript.

Hour, Date, Place		Summary of Events and Information	Remarks and references to Appendices
Oct 16	4 a.m.	Moved out of billets at his bases to occupy positions, which had been evacuated by H.Q.R.R.	
	7.30 a.m.	Advance resumed. 107 Bty in action R of LA COUTURE, 109 Bty at X roads W of Du of PONT du HEM.	
		107 accompanied Mgr's column at Brigade	
		109 " " " left	
		108 in Reserve	
this day	4 pm	Columns held up short of AUBERS	
	5 pm	The attack not proceeded with on account of the mist	
		Bivouacked on RUE DE BACQUEROT	
17th	6 am	Moved without opposition on AUBERS	
	noon	On seetin 180 (?) Bde came into action against FROMELLES	
		In the afternoon the whole Brigade was in action between AUBERS and HAUT POMMEREAU, supporting the attack on HERLIES	
	7 pm	Billetted near PIETRE	

WAR DIARY or INTELLIGENCE SUMMARY.

Army Form C. 2118.

Hour, Date, Place		Summary of Events and Information	Remarks and references to Appendices
Oct 18th	5 a.m.	Moved out of Bivouac to positions hld overnight.	
	7.30 a.m.	Firing opened.	
		109 Battery in support of Left attack	
		107 - the centre -	
		108 - advanced to L'AVENTURE.	
		Remained in action all day	
	6 pm	108 Battery supports attack by R. Sc. Fusiliers -	
	8 pm	Returned to Bivouacs. Expenditure of Ammunition 1500 Rds.	
Oct 19th	5.30 a.m	Resumed positions in action 8"/170 with 9"/30"170 at LA CLIQUETRIE.	
		A quiet day.	
		Returned to bivouac at dark.	
Oct 20th	5.30 a.m	Resumed positions.	
	mid day	Brigade firing on Infantry	
		frequent targets and a large expenditure of ammunition (1500 Rds).	
		Returned to bivouac at night leaving 2 guns 107 Battery	
		and two guns 130 Battery in action.	
Oct 21st	5.30 a.m	Resumed positions	
		A quiet day. 108 Battery fired late in the day with effect on	
		enemy S of LE PILLY. Returned to bivouac at dark. 1 Section 107 Battery remaining out -

WAR DIARY or INTELLIGENCE SUMMARY

Army Form C.2118.

Hour, Date, Place		Summary of Events and Information	Remarks and references to Appendices
Oct 22nd	5.30 a.m.	Line of infantry trenches withdrawn. 107 Battery in Reserve. 109 Battery in position near AUBERS. 108 in position near HAUT POMMEREAU. A quiet day -	
	7 p.m.	Retired withdrawn to bivouac near CHAPIGNY at dusk, leaving 4 guns 108 Battery in action.	
	9.20 p.m.	Received orders to retire towards ROUGE CROIX.	
Oct 23rd	2 a.m.	107 Battery in action on RUE de BACQUEROT. 108 & 109 Batteries bivouacked at ROUGE CROIX.	
	5.30 a.m.	108 Battery occupies 2 gun position on RUE de BACQUEROT, with two guns forward just behind the infantry trenches - 109 Battery in Reserve.	
	5.30 p.m.	Withdrawn to bivouac just N.W. of PONT du HEM.	
Oct 24	5.30 a.m.	Position resumed - 108 Battery in Reserve.	
	5.30 p.m.	Returned to billets 2 miles E. of VIEILLE CHAPELLE, leaving 4 guns in action.	
" 25th	5.30 a.m.	Resumed position - 107 Battery in Reserve - A good deal of shell fire during the morning -	
	5.30 p.m.	Returned to bivouac leaving in action 4 guns 108 Battery and two guns 109 Battery -	

Extracts from Battery
Diaries to be inserted
under Bde heading

10th		108th	
Oct. 11th		108th	
12th			
13th			
14th			
15th	107th		
16th	107th		109th
17th	107th	108th	109th
18th	107th	108th	~~109th~~
19th	107th		109th
20th	107th		109th
21st	107th		109th
22nd	107th	108th	109th
23rd	107th	108th	
24th	107th		109th
25th	107th	108th	109th
26th	107th	108th	
27th	107th		109th
28th		108th	109th
29th	107th		
30th	107th		109th
31st	107th	108th	109th

WAR DIARY or INTELLIGENCE SUMMARY

Army Form C. 2118.

(Erase heading not required.)

Hour, Date, Place		Summary of Events and Information	Remarks and references to Appendices
Oct 26th	5.30 a	Resumed position 109 Battery in Reserve.	
	3.30 pm	On of the advanced guns shelled about 3.30 pm and rendered unserviceable (casualties 1 Officer wounded O.R. 1 killed 1 wounded)	
	6 pm	Returned to bivouac, leaving in action 3 guns 108 & 2 guns 109 Bty.	
27	5.30 a	Resumed position (108 Bty in Reserve)	
		109 battery brought a 3rd gun into action in new position.	
		A quiet day	
	5.30 p	Returned to Bivouac, leaving in action 3 guns 109, & 2 gun 107 Battery.	
	6 p	5th attempt went across to look at damaged gun and was lost.	
28	5.30 a	Resumed position 107 Battery in Reserve.	
		A quiet day	
	5.30 p	Return to Bivouac leaving in action 2 guns 109, 3 guns 108 Bty.	
29	5.30 a	Resumed position - 109 Battery in Reserve.	
	5.30 p	Returned to Bivouac leaving in action 3 guns 108, 2 guns 109 Bty.	
30	5.30 a	Resumed position - 108 Battery in Reserve.	
	4.30 p	Relieved W.B. 10 Bde. R.H.A.	

WAR DIARY
or
INTELLIGENCE SUMMARY.

(Erase heading not required.)

Army Form C. 2118.

Hour, Date, Place	Summary of Events and Information	Remarks and references to Appendices
Feb 24th 5.30a.m.	107 Bty in position N of CROIX BARBEE HQ – SW of RICHEBOURG ST VAAST. Resumed position. 108 battery back in their position in RUE DU BACQUEROT. Bde HQ 1 MLE SW of CROIX BARBEE. One section from each battery remained at at midnight.	
6 pm.	remainder to remain as before.	

23rd Bn. R.F.W.

Date	Officers			Other Ranks		
	Killed	Wounded	Missing	Killed	Wounded	Missing
4.10.14				1		
15.10.14						
19.10.14		Lt. J.M. Ferguson		2	2	
20.10.14		Major F. Metcalfe		2	1	
25.10.14					2	
26.10.14	Lt. E.J.B. Anderson				2	1
27.10.14		Lt. B.F. Rhodes				
28.10.14					2	1
1.11.14		Capt E. Herbert			2	1

3rd Divisional Artillery½

23rd BRIGADE R. F. A.

NOVEMBER 1914.

Army Form C. 2118.

WAR DIARY
or
INTELLIGENCE SUMMARY.
(Erase heading not required.)

Instructions regarding War Diaries and Intelligence Summaries are contained in F.S. Regs., Part II. and the Staff Manual respectively. Title pages will be prepared in manuscript.

Hour, Date, Place	Summary of Events and Information	Remarks and references to Appendices
NOVEMBER 1st 6.30 am	Brigade in support of trenches occupied by Seaforth Highlanders 2nd and 9th Gurkhas.	
2nd	All guns were manned during the night as an attack was expected.	
6 am	Relieved by 42nd Bde R.F.A, and retired to billets NEUF MEILLE CHAPELLE.	
3rd 2 pm	Bde & Bty Commanders reconnoitred positions near LA FLINQUE.	
4th		
5. 30 am	Relieved 10th Bde R.F.A. 107 Bty at MANGERIE, 108 at Fm L'ÉPINETTE and 109 Bty at A of RUE du BACQUEROT. The whole in Support of 8th Bde.	
5th	Brigade in action as on 4th Inst.	
6th	" " " " " " "	2 Guns 108 Bty in support of 7th Indian Bde.
7th	" " " " " "	The whole of 108 Bty " " " "
	1st Bde relieved 8th Brigade in the trenches.	
8th 6.0 am	Relieved by 42nd Bde R.F.A. going to billets near Fm MARAIS.	
9th 2 pm	Reconnoitred positions	

Army Form C. 2118

WAR DIARY
or
INTELLIGENCE SUMMARY.
(Erase heading not required.)

Instructions regarding War Diaries and Intelligence Summaries are contained in F.S. Regs., Part II. and the Staff Manual respectively. Title pages will be prepared in manuscript.

Hour, Date, Place	Summary of Events and Information	Remarks and references to Appendices
NOVEMBER		
10th		
6.0 a.m.	Occupied positions 107 near PONT DU HEM, 108 near CROIX BARBEE 109 S.E. of LA COUTURE — The whole in support of N° MEERUT B°.	
12 m.n.	A burst of fire & ¾ hour against NEUVE CHAPELLE — A tremendous cannonade	
11th	Position occupied as on 10th Inst.	
12th	" " " " " "	
	Part of 19th Meerut B° relieved by 8th B°.	
13th	Positions occupied as on 10th Inst.	
9 pm – 12.10 am	Supports operation against German trench in front of Garhwal Brigade.	
14th	Position occupied as on 10th Inst. 33rd Brigade arrived about 11.30 pm.	
15th		
6.0 am	Relieved by 33rd B° Brigade assembled at FOSSE and marched to bivouac near OUTERSTEENE arriving there about 1.30 pm.	
16th	Rested in billets.	

Army Form C. 2118.

WAR DIARY
or
INTELLIGENCE SUMMARY.
(Erase heading not required.)

Instructions regarding War Diaries and Intelligence Summaries are contained in F.S. Regs., Part II. and the Staff Manual respectively. Title pages will be prepared in manuscript.

Hour, Date, Place	Summary of Events and Information	Remarks and references to Appendices
NOVEMBER 17th	Reconnoitred positions under C.R.A. around YPRES	
18th	Reconnaissance by Battery Commanders	
19th 7.45 a.m.	Marched to RENINGHELST where it remained till 3 p.m., at which hour it proceeded to Billets at RENINGHELST. B" and Battery Commanders reconnoitred position near KEMMEL.	
20th 4.30 a.m.	Marched from RENINGHELST and sent to KEMMEL where positions were reconnoitred and occupied by 8.0 a.m.	
21st	Position occupied as on 20th. A quiet day.	One section from each Battery was moved during the night
22nd	" " " "	
23rd to Dec 2nd	" " " "	

M.M.Hammond
Captain & Adjt. XIX R.F.A.

3rd Divisional Artillery.

23rd BRIGADE R. F. A.

DECEMBER 1914.

Copied from diary for November 1914.

23rd November to
2nd December 1914.   Positions occupied as on 20th.

WAR DIARY
INTELLIGENCE SUMMARY.
(Erase heading not required.)

Army Form C. 2118.

Hour, Date, Place	Summary of Events and Information	Remarks and references to Appendices
DECEMBER. 3rd	Brigade withdrawn from position being relieved by 40th D.R.T.A. The King's Visit – Major Tooke with a guard of honor of 100 men proceeded to LOCRE – The remainder of the Bty. quartered in MONT NOIR – His Majesty at MONT NOIR –	40th D.R.T.A.
4th & 5th	Brigade in Reserve.	
6th	Reinoculated for serum.	
7th	Relieves 42nd Bty. in position W. of KEMMEL.	
8th – 13th	Were in occupation of this position – A quiet time –	
14th	Commencing at 7. a.m. a continuous bombardment was kept up throughout the day. General direction being WYTSCHAETE, Mars and Pts. 73 and 74.	
15th	A continuous fire against the same points.	
16th	Bty. HQ., 107 and 108 Batteries were relieved by 40th R.A. at 4 p.m., and went into newn at BERTHEN	
17th	109 Battery relieved at dawn – Brigade in Reserve –	
18th & 19th	Recon. airplanes carried out of position round KEMMEZ	
20th		
21st	Relieved 107 Bty. R.T.A. in position round KEMMEL.	

Army Form C. 2118.

WAR DIARY
or
INTELLIGENCE SUMMARY.
(Erase heading not required.)

Instructions regarding War Diaries and Intelligence Summaries are contained in F.S. Regs., Part II. and the Staff Manual respectively. Title pages will be prepared in manuscript.

Hour, Date, Place	Summary of Events and Information	Remarks and references to Appendices
DECEMBER 22nd — 31st	Remains in occupation of the position — German Trench being intermittently engaged throughout the period.	

J. M. Hammond
Captain
23rd B. Regt.

3RD DIVISION
DIVL ARTILLERY

23RD BRIGADE R.F.A.
107TH, 108TH & 109TH BATTERIES
AUG - OCT 1914

3rd Divisional Artillery.

23rd Brigade R.F.A.

107th BATTERY R. F. A.

AUGUST 1914.

I.

107th Battery R.F.A.
23rd Brigade R.F.A.
IIIrd Division

WAR DIARY
or
INTELLIGENCE SUMMARY.
(Erase heading not required.)

Army Form C. 2118

Instructions regarding War Diaries and Intelligence Summaries are contained in F.S. Regs., Part II. and the Staff Manual respectively. Title pages will be prepared in manuscript.

Hour, Date, Place	Summary of Events and Information	Remarks and references to Appendices
1914		
Aug. 5. Bulford Camp	Order to Mobilize received.	
17th — 11 p.m.	Entrained at 11 p.m.	
18th Southampton 7 p.m.	Embarked on S.S. Minneapolis, American Transport. Fine. Sailed.	
19th HAVRE —	Disembarked & marched to No. 2 Rest Camp — men billeted.	
20. — 6.15 p.m.	Marched to Dock Station & entrained.	
21. — 12.15 a.m.	Train left — via ROUEN to AUMOIS (AULNOIS)	
AULNOIS 5 p.m.	Detrained & marched to LONGUEVILLE to bivouac.	
22. LONGUEVILLE — 5.30 a.m.	Marched behind 9th Inf[ty] B[de] via MALPLAQUET + FRAMERIES to CUESMES + bivouac. Horses watered & fed before dark to fuel. Bivouac up on the hill 1 mile S.E.	
23. CUESMES —	Horses almost foundered to hide from aeroplanes. Reconnoitred positions.	
1 p.m.	Moved to Mt EREBUS. Could see into a section in a close evening attempt to bridge over canal — but not fire. Retired to positions under cover S.D CUESMES — taking M[t] EREBUS. Did not fire — hostile attack to (turn?) W.D. GENLY road	
24.	Occupied same position at 3.0 a.m. Shell came from spot beside N[D] FRAMERIES. Battery was ammed. to the left & brigade staff moved forward to find a lot at a[?] attacking German infantry North of the shield trench	

WAR DIARY
or
INTELLIGENCE SUMMARY.
(Erase heading not required.)

Army Form C. 2118

Hour, Date, Place	Summary of Events and Information	Remarks and references to Appendices
1914 August 24 Cont. p.m.	Ordered to retire - hindered up under heavy musketry & rifle & gun [?]. and S. Pre's & gun - 11 horses killed before the first one wagon - batteries unlimbered with intention of our guns [?] with another fresh [?]. Retired to hands N.W. of NOIRCHAIN & had a fresh at infantry advancing on to our left [?].	
p.m.	Retired again to QUEVY LE PETIT — BLAREGNIES — BAVAI — to bivouac at BERMERIES.	
25th BERMERIES	Marched to TROISVILLE. Met horses S. of MOULIN ST MARTIN. Prepared entrenchment for one section to cover road state N.W. of the MOULIN, where one company infantry trench, facing INCHY. The centre section went to the S. of entrenchments. Remaining 2 guns under cover of the ridge - west of the MOULIN. Shelled German infantry advancing down hill west of INCHY and then in the village of INCHY which [?] retired. In action at LE MOULIN but did not fire.	
26	Retired through BERTRY with 9th Inf. Bde - bivouacked all night.	
27. HARGICOURT.	to HARGICOURT - short halt for breakfast. Then moved forward occupying rear guard position to JEANCOURT & VENDELLES. in after dinner guard position - did not fire - camped VERMAND. 7pm.	
28. VERMAND. 7p.m. 12:30 A.M.	Marched to HAM. remounted [?] head positions [?] did not come into action after.	

Army Form C. 2118

WAR DIARY
or
INTELLIGENCE SUMMARY.
(Erase heading not required.)

Instructions regarding War Diaries and Intelligence Summaries are contained in F. S. Regs., Part II. and the Staff Manual respectively. Title pages will be prepared in manuscript.

Hour, Date, Place	Summary of Events and Information	Remarks and references to Appendices
August—		
28. HAM. 2.pm	Marched to bivouac just N. of NOYON — arriving 7.30 pm	
29. NOYON. 12.15 p.m	Marched out to support Cavalry retirement — did not come into action	
8.p.m	Marched via MOULIN-COURT to MORSAINS	
30. MORSAINS — 2.p.m	continued march through VIC-SUR-AISNE to MONTOIS	
31. MONTOIS. 7.a.m.	Marched via VILLERS COTERETS to VAUCIENNES —	

3rd Divisional Artillery.

23rd Brigade R. F. A.

107th BATTERY R. F. A.

28th AUGUST - 30th SEPTEMBER 1914.

September 1914

87th Battery RFA
23rd Brigade
III tier.

WAR DIARY
or
INTELLIGENCE SUMMARY.
(Erase heading not required.)

Army Form C. 2118

Instructions regarding War Diaries and Intelligence
Summaries are contained in F.S. Regs., Part II.
and the Staff Manual respectively. Title pages
will be prepared in manuscript.

Hour, Date, Place	Summary of Events and Information	Remarks and references to Appendices
Aug 28th HAM.	Marched to Livermez first N. of Noyon - arriving 7:30 p.m.	
29. NOYON 12:45 p.m.	Marched 12:15 p.m. to support Cavalry + RHA retirement - Back to bivouac 4 pm	
8 pm	Marched thro' MOULIN COURT to MORSAINS	
30. MORSAINS 2 pm	Continued march through VIC-SUR-AISNE to MONTOIS.	
31. MONTOIS 7.0.	Marched via VILLERS-COTERETS to VAUCIENNES.	
September 1. VAUCIENNES 9:30 a.m.	Marched to BOUILLANCIE.	
2nd BOUILLANCIE 3:45 a.m.	Marched to PENCHARD.	
3rd PENCHARD 9:15 a.m.	Marched through MEAUX to bivouac between HAUTE MAISON + LOGE ARTUS.	
	Lt Wright gazetted Major in Battery - He joined up in trenches on DAVAL on Aug. 24"	
4th HAUTE MAISON 2 pm	Marched about 2 miles to S. of MONTANSON farm.	
10:30 pm	Marched via CRECY - FORET de CRECY to LIVERDY - 7:50 AM 5th	
5. LIVERDY -	Halt	
6. " 6:30 a.m	Marched via LA HOUSSAYE to LUMIGNY.	

WAR DIARY or INTELLIGENCE SUMMARY.

Army Form C. 2118.

(Erase heading not required.)

Hour, Date, Place	Summary of Events and Information	Remarks and references to Appendices
Sept		
7. LUMIGNY. 12.30 p.m.	Marched via COULOMMIER to Chateau LE BUISSON.	
8. Chateau LE BUISSON. 5.30 a.m.	Marched via REBAIS – BUSSIERES to LES FEUCHERES.	
9. LES FEUCHERES. 5 a.m.	Marched with 9th Bde to NANTEUIL – Cavalry action at (GF.?) old road north of town – Left section enfiladed a battery in action & silenced it – (Battery subsequently captured by Lincoln Regt). Battery was firing from 9.I. & Montagne shooting at troops moving down the road in front of position – Casualties 2 men wounded – 1 horse killed & 3 wounded. In action till dark – then marched to bivouac at VENTELET farm.	
10. VENTELET. 5 a.m.	Marched with van guard (Royal Fusiliers) to MARIGNY. Left section in action against retiring infantry & transport, also the right section – To bivouac at DAMMARD.	
11. DAMMARD. 7.30 a.m.	Marched to GRAND ROZOY.	
12. G. ROZOY. 6 a.m.	——— BRAINE – crossed river – Right section in action & shelled woods under BRENELLE. Bivouac S. of BRENELLE.	
13. BRENELLE. 8 a.m.	Marched to @ 164 on CHASSEMY road. In action facing (val?) behind ??. Then moved to the right to a position (in) VAILLY shelled infantry retiring from bridge & village – ?? at dusk to bivouac just north of BRENELLE	

WAR DIARY
or
INTELLIGENCE SUMMARY.
(Erase heading not required.)

Army Form C. 2118

Instructions regarding War Diaries and Intelligence Summaries are contained in F.S. Regs., Part II. and the Staff Manual respectively. Title pages will be prepared in manuscript.

Hour, Date, Place		Summary of Events and Information	Remarks and references to Appendices
14. BRENELLE	4 a.m.	Marched out of camp - In reserve all day - Returned to same bivouac at dusk -	
15. "	4.45 a.m.	Into action on right of 108th Battery at O164 on CHASSEMY Rd. Fired on Infantry heads NE of VAILLY + on to FOLEMPRISE Farm, which caught fire + was burnt - To same bivouac at dusk -	
16. "	2.30 a.m.	Re-occupied same position. Fired a few rounds at a hayrick on which there was apparently an observation party.	
	4 p.m.	Relieved by 40th Bty (23rd Battery) + moved to bivouac W. of BRAINE -	
17. BRAINE		Rest day	
18. "	3 p.m.	Marched to old bivouac N. of BRENELLE.	
19. BRENELLE		107th in reserve all day - but moved	
20. "	11.55 a.m.	Ordered to occupy own position at O164 - Fired 51 rounds at wood S. of ROUGE MAISON + at haystacks -	
	6.30 p.m.	Left guns in position with a guard + retired to bivouac	
21. "	5 a.m.	Took post on the guns - Shelled [illegible] of [illegible] farm - others Did nothing all day	
	6.30 p.m.	Left guns + went to bivouac	

WAR DIARY
or
INTELLIGENCE SUMMARY

(Erase heading not required.)

Army Form C. 2118.

Instructions regarding War Diaries and Intelligence Summaries are contained in F. S. Regs., Part II. and the Staff Manual respectively. Title pages will be prepared in manuscript.

Hour, Date, Place		Summary of Events and Information	Remarks and References to Appendices
September			
22. BRENELLE	5.a.m.	Took post on the guns	
	8.30.a.m	Shelled N. edge of wood West of FOLEMPRISE farm, at the same time as several other Batteries	
	6.30 pm	Limbered up & took guns back to bivouac.	
23. — " —	7.a.m.	Marched to Bivouac just West of BRAINE	
24. BRAINE		In reserve	
25. — " —	2 pm	Reconnoitred position occupied by 40th & 73rd South of BRENELLE — CHASSEMY road	
	4 pm	Moved to Bivouac just South of BRENELLE	
26. BRENELLE	3.a.m.	Occupied position between 4 guns West of road South of CHASSEMY road & BRENELLE ½ mile North of the road. Left section fired occasionally during the day at Infantry in neighbourhood of OSTEL. Rest of Battery did not fire.	
	6.30 pm	Horses returned to bivouac S. of BRENELLE. Bivouac in same.	
27. Position at CHASSEMY BRENELLE road	6.30 a.m	Manned the guns	
	4 pm	Fired on Trench West of ROUGE MAISON	
	5.30 pm	Fired on to shell S. end of Bois de VERVINS. Tried, but it was out of range	
	6.30 pm	Bivouac in same	

WAR DIARY
or
INTELLIGENCE SUMMARY

(Erase heading not required.)

Army Form C. 2118.

Hour, Date, Place	Summary of Events and Information	Remarks and References to Appendices
September		
28. Porters S. of CHASSEMY BRENELLE Road – 6.30am	Manned guns. Did not fire at all	
6.30 p.m.	Bivouac in camp	
29. — " — 6.30 am	Manned guns "	
3 p.m.	Shelled RAVIN W. of ROUGE MAISON for ten minutes	
4.30 p.m.	" " " " "	
6.30 p.m.	Bivouac in camp	
30. — " — 6.30 am	Manned guns – did not fire all day	
6.30 p.m.	Bivouac in camp	
	(Left Section fired 125 rounds at infantry in OSTEL Valley)	

3rd Divisional Artillery.

23rd Brigade R.F.A.

107th BATTERY R. F. A.

OCTOBER 1914.

107th Battery R.F.A.
23rd Bgde. R.F.A.
III Division

Army Form C. 2118.

WAR DIARY
or
INTELLIGENCE SUMMARY

(Erase heading not required.)

Instructions regarding War Diaries and Intelligence Summaries are contained in F. S. Regs., Part II. and the Staff Manual respectively. Title pages will be prepared in manuscript.

Date	Hour, Date, Place	Summary of Events and Information	Remarks and References to Appendices
October			
1.	Position south of TRENEHE – CHASSEMY Road. 6.30am	Received guns. Fired a few shells during the day at German Infantry patrols East of ROUGE MAISON	
	6.30pm	Bivouac in same.	
2.	6.30 am	Received guns. Thick fog all day. No batteries. Various patrols returned by	
	6pm	Marched via BRAINE – ARCIS – Buzancy to CRAMAILLE arriving 12.30am. Bivouac	
3. CRAMAILLE	5.30 am	Move 2 miles to bivouac alongside road under cover from aeroplanes	
	6pm	Marched (behind 9th Hy Bridge) via BEUGNEUX – GRAND-ROZOY – TIBLY sur OURCQ [?] – No Rate to TROESNE	
4. TROESME	1.30 am	Bivouac alongside road. Twenty by River.	
	6 pm	Marched (behind 9th Hy Bde) via LA FERTÉ MILAN – BOIS DE RETZ – COYOLLES – VAUCIENNES to CREPY.	
5. CREPY.	2.30 a.m	Billeted in large farm	
	6 pm	Marched (behind 9th Hy Bde) via BOUY – RULLY – VILLENEUVE to ROBERVAL.	
6. ROBERVAL	12.30 a.m	Bivouac	

Army Form C. 2118.

WAR DIARY
or
INTELLIGENCE SUMMARY

(Erase heading not required.)

Instructions regarding War Diaries and Intelligence Summaries are contained in F. S. Regs., Part II. and the Staff Manual respectively. Title pages will be prepared in manuscript.

Hour, Date, Place	Summary of Events and Information	Remarks and References to Appendices
October		
6. CM ROBERVAL. 9.a.m.	Ordered to entrain at PONT ST MAXENCE - 4.15 p.m.	
1.p.m.		
1.30 pm	marched to PONT ST MAXENCE	
PONT ST MAXENCE. 3.30 pm	arrived and entrained close to station	
4.10 pm	orders to entrain at LONGUEIL ST MARIE (7 miles) at 5 pm	
LONGUEIL ST MARIE 6 pm	arrived at station. No train ready.	
7 pm	train arrived - all to have been fitted for infantry remains	
	+ things of entrained	
10.5 pm	Train started	
7th NOYELLE 7.a.m.	arrived	
8.30 am	started detraining	
11.am	marched to BUIGNY ST MACLOU	
BUIGNY ST MACLOU 2 p.m.	bivouacked at BONNEVAL farm.	
8	Remained in Bivouac	

Army Form C. 2118.

WAR DIARY
or
INTELLIGENCE SUMMARY
(Erase heading not required.)

Instructions regarding War Diaries and Intelligence Summaries are contained in F. S. Regs., Part II. and the Staff Manual respectively. Title pages will be prepared in manuscript.

Hour, Date, Place	Summary of Events and Information	Remarks and References to Appendices
October		
9th BONNEVAL Farm 2am.	Marched (rear Bde. 9th Brigade) via LE PLESSIEL — CANCHE — LE BOISLE to TOLLENT. Arrived 8 a.m.	
BUIGNY ST: MACLOU		
TOLLENT 8 a.m.	Bivouac till 5.30 p.m.	
5.30 p.m.	Marched to TANGRY	
10th TANGRY 9 a.m.	arrived + billeted	
11th —		
7 a.m.	Marched with 9th Inf. Bde. (9th Bde. left flank guard to 7th[?] Division) via PERNES — FLORINGHEM — BURBURE & HAUTERIEUX (long halt, water + food) then march along — a mile to billets in GUISE farm.	
12th HAUTERIEUX 6.45 a.m.	Marched behind 9th Inf. Bd. to ROBECQ. Long halt, then along tram track towards VIEILLE CHAPELLE. Long halt. Fighting going on in front + night 6 p.m. — back about a mile to billets in small farm in ROBECQ.	
13th ROBECQ 6 a.m.	Marched to LES LOBES & remained there in reserve	
6 p.m.	Bivouac in LA PILATERIE Farm	
14th " LES LOBES	In reserve — Remained in billets — 9 remounts arrived. Sent 5 horses to Vety Hospital. Bright sun and 50.	
15th " 6 a.m.	107 in reserve — marched to[?] ZELOBES & remained there till 10 a.m. then back to billets in LA PILATERIE Farm	
	2 pm Reconnoitred positions round VIEUX CHAPELLE	

Army Form C. 2118.

WAR DIARY
or
INTELLIGENCE SUMMARY

(Erase heading not required.)

Instructions regarding War Diaries and Intelligence
Summaries are contained in F. S. Regs., Part II.
and the Staff Manual respectively. Title pages
will be prepared in manuscript.

Hour, Date, Place	Summary of Events and Information	Remarks and References to Appendices
October 16th LA PLATERIE. 4.a.m	Marched via VIEUX CHAPELLE to CROIX BARBÉE	
8.30 am	Short march in trucks fog via CROIX ROUGE — CHAPIGNY to PIETRE — to attack AUBERS — heavy fire but heavy dash — infantry digging in + battery withdrew to within ½ mile of CROIX ROUGE.	
17. CROIX ROUGE 5.30 am	Marched to St PIETRE	
8.30 am	On little knoll Rgt up the hill to Ht POMMEREAU from Right section coming into action + firing at Infantry at German digging trenches on LILLE — LA BASSEE road. Rhodes Lut 1 gun to LA CLICQUETERIE farm + remainder of battery came into action alongside English Battery.	
1.p.m	Lincoln Rgt attacked + took HERLIERS village supported by Rt battery + centre of 1/130 R.5 (Howitzers)	
7.pm	Battery withdrew to billets on PIETRE road.	
18. Ht POMMEREAU 5.30 am	to occupy position. Known to be taken with Lt Section to LA CLICQUETERIE. Moved forward to LA VENTURE with Scots Guards, who were together with Suffolks going on ahead to give us rest to take La FOURNES. On the South beyond them + were heavily engaged by LA CHATEAU WOOD + recalled with thinly engaged.	
8.pm	Rgt withdrew to same billet	

Army Form C. 2118.

WAR DIARY
or
INTELLIGENCE SUMMARY
(Erase heading not required.)

Instructions regarding War Diaries and Intelligence Summaries are contained in F. S. Regs., Part II. and the Staff Manual respectively. Title pages will be prepared in manuscript.

Hour, Date, Place	Summary of Events and Information	Remarks and References to Appendices
October		
19. H⁴ POMMEREAU 5.30 am	Reoccupied gunpits D.S. gave instructions to LAVENTURE with LINCOLN regiment.	
	Captain Fiske left us to command 109th Battery vice Major Mitchell wounded.	
10 am	Left section shelled LA MAIN road NE of CHATEAU	
11 —	— Centre & Right —	
noon	— — — —	(?) South Local [illegible] —
1 pm	— — — —	(?) — CHATEAU.
2 pm	— — — Shelled Left of CHATEAU briskly	19th killed 'g' COTTERELL D⁰ NOLAN wounded g: FINDLAY (died in Hospital later)
	HERLIES. Battery briskly shelled by long howitzers - No damage - A wagon returning from left section came by & down & one horse were killed & [illegible] 2/Lt H Symons & some gunners went out to clear the team & another shell came & wounded g: Findlay -	
7 pm	Z=1 back to same [illegible]	
20th 5.30 am	Occupied a third position in the gully behind the main one. Observing by telephone from house in LAVENTURE Shelled S.E. of HERLIES. To German attack at various times during afternoon. Repeated gun attempts to support infantry in area of [illegible] to [illegible] attack - but not often fire	

Army Form C. 2118.

WAR DIARY
or
INTELLIGENCE SUMMARY
(Erase heading not required.)

Instructions regarding War Diaries and Intelligence Summaries are contained in F. S. Regs., Part II. and the Staff Manual respectively. Title pages will be prepared in manuscript.

Hour, Date, Place	Summary of Events and Information	Remarks and References to Appendices
21st POMMEREAU	Returned from LAVENTURE & Billetted in same quarters.	
2 am	Guns on trenches in front of CHATEAU moved	
7.60	— German attack returned fire Night	
3 pm	Searches behind hills near the attack repaired to Co.	
	Coy got against our left.	
7 pm	returned to billets leaving Cmdt section out at night to support infantry in advance to own trenches.	
22nd LA PIETRE 5.30 am	In action [L] the entire under Lt Ritchie's & Whitfield (E Sect) in command, 3 battery back to gun Lister at farm a mile back in NEUVE CHAPELLE. Remained there all day.	
	Proceeded to punish [Grade Route CROSS] Withdraws & reached fields on RUE DU PACQUEBOT	
10 pm		
23rd RUE DU PACQUEBOT 5.30 am	After night section to another position near Hamilton, station moved to Seek further H.Q. 7 RA left division attempt a advance on Battle at PONT DU HEM.	

Army Form C. 2118.

WAR DIARY
or
INTELLIGENCE SUMMARY
(Erase heading not required.)

Instructions regarding War Diaries and Intelligence Summaries are contained in F. S. Regs., Part II. and the Staff Manual respectively. Title pages will be prepared in manuscript.

	Hour, Date, Place	Summary of Events and Information	Remarks and References to Appendices
24	PONT DU HEM 5:30 am	5.30 a.m. moved off from position	
	6.30 pm	and after staying in village went to set the trenches to (?) or PONT DU HEM, leaving our section in actn.	
25	5:30 am	Occupied same position - did not fire all day	
	6.30 pm	Lt. Symons went to 3° Ammunition column. To Billets leaving our section in actn.	
26	5:30 am	Occupied same position - did not fire	
	6.30 pm	To Billets leaving our section in actn. Lt. Rhodes wounded during night by bullet.	
27	5:30 am	Occupied same position - fired a few shells at a	
	6.30 pm	target in which Germans were assembling. To Billets leaving our section in actn.	
28	5:30 am	109" Battery occupied our position - retiring at the	
	6.30 pm	left our the night — Battery in reserve in billets all day.	
29	5:30 am	Occupied same position - did not fire	
	6.30 pm	To Billets - leaving our section in actn.	

Army Form C. 2118.

WAR DIARY
or
INTELLIGENCE SUMMARY

(Erase heading not required.)

Instructions regarding War Diaries and Intelligence Summaries are contained in F. S. Regs., Part II. and the Staff Manual respectively. Title pages will be prepared in manuscript.

Hour, Date, Place	Summary of Events and Information	Remarks and References to Appendices
Oct 1917		
30. PONT DU NEM — 5.30 a.m.	Occupied gun positions — there after a few shells of a similar in a village close to Suffolk Reg Trenches	
5 p.m.	Relieved 41st Battery in position just West of CROIX BARBEE, looking across Northern in town behind greater	
31. CROIX BARBEE 5.30 a.m.	Occupied position — just past the A Barracks Cottle (whose position seems) on Section in centre	
6.30 p.m.	Received R. orders attached to Battery (infantry from 49th R. Battery)	

3rd Divisional Artillery.

23rd Brigade R.F.A.

108th BATTERY R. F. A.

AUGUST 1914.

Army Form C. 2118

WAR DIARY
or
INTELLIGENCE SUMMARY.
(Erase heading not required.)

Instructions regarding War Diaries and Intelligence Summaries are contained in F. S. Regs., Part II. and the Staff Manual respectively. Title pages will be prepared in manuscript.

Hour, Date, Place	Summary of Events and Information	Remarks and references to Appendices
	Confidential	
	War Diary of 108th Battery. R.F.A. 23rd Bde F.A III Div N	
	from Mobilization to 31.8.14	
	Volume I	
	W. S. Carey, Major R.F.A	
	Comdg.	

WAR DIARY
or
INTELLIGENCE SUMMARY.
(Erase heading not required.)

Army Form C. 2118

Instructions regarding War Diaries and Intelligence Summaries are contained in F.S. Regs., Part II. and the Staff Manual respectively. Title pages will be prepared in manuscript.

Hour, Date, Place	Summary of Events and Information	Remarks and references to Appendices
6th to 17th August	Mobilisation orders were received on evening of 5th. Mobilisation proceeded very smoothly. Considerable delay was experienced in obtaining Mech-Transport for heavy Draught horses, and the patterns supplied were too large and of inferior workmanship – A.B. 67 for canvas and A.F. B 122 & 103 also were never received in full.	
18th August	Battery entrained for Southampton in 2 trains leaving AMESBURY 1.22 A.M. and 2.22 A.M. Arrived SOUTHAMPTON soon after dawn: Embarkation on board A.T. Co. S.S Minneapolis was completed about midday. The Ship sailed about 8 P.M.	
19th August	Minneapolis entering out of 23rd Bde (less Bde Staff) and other details, Arrived off HAVRE 7.0 A.M. Disembarkation was completed early in the afternoon and troops marched to rest camp No.2, about 8 P.M. No casualties occurred during voyage.	
20 August	Marched to station in HAVRE docks at 6. P.M and entrained. Left about midnight. Sealed orders (BUSIGNY)	

WAR DIARY
or
INTELLIGENCE SUMMARY.

(Erase heading not required.)

Army Form C. 2118.

Instructions regarding War Diaries and Intelligence Summaries are contained in F.S. Regs., Part II. and the Staff Manual respectively. Title pages will be prepared in manuscript.

Hour, Date, Place	Summary of Events and Information	Remarks and references to Appendices
21st August	Situation having been changed to LANDRECIES battery detrained there at 5.30 P.M. and at 7.30 P.M marched in order, in company with 109th Battery for BAVAI. a No Casualties during train journey.	
22. August	Battery arrived LA LONGUEVILLE 3.AM. and resumed it's march at 4.45am for QUESNES arriving there at about 2.P.M. Position were reconnoitred on heights N of FRAMERIES. and Battery BIVOUACED there.	
23. August	Battery proceeded in early afternoon to Mt EREBUS with 107 of Brigade. 2 guns, Mr. Nectar, Lieut Smith were entrenched in pits with commander trench, forming NW to support infantry. The whole Brigade withdrew about 5. P.M. 108th Cd. did not open fire this day. Battery retired to position of higher before, about 1½ mile. S.W. of CIPPY.	
24 August	After engagement of FRAMERIES where 4 guns shelled Mt EREBUS and under Lieut. SMITH, covered the withdrawal of rest of Brigade, Battery came into action about 1200 yds further back and fired in advancing infantry for about ½ hour, then continued retirement on BERMERIES.	

WAR DIARY or INTELLIGENCE SUMMARY.

Army Form C. 2118

(Erase heading not required.)

Hour, Date, Place	Summary of Events and Information	Remarks and references to Appendices
August 25th	Arriving there at dusk via RAVAI. Casualties in this action No. 76635. Pte. Biddlecombe F.W. (Miller, Coy of Rgt) and 2 horses killed, 2 wounded. No of Wounded. Fined at FRAMERIES 249. Battn. marched at dawn and arrived at 7.10 P.M. at TROISVILLES. Bivouacked near Maples, St MARTIN. Positions for 1 section of 108th and also of 107th which could sweep ravine toward INCHY, were selected and entrenched. Very cold wet night —	
August 26	Action at TROISVILLES Commenced, called LE CATEAU. The 4 guns of 108th under Lt. Bally fired continually on advancing infantry toward INCHY from dawn till 3 P.M. One hundred rounds a gun were allotted L "section under Lieut Anderson entrenched as above for local defence. When general retirement was ordered 4 guns retired at once and thereafter heavily fired at her 100 rounds per gun. formed the retiring infantry. By order of O.C. 23 Bde. The guns were left in their pits. 2 guns, 1 carriage limber, 1 wagon limber, 2 brakes. Parts of breech mechanism to been removed.	

WAR DIARY
or
INTELLIGENCE SUMMARY.
(Erase heading not required.)

Army Form C. 2118

Hour, Date, Place	Summary of Events and Information	Remarks and references to Appendices
August 26 Continued	Infantry casualties during their retirement up to the Guns were almost Nil. and after passing the guns came out of view of enemy — The 4 guns fell into about 200 yards short ranged on enemy position at about towards AUDINCOURT — The horses appearing after 2 hours retirement were withdrawn and although pretty close into action area two's No horse shell were fired. In the action battery and it seems stations were not concealed casualties I have recorded — In battles road M# HOWIN & MARTIN No 34673 — From No 3 A Corpl JOHNSON & No 67316 Corpl NORMAN G. No 57300 B# MITCHELL S.H. and No 55055 B# GARDNER W.F. were employed at patrol work during retirement by order of R.H.C. 9th Inf. Bde, All the above L/c GARDNER? are still missing (24.9.14) B. Gardner rejoined 15 Sept. No 19 rounds fired 697 with L/cp of patrol No. 3 Accurate was lost — First that evening, Mill. Captain ALLsup. became separated from Jenny Battery this evening, but rejoined on 2 nd Inst.	

Army Form C. 2118.

WAR DIARY
or
INTELLIGENCE SUMMARY.
(Erase heading not required.)

Instructions regarding War Diaries and Intelligence Summaries are contained in F. S. Regs., Part II. and the Staff Manual respectively. Title pages will be prepared in manuscript.

Hour, Date, Place	Summary of Events and Information	Remarks and references to Appendices
27 August	Retirement continued MAGNICOURT day, through	
28	VERMANDES	Very hot in day
29	Night march through Noyon HAM & NOYON	
30	Crossed river and Bivouacked 5 of it. Received baggage and Mail. VIC SUR AISNE	
31	Battn. arrived at Sunrise VAUCIENNES. About 5 PM Three horses were destroyed during above retirement -	

3rd Divisional Artillery.
23rd Brigade R.F.A.

108th BATTERY R. F. A.

SEPTEMBER 1914.

Army Form C. 2118.

WAR DIARY
or
INTELLIGENCE SUMMARY.

108th Battery RFA

(Erase heading not required.)

Instructions regarding War Diaries and Intelligence Summaries are contained in F.S. Regs., Part II. and the Staff Manual respectively. Title pages will be prepared in manuscript.

Hour, Date, Place	Summary of Events and Information	Remarks and references to Appendices
1914 Sept 1.	Marched to BOUILLANCY with 9th Bde. Rear guard battery. Battery was not engaged.	
2	Marched to PENCHARD with 9th Inf. Bde.	
3	" " PRÉVILLIERS " " "	
4	" " E.of CRÉCY " " " and there bivouaced	
5	Right moved to LIVERDY arriving there 2 AM on 5th. Rested there for 6th.	
6	The afternoon being claimed by the allies, Battery marched with 5th Inf. Bde. to LUMIGNY.	
7	Marched via COULOMMIERS to CHATEAU LE BUISSON	
8	To FEUCHÈRES with action against enemy's rear guard near GIBRALTAR. German forces had 6-2 horses wounded by shell fire against wagon-line.	
9	To VENDELET FERME via BEZU with action against enemy rear guard at latter place.	
10	To CHOUY HARD with action against enemy rear guard at VEUILLY LE POTERIE. This day battery did not fire.	

Army Form C. 2118.

108th Battery R.F.A.

WAR DIARY
or
INTELLIGENCE SUMMARY.
(Erase heading not required.)

Instructions regarding War Diaries and Intelligence Summaries are contained in F. S. Regs., Part II. and the Staff Manual respectively. Title pages will be prepared in manuscript.

Hour, Date, Place	Summary of Events and Information	Remarks and references to Appendices
Sept. 11.	To GRAND ROZOY. Commencement of very wet weather	
12	To BRAISNE in support of Cavalry	
13	BRENELLE. One section Lieut Anderson in action	
14	above CHASSEMY against CHIVRES heights. BRENELLE in action near point junction of roads point 184. The section killed two wounded by Shell fire.	
15	— do —	
16	— do —	
17		
18	Rest in BRAISNE returned to BRENELLE night of 18th	
19		
20	In action near Queu de LIEU. 3 mile east of old position.	
21		
22	On 22nd German aeroplane gave away position by signals and adversing batteries 40th suffered considerably in this position.	

Army Form C. 2118.

WAR DIARY
or
INTELLIGENCE SUMMARY.

(Erase heading not required.)

Instructions regarding War Diaries and Intelligence Summaries are contained in F.S. Regs., Part II. and the Staff Manual respectively. Title pages will be prepared in manuscript.

10 G.H. Batty. R.F.A.

Hour, Date, Place	Summary of Events and Information	Remarks and references to Appendices
Sept 23 1914	Rest in BRAISNE	During the latter period of this portion of the AISNE battle Lieut Anderson & Lieut Campbell took turns to go forward to the Infantry trenches about VAILLY.
24	" " "	
25	" " "	
26	" " "	
27		
28		
29		
30	Unaided battery, concealed in small wood 500 W of point 164. Observing station near point 164.	
1 October		
2	Marched in 2nd October to CRAMAILLE.	
3	To TROESNES	
4	CREPY	
5	RHUIS	
6	Entrained 6 PM at LA LONGUEIL for ABBEVILLE. Detrained then 5 AM on 7th	
7	to BUIGNY. (Bonneval farm) marched at 2.0 AM on 9th	
9	BONNEVAL FARM to TOLLENT marched at 5.30 PM –	
10	To TANGRY arrived there 9.0 AM. 25 miles in 16 hours. road bad, but marching was worse –	

WAR DIARY or INTELLIGENCE SUMMARY

Army Form C. 2118.

108th Battery RFA

Hour, Date, Place	Summary of Events and Information	Remarks and references to Appendices
11 October 1914	to RUBEDDE Advanced Guard Halting with 7s Fusiliers	
12	to LOGON	
13	LES LOBES	
14	at " " } in Reserve	
15	" "	
16	" "	
17	1 Rue de Bacquerot	
18	Near AUBERS in action against HERLIES 2.30 PM till dusk supporting 9th Bde attack. Bivouacked at PIETRE. AVENTURE Convoy main road between HERLIES & 8° left of CHATEAU WOOD. Two teams went forth to advanced position near front inclines station. The other section in & were relieved Position near LA QUIVETERIE farm - Another took to remove by disposal late very slightly wounded by shell fire.	
19	} taken as above except that on 20 & 21	Pte 19th Gunner Taylor very slightly wounded by shell fire.
20	} only 19un was left in general position	
21		
22	Withdrew our section to HAUT-POMMEREAU Waller Lieut Smith, and LIEUT CAMPBELL's section went back to come into action near PIETRE crossroads. The gun of this section was centrally killed by LIEUT ANDERSON from HAUT-POMMEREAU — about 7 PM the latter retired	Advanced section supported R.C. Fusiliers. Rear section supported LINCOLNS.

Army Form C. 2118.

WAR DIARY
or
INTELLIGENCE SUMMARY.
(Erase heading not required.)

108th Battery RFA

Hour, Date, Place	Summary of Events and Information	Remarks and references to Appendices
22 Sept. 15/14 Continued	The battery retiring as ordered reached ROUGE CROIX about 1. AM on 23rd.	
23	Inl. cellar near M.N. near V in RUE DU BACQUEROT. Horse shown Kept observing station in that house until cooperns blew off. Then observing station near haystack up road. Against enemy's attack on our trenches began two hours shelled. I had to be shifted with two howrs & 2 Neuberands cent shells, fore, bangs, & from F.M. B.o.M.S. & Prussian booked with us in direction of the bazar line.	⁂ 8mm Rock Geneva Shrapnel
	Lieut Andersen had one gun in Infantry front line on LINCOLNS right, Lieut Campbell also on LINCOLNS LEFT near a large BARN a main road. Running E & NEUVE - CHAPELLE	These forward guns were relieved as from Detachments as increased by other batteries of the Brk either daily or every two days

Army Form C. 2118.

108th Battery, RFA

WAR DIARY
or
INTELLIGENCE SUMMARY.
(Erase heading not required.)

Hour, Date, Place	Summary of Events and Information	Remarks and references to Appendices
24 Sept 1914	Battery noted PONT DU HEM moves in convoy to near BOUT DEVILLE. LIEUT CAMPBELL went sick with heart trouble (Sent to BHSE)	
25.	In action on 23rd Inst. Situation the day previous acute, as enemy pushed in front but were driven back. LIEUT Smellie left advanced gun (was shelled on its rear) his evening station, & was caught for (gr: horses was wounded. + horses 3 horses able to return fire. In action on 25th on the day Lieut Anderson was wounded, Br. Powell killed, Sergt. Harry towards. Gr. Johnson wounded. The second where Lieut Anderson was attached became the night advanced gun from its emplacement to give a sweep attack. The gun (4th Howitz) it hit closed by H.E. shell – Lieut Anderson was sent to BHSE	
27.	BOUT DE VILLE Capt. Lewis STONES joined from Reft H.Q for temporary duty –	

Army Form C. 2118

WAR DIARY
or
INTELLIGENCE SUMMARY.
(Erase heading not required.)

108th Battery RFA

Hour, Date, Place	Summary of Events and Information	Remarks and references to Appendices
28. Oct. 1914	Battery in same position. Lieut DAWES was with Left Advanced Gun. — The other gun was now in "no man's land" —	Battery was made up to 6 guns to replace 2 guns lost at LE CATEAU
29	In action in same position. Sergeant Gunner ELY was wounded with forward gun. ? Pivot near BOUT DEVILLE	
30		
31	Moved back to old positions about 11 AM with 3 guns in the rear position & one in the rd. crescent. The Regist the left forward gun was safely withdrawn by Lieut SMITH and Sergeant Smith with C.R.B.? I was unable to approach the right forward gun which had now between the opposing firing lines.	

J V Bland
Major RFA
Cmdg. 108th Bat'y RFA

FOSSE. 9/11/14.

3rd Divisional Artillery.

23rd Brigade R. F. A.

109th BATTERY R. F. A.

AUGUST 1914.

Army Form C. 2118.
109th Battery R.F.A.
23rd Bde R.F.A.
III DIVISION

WAR DIARY
or
INTELLIGENCE SUMMARY.
(Erase heading not required.)

Instructions regarding War Diaries and Intelligence Summaries are contained in F. S. Regs., Part II. and the Staff Manual respectively. Title pages will be prepared in manuscript.

Hour, Date, Place			Summary of Events and Information	Remarks and references to Appendices
1914				
Aug 5	Bufford Camp		Order to Mobilize Received	
" 18	Entrained	1.30 a.m.	Entrained	
" "	Southampton	7 p.m.	Embarked on S.S. hinneapolis. Sailed	
" 19	Havre		Disembarked and marched to No 2 Rest Camp near BLÉVILLE	
" 20	"	10.30 p.m.	Entrained. Travelled via ROUEN and AMIENS to LANDRECIES.	
" 21	LANDRECIES		Detrained	
" 22	LA LONGUEVILLE	7.30 p.m.	Marched via BAVAI to LA LONGUEVILLE	
" "		5.30 a.m.	Marched behind 9th INF BDE via MALPLAQUET + FRAMERIES to CUESMES and bivouacked thirty
" 23	CUESMES	7.15 p.m.	Moved off N. towards MONS. Right and Centre Sections in action in the Streets in the outskirts of MONS. Left Section in action 800x in rear. Right Section fired 2 rounds against Infantry. Retired to position under cover S. of CUESMES facing Mt. EREBUS.	
" "		p.m.	Fire Withdrew at dusk to Bivouac W. of GENLY Road.	
24		Dusk		
" "		30 m.	Moved off to FRAMERIES. Twenty mile action facing W. in an orchard under cover, Battery under Shrapnel fire. Dismounted Guns and 3 Burounds of Enemy invisible	
" "	FRAMERIES	7.30 a.m.	Came out of action. Centre Section in action in covered position facing N., observation station in neighbouring house. Fired continuously against Infantry by Sections and a Battery.	
" "		7.35 a.m.		
" "		9.30 a.m.	Section withdrawn. LtD. HILL wounded in right arm 3 men killed	
" "			Retired South from FRAMERIES. Left Section came into action to cover retirement of rear guard, but did not fire. 4 guns later came into action at LA BRUYERE covering retirement. No sign of enemy.	

Army Form C. 2118.
109th Battery R.F.A.
23rd Bde. R.F.A.
III Division

WAR DIARY
or
INTELLIGENCE SUMMARY.
(Erase heading not required.)

Instructions regarding War Diaries and Intelligence Summaries are contained in F.S. Regs., Part II. and the Staff Manual respectively. Title pages will be prepared in manuscript.

Hour, Date, Place		Summary of Events and Information	Remarks and references to Appendices
August 24th	5 p.m.	Continued retirement via HOUDAIN to WAAST LE BAVAYE. Bivouac.	
" 25th	4.30 am	Joined 107th & 108th Batteries at starting front near BERMERIES. Reached TROISVILLE 5.30 pm. Bivouac South of MOULIN ST. MARTIN. Reconnoitred position over night.	
26th TROISVILLE		Took up covered position on left of 108th Battery, to cover front occupied by Royal Scots Fusiliers. Shelled German infantry moving across our front W. of INCHY, & kept sunken road under fire all day. Enemy	
"	3 p.m.	never advanced beyond this road while battery in action. Order to retire given. Retired via BERRY - marched all night.	
" 27th	"	Reached HARGICOURT at 9 am. Bivouac to the bed taken over duties of rear guard battery from 107th at BEAUREVOIR. Came into action covering retirement. A few Uhlans approached battery position but were driven off by rifle fire of detachments. Arrived VERMONT about 6 pm.	
" 28th VERMONT	12.30 am	Marched to HAM. Arrived 5.30 am. Took up position N. of canal.	
	12 noon	Retired over canal without firing. Continued retirement to CLISSOLES	
		W. of NOYON, reached at 9 pm.	
" 29th NOYON	12 noon	Came into action N.E. of CLISSOLES in support of 2nd Cav. Bde. & "L" Bty. R.H.A. Did not open fire. Retired at 6 pm.	
	6 p.m.	Commenced night march via LANDRIMONT & VERESNES & CUTS Halt & bivouac till 2 p.m. of MORSAINS (inserted: MAREST AM)	
" 30th MORSAINS	9.30 am	Arrived in bivouac at BERNY-RIVIERE.	
" 31st BERNY-RIVIERE	7 am	Marched via VILLERS - COTTERETS to VAUCIENNES. Bivouac 5.30 pm. Devoted improvement in general situation.	

3rd Divisional Artillery.
23rd Brigade R.F.A.

109th BATTERY R. F. A.

SEPTEMBER 1914.

109th Bty RFA

WAR DIARY
or
INTELLIGENCE SUMMARY.
(Erase heading not required.)

Army Form C. 2118.

Hour, Date, Place	Summary of Events and Information	Remarks and references to Appendices
September 1st VAUCIENNES 9.30am	Marched via LEVIGNEM + FRESNOY & BOUILLANCY. Delayed en route by Army of 6th Divn around CREPY. Bivouac about 6.30 pm.	
2nd BOUILLANCY 5.30am	Marched via BARCY to bivouac at PENCHARD. Arrived about 2 pm.	
3rd PENCHARD 9 am	Moved off via MEAUX to bivouac at LA LOGE D'ART US. Arrived at 3.30 pm.	
4th LA LOGE D'ARTUS	Reconnoitred position to occupy if attacked. Moved bivouac about 2 miles to MAUPERTIUS during the afternoon.	
10.30 pm	Germans reported to have crossed MARNE. Marched by night via CRECY.	
5th 9.15 am	Arrived in bivouac at LIVERDY.	
6th LIVERDY	Information received that French troops about to take offensive.	
"	5 am Broke up from bivouac to join Vanguard at CHÂTRES. Marched via LA HOUSSAYE to LUMIGNY. No opposition. Capt HARRIS went sick.	
7th LUMIGNY 12.30 pm	Marched via COULOMMIER, where 3rd Divn was concentrating, to bivouac at CHATEAU LE BUISSON.	
8th LE BUISSON 6.30 am	Marched via CHAUFFRY & REBAIS. Advanced through advanced Adv guard with Royal Scots Fusiliers + took up a position N of ORLY with right + centre Sections. Shelled retreating Germans. Camped at LES FEUCHERES.	
" 9th 4.30 am	Moved off to the Van Guard Battery. Came into action S of NANTEUIL but did not fire. Crossed the MARNE at NANTEUIL without opposition. Held up for some at LUCAS. Went forward to BEZU, but did not come into action. Bivouac 1½ miles N. of BEZU.	

109th Bde RFA

Army Form C. 2118

WAR DIARY
INTELLIGENCE SUMMARY
(Erase heading not required.)

Hour, Date, Place		Summary of Events and Information	Remarks and references to Appendices
September 10th BEZU		Marched via MARIGNY on VEUILLY, where advance guard was held up by enemy in position S of CHEZY. Position on were ably held. Bivouac at DAMMARD.	
" 11th DAMMARD	7 a.m.	Marched via NEUILLY to GRAND ROZOY. Arrived 3.30 p.m.	
" 12th ROZOY	5.45 a.m.	Vanguard battery. Marched via MAAST on BRAINE. Came into action 1½ miles S of BRAINE to cover advance of infantry. Very heavy ground. Did not fire.	
" 13th BRENELLE		Bivouac at BRENELLE. Passage of AISNE disputed about VAILLY. Bridges destroyed, enemy occupying strong position. Halted NW of BRENELLE in readiness to support infantry crossing. Did not come into action. Infantry (9th Bde) all across by dusk. Returned to bivouac at BRENELLE.	
" 14th	4.45 a.m.	Moved off. Remained in readiness at a point ½ mile N of BRENELLE	
	11.30 a.m.	Came into action near PEUPLIER. Position & range found by enemy; heavy howitzers guns withdrawn after nightfall. Two guns put out of action. 6 men wounded. Returned to old bivouac	
" 15th		In reserve all day.	
" 16th		Again in reserve. Brigade relieved by 40th Bde at 4 pm. Moved to BRAINE for 2 days rest.	
" 17th BRAINE		In reserve.	
" 18th "		In reserve. Relieved 40th Bde in action at 4.30 pm. Bivouac at BRENELLE.	
" 19th BRENELLE		In action at daybreak in position ½ mile NE of PEUPLIER. Fired at FOLEMPRISE FARM. Returned to bivouac at dusk.	
" 20th "	5 a.m.	In action in same position as yesterday. Shelled enemy's trenches & wood. Bivouac as before.	
" 21st "	"	In action in same position. Very quiet day. Fired at guns NE of FOLEMPRISE. Bivouac as before.	
" 22nd "	"	In action in same position. Very little firing. Returned to bivouac after dark.	
" 23rd "	7 a.m.	Went into bivouac at BRAINE in reserve.	

109th B.g. R.F.A.

Army Form C. 2118.

WAR DIARY
or
INTELLIGENCE SUMMARY.

(Erase heading not required.)

Instructions regarding War Diaries and Intelligence Summaries are contained in F. S. Regs., Part II. and the Staff Manual respectively. Title pages will be prepared in manuscript.

Hour, Date, Place		Summary of Events and Information	Remarks and references to Appendices
September 24th	BRAINE	In reserve at BRAINE.	
" 25th	"	In reserve. Moved at 6 p.m. to new bivouac S of BRENELLE.	
" 26th	BRENELLE	3.45am moved off & took up position 2 miles N.W of BRENELLE, to relieve 40th Bde. Fired very little.	
" 27th	"	5.30am Left guns in position & withdrew teams to bivouac 1 mile S of BRENELLE.	
" 28th	"	In same position. Fired at enemy's trenches.	
" 29th	"	Same as previous day.	
" 30th	"	"	

J. L. J. Johnson Capt RFA
Comdg 109th Bde RFA

3rd Divisional Artillery.

23rd Brigade R.F.A.

109th BATTERY R. F. A.

OCTOBER 1914.

109th Bty

Army Form C. 2118

WAR DIARY
or
INTELLIGENCE SUMMARY.
(Erase heading not required.)

Instructions regarding War Diaries and Intelligence Summaries are contained in F.S. Regs., Part II. and the Staff Manual respectively. Title pages will be prepared in manuscript.

Hour, Date, Place			Summary of Events and Information	Remarks and references to Appendices
October	1st BRENELLE	5.30 am	Guns in same position 2 miles N.W. of BRENELLE. Teams in bivouac 1 mile S. of BRENELLE. Very little firing.	
"	2d "		In same position. To mostly to fire. Left position at 6.30 p.m. & marched via BRAINE to CREMAILLE. Arrived in bivouac at midnight.	
"	3d CREMAILLE	5.30am	Moved halfway across road to bivouac under cover of wood. Moved at 6 p.m. via ROZOY à BILLY-SUR-OURCQ to TROESNES. Bivouac.	
"	4th TROESNES		Remained in bivouac all day.	
"	5th "	7.45am	Arrived at CREPY. Bivouac. Moved off at 6 p.m. & marched through VAUCIENNES to CREPY.	
"	6th ROBERVAL		Moved off at 3.30 am via RHUIS & VERBERIE to LE MEUX. Arrived at 6 pm & entrained. Left at 12 midnight.	
"	7th "	7.30am	Arrived ABBEVILLE & detrained. Marched to bivouac at GRAND LAVIERS, but off after 1 hour, to proper bivouac at BONNEVAL FARM near BUIGNY.	
"	8th BONNEVAL		Remained in bivouac all day.	
"	9th "	2 am.	Marched off via FROYELLES & LABROYE to TOLLENT. Bivouac 7.30 a.m.	
"	10th TANGRY	9.45am	Moved off at 5.45 pm & marched via BERNATRE & MONCHY Arrived TANGRY, having covered 28 miles in 16 hours. Remained in bivouac during the day.	
"	11th "	7 am	Marched via PERNES, FLORINGHEM, & BURBURE to ROBECQ. Halted for 2 hours & then went back to bivouac at LECLEME	
"	12th LECLEME	6.45am	Moved off via ROBECQ & LE CORNET MALO. Afterwards on to LACON. 9th Inf Bde in touch with enemy. Bivouac.	
"	13th LACON	5 am	In reserve. Ready to move. Moved about 1 mile up the road. Bivouac.	
"	14th "	6.30 am	In reserve. Ready to move.	

109th Bty RFA

WAR DIARY
or
INTELLIGENCE SUMMARY.
(Erase heading not required.)

Army Form C. 2118.

Hour, Date, Place		Summary of Events and Information	Remarks and references to Appendices
October 15th LACON		Again in reserve. Reconnoitred positions to take over from 40th Bde.	
" 16th	4am	Moved off. One section in action at LA BOUDEVILLE. Remaining section waited near PONT DU HEM. Joined by other section. Moved on about 2 p.m & halted just S of LAVENTIE at 5 p.m. 1 section came into action 1½ miles W of Aubers. Fired a few rounds. Bivouac at ROUGE CROIX.	
" 17th ROUGE CROIX	5:30am		
	9:30am	Came into action near position of yesterday. Moved on to AUBERS. Came into action just S of village at 4 p.m. Bivouac about 1 mile W of AUBERS.	
" 18th AUBERS	5:30am	In action in same position as previous day. Very little firing. Same bivouac.	
" 19th	"	In same position. Major Metcalfe observing in infantry firing trench, hit in side. Captain Fisher took over battery. Fired about 100 rounds at enemy's infantry. Same bivouac.	
" 20th	"	Same as yesterday. Very little firing. Same bivouac.	
" 21st	"	Same as yesterday. Infantry to retire during night about 1 mile to stronger line. Same bivouac. Not much firing.	
" 22nd	"	Same position. Very little firing. New bivouac at CHAPIGNY. Moved out again about 10 pm to ROUGE CROIX.	
" 23rd ROUGE CROIX		In reserve. Moved back & took bivouac at PONT DU HEM.	
" 24th PONT DU HEM	4:30	Took over 2 guns of infantry firing line near LAVANTIE from 108th Battery. Section in action 1 mile N of ROUGE CROIX. Moved to new bivouac at VIEILLE CHAPELLE.	
" 25th VIEILLE CHAPELLE		Took over from 108th Battery 1½ miles N of ROUGE CROIX at dawn. 1 section left out all night. Remainder to old bivouac.	

107th Bde RFA

VIII

Army Form C. 2118.

WAR DIARY
or
INTELLIGENCE SUMMARY.
(Erase heading not required.)

Hour, Date, Place		Summary of Events and Information	Remarks and references to Appendices
6 Oct 26th VIEILLE CHAPELLE		In reserve.	
" 27th "	5.30p	Relieved 108th Battery. Very little firing. It Herbert went to look at forward gun position, had been left, & did reconnaissance. Three guns left out all night.	
" 28th "	"	Relieved by 108th & took over guns of 107th. One section left out during night.	
" 29th "	"	Very little firing.	
" 30th "	"	Relieved by 107th. Returned to bivouac for a rest.	
" "	10am	Took over guns of 108th Battery. After dark one section sent to pros team near	
" "		LA COUTURE.	
" 31st LA COUTURE	5.30a	Whole battery in action near LA COUTURE. One section left out during night. Very little firing.	

J.E. Seton Major RFA
Comdt 108th Bty RFA

Index

SUBJECT.

3RD DIV

No.	Contents.	Date.
	R.F.A., 23RD BRIGADE, WAR DIARY, JAN - DEC, 1915	

A.2

121/4566

3rd Division

23rd Brigade R.F.A.

Vol V. 1.1. — 28.2.15

Nil

WAR DIARY or INTELLIGENCE SUMMARY

Army Form C. 2118.

2nd Brigade R.F.A

Hour, Date, Place	Summary of Events and Information	Remarks and references to Appendices
1915		
Jan 1st	Brigade relieved by H.Q. 7 A.F.B., and went into rest at ST JANS CAPPEL.	
Jan 2nd, 3rd, 4th, 5th	In Reserve. On Jan 5th B" and Battery Commanders made a Reconnaissance in the direction of DICKEBUSH.	
Jan 6th	Positions reoccupied 107 & 108 Bty's about 1½ miles NW of KEMMEL, 109 Battery 1 Mile W of KEMMEL. All three in Support of 8th If Bde.	
Jan 7th – 14th	Remained in action, but little firing was done.	
Jan 15th	Bde relieved by H.Q. 18th B", and went into Reserve at ST JANS CAPPEL.	
Jan 16th – 20th	In Reserve	
Jan 21st	Relieved 42nd Bde in positions W of KEMMEL	
Jan 22nd – Feb 6th	Remained in action; little firing was done. Batteries now linked up by Telephone with trenches.	

Capt & Adjt 2nd Bde [signature]

WAR DIARY
or
INTELLIGENCE SUMMARY.

(Erase heading not required.)

Army Form C. 2118.

23rd Brigade R.F.A.

Hour, Date, Place	Summary of Events and Information	Remarks and references to Appendices
Feb 6th 6.30 am	Relieved by 42nd Bde R.F.A. and went into rest at ST JANS CAPPEL.	
Feb 7th and 8th	In Reserve.	
Feb 9th	Relieved 42nd Bde in position near KEMMEL.	
Feb 10th, 11th, 12th, 13th	Remained in action.	
Feb 14th, 15th, 16th	Relieved at 3.30 pm by 42nd Bde R.F.A. and went into Reserve at ST JANS CAPPEL.	
Feb 17th	In Reserve at ST JANS CAPPEL.	
Feb 18th, 19th, 20th, 21st	Relieved 42nd Bde R.F.A. but subsequently relief was cancelled and Bde returned to ST JANS CAPPEL. In Reserve at ST JANS CAPPEL.	
Feb 22nd	Relieved 42nd Bde at 3.30 pm in positions near KEMMEL.	

Army Form C. 2118.

WAR DIARY
or
INTELLIGENCE SUMMARY.
(Erase heading not required.)

Instructions regarding War Diaries and Intelligence Summaries are contained in F.S. Regs., Part II. and the Staff Manual respectively. Title pages will be prepared in manuscript.

Hour, Date, Place	Summary of Events and Information	Remarks and references to Appendices
Feb 23, 24, 25.	23rd Brigade R.F.A. In action but very little firing.	
26.	Relieved at 3.30pm by 42nd Bde R.F.A. and went into Reserve at St JANS CAPPEL.	
27, 28.	In Reserve at St JANS CAPPEL.	

John Hammond
Captain H.Q.
23rd Bde R.F.A.

3rd Division

23rd Bde RFA

Vol VI 1 - 31.3.15

Army Form C. 2118.

WAR DIARY
or
INTELLIGENCE SUMMARY
(Erase heading not required.)

23rd Brigade R.F.A.

Hour, Date, Place	Summary of Events and Information	Remarks and references to Appendices
March 1st – 4th.	In Reserve at ST JANS CAPPEL.	
5th.	Relieved 42nd Bde in action occupying positions west of KEMMEL.	
6th.	A quiet day.	
7th.	Fired under orders of C.R.A. at 3 p.m.	
8th.	" " " " " " "	
9th.	" " " " " " "	
10th.	" " " 8 a.m.	
	" " " 8 a.m. [on	
	Section 107 Battery pushed forward to patrol	
	East of LINDENHOEK – fr Wine Cutting.	
11th.	A quiet day.	
12th.	Bombardment which was timed to commence at 9.0 a.m. was delayed by fog, and could not take place till 2.30 p.m. Supported the attack by WLTSh WORCESTERs on SPANBROEK MOLEN.	

Army Form C. 2118.

WAR DIARY
or
INTELLIGENCE SUMMARY.
(Erase heading not required.)

23rd Brig a/v R.F.A.

Hour, Date, Place	Summary of Events and Information	Remarks and references to Appendices
March 13th	A quiet day	
" 14th 5.30pm	Fired on trenches opposite 85th Bde., during the German attack on St. Eloi.	
" 15th – 24th	Remained in positions, but nothing of any imp[ortance] occurred.	
March 25th 9.pm	1 Section from 107 & 109 Batteries and two Sections 108 Battery relieved Sections of 27th Divl Arty near Dickebush.	
26th	Detached Sections rejoined their Batteries.	
March 27th 28th 29th 30th 31st	Quiet days. Two sections from 107 and 108 B altered, and one section 109 Bty relieve corresponding two sections of 19th & 20th B. 27th Div	

Paul Hammond
14/4/15

121/5318

3ᵈ Division

23ʳᵈ Bde. R.F.A.

Vol VII 1 — 30.4.15

Army Form C. 2118.

WAR DIARY
or
INTELLIGENCE SUMMARY. 23rd Army Bde. R.F.A.
(Erase heading not required.)

Instructions regarding War Diaries and Intelligence Summaries are contained in F. S. Regs., Part II. and the Staff Manual respectively. Title pages will be prepared in manuscript.

Hour, Date, Place	Summary of Events and Information	Remarks and references to Appendices
April 1st	Relief of Batteries of 19th & 20th Brigades completed, and Bde. HQ established at DICKEBUSH. [1 Section pr Battery]	
3rd	Still in action at KEMMEL	
	Detached Sections rejoined.	
10th	A Zeppelin passed over DICKEBUSH	
14th 11.30pm	Germans exploded a mine near St Eloi; the Brigade opened fire; this in the opinion of GOC 3rd Div. prevented the Germans attacking	
17th 7 pm	Bde stood by to assist 5th Div in the attack on Hill 60.	
Rn 8 am	Bombs dropped near DICKEBUSH Lake from an aeroplane	
9.30 am	108 Battery assisted 5th Division with its fire.	
30th 9 pm	One gun Gun 109 Ry battery placed in dummy gun position	

Brigade in action in DICKEBUSH

John Stewart
Captain 23rd Bde RFA

121/5610

A2
186

3rd Division

23rd Bde R.F.A.

Watson 6 — 31.5.15.

Nil

WAR DIARY
or
INTELLIGENCE SUMMARY. Q 3rd Bring adc R.F.A.

Army Form C. 2118.

(Erase heading not required.)

Instructions regarding War Diaries and Intelligence Summaries are contained in F.S. Regs., Part II. and the Staff Manual respectively. Title pages will be prepared in manuscript.

Hour, Date, Place	Summary of Events and Information	Remarks and references to Appendices
MAY.	The Brigade in action 1/2 Mile E. N.E. of DICKEBUSH.	
6th	108 Battery cooperated with 5th Div Arty by shelling Wood in I.35. One of Night two guns were pushed forward to engage at closer range. These were also supposed to be a line of approach for the enemy to Hill 60. The forward guns were withdrawn at dawn.	Ref /20000 SW 28 NW
9th	109 Battery moved to a position just E of DICKEBUSH Lake.	
13th	Searching hostile guns which were firing to the South against 5 Corps. 109 Battery pushed forward to engage hostile advance as a the range in case of a bombardment of the line.	
	Great aerial activity on the part of the Germans.	
	Considerable firing Sep 5 1915 and 11:15pm. 18 Battery fired in support about 150 rounds at was some just again.	
	Desultory shelling.	
15th	Desultory shelling in the Afternoon.	
22nd	Enemy bombarded Aug YPRES. the asphyxiating gases was distinctly noticeable at DICKEBUSH	
23rd	Desultory fire throughout the day.	
25th	12:30pm German aircs above 4/5 Div Arty	
26th	In the evening a section 107 Batt'y and 1 section Gun & A 1/1/g Battery	
29th	moved by A7 R 27 to HDU.	
30th	The section withdrawn on 31st and moved section of 18th Pr. 27 M. Bde S.E. of YPRES	
31st	Enemy shelled part of 19:05 1/2 my SE of YPRES	

(9 29 6) W 3552-1107 100,000 10/13 H W V Forms/C. 2118/10

3rd Division.

23rd Bde R.F.A.

Vol IX 1 — 30.6.15

Army Form C. 2118.

WAR DIARY
or
INTELLIGENCE SUMMARY.
(Erase heading not required.) 2nd Brigade R.H.A.

Instructions regarding War Diaries and Intelligence Summaries are contained in F. S. Regs., Part II. and the Staff Manual respectively. Title pages will be prepared in manuscript.

Hour, Date, Place	Summary of Events and Information	Remarks and references to Appendices
Jan 1st	In positions S.E. of YPRES.	
2^h 10.0 m	108 Battery shelled losing 2 killed & 5 wounded.	
	Fighting at HOOGE.	
11th — 11th	Nothing of moment. B^{de} H.Q. and Battery positions were shelled intermittently.	
12th — 15th	B^{de} came under orders of 50th Div Arty. Nothing of note.	
16th	Cooperated with 7th and 9th Brigades in their successful attack.	
17th — 25th	Nothing of note — All positions shelled intermittently.	
22nd	Cooperated with 7th & 9th in their attack on HOOGE.	
25th — 29th	Nothing of note. All positions shelled intermittently.	
30th	107 B^y Wagon line hit — 6 killed 3 wounded.	
	Total Casualties for the month about 15 killed & 25 wounded	

121/6356

3758 Karrivion

92nd Bde. R.T.N.

Vol X

1-31-4-11

Army Form C. 2118.

WAR DIARY
or
INTELLIGENCE SUMMARY.   23rd Bing ade. R.F.A.

(Erase heading not required.)

Instructions regarding War Diaries and Intelligence
Summaries are contained in F.S. Regs., Part II.
and the Staff Manual respectively. Title pages
will be prepared in manuscript.

Hour, Date, Place	Summary of Events and Information	Remarks and references to Appendices
July 1st – 6th.	Brigade in Action ½ mile S. of YPRES, Bde. HQ at S.W. Corner of ZILLEBEKE Lake. A good deal of German shelling during the period.	
4th & 8th.	108 and 109 Batteries and Bde HQ relieved by H.6th Div. Arty. 107 Battery remaining in action.	
8th – 13th.	Bde HQ, 108 and 109 Batteries in rest at Poperinghe. 107 Battery in action.	
14th & 15th	Bde HQ 108 & 109 Batteries relieve H6th Div Arty Batteries and resume positions evacuated on 7th & 8th. Bde Comes under the orders of H6th Div Arty.	
16th, 17th 18th. 18th	Nothing of importance. 129 (Army Battery) 3.6"15 and 5" Straff Battery come under orders of this Bde. The whole composing Siffr. Group H6th Div Arty.	
19th.	The Group cooperates with 3rd Div Arty in bombardment of German Redoubt.	

Army Form C. 2118.

WAR DIARY
or
INTELLIGENCE SUMMARY.
(Erase heading not required.)

O3rd Brigade RFA JULY (contd)

Hour, Date, Place	Summary of Events and Information	Remarks and references to Appendices
July 20th.	Bgr HQ and all Batteries came under fairly heavy Shell fire - but retaliation on French CO and C1 when German attack was expected.	
21st. 22nd. 23rd.	Nothing of importance German trenches mined opposite A and A1, but their retaliation was meagre -	
24th & 25th.	Nothing of Importance - German Artillery active. Bgr HQ moved to KRUISSTRAAT ½ mile S.W of YPRES.	
26th.	Nothing of importance.	
27, 28, 29th. 30th.	German Attack at 3.0 am on left of 46th Div. 14th Div losing ground - 107, 109 and 129 Batteries fired with effect and 7.0.0 168 Battery was of great use supplying information to 46th Div -	

Army Form C. 2118.

WAR DIARY
or
INTELLIGENCE SUMMARY.
(Erase heading not required.)

2 3 rd B? O.H. July (contd)

Hour, Date, Place	Summary of Events and Information	Remarks and references to Appendices
July 31st	In the afternoon the Brigade supported the counter attack which was only partially successful. The Brigade came under heavy shell fire during the day, but casualties are light. At 2.0 am the German attack was reported to have been renewed. 107, 109 and 129 Batteries cooperating in the Defense - 108 & 5th Staff watching the remainder of front of 69 Brigade — By 7.0 am all was again quiet At 7pm German Artillery became very active, shelling all roads and approaches —	

WAR DIARY
or
INTELLIGENCE SUMMARY 2nd Bde R.F.A July (cont)
(Erase heading not required.)

Army Form C. 2118.

Hour, Date, Place	Summary of Events and Information	Remarks and references to Appendices

About 7.30 pm 14 Div on our left started an
S.O.S scare, but did not localise the
dangerous quarter.
At 8.30 pm S.O.S call was received from
139 Inf. Bde.
All Batteries opened fire, the 108 Battery
opening very promptly on a 'call' from the
trenches in B sector.
The fire of the Brigade was most effective
and the Infantry reported that the German
attack had been driven off.
The Div Commander, the Corps Commander,
and the Army Commander all expressed
themselves their appreciation of the
work carried out on July 30th & 31st. David Warner Lt.
Capt & adj

121/6737

3rd Division

23rd Bde R+M.
Vol XL
August 15

Army Form C. 2118.

WAR DIARY
or
INTELLIGENCE SUMMARY.

(Erase heading not required.)

23rd Brigade R.F.A.

Hour, Date, Place	Summary of Events and Information	Remarks and References to Appendices

Bde in positions 1/2 Mile S.E. of YPRES
Bde HQ at KRUISTRAAT

Under Orders of 46th Div Arty.
Left Group. { 107, 108, 109 Batteries
                129 (How) Battery
                5th Staff Battery

Aug 1st to 3rd: Nothing of Importance.

4th:
5th: 107 Battery and 129 Battery came under 6th Div Arty. Forming "F" Group under orders of OC 23rd Bde R.F.A.
    108 Battery bring a gun into action in SANCTUARY WOOD.

6th: 1 Section 5th Mountain Battery joins Left Group.

7th: Forward gun of 109 Battery and section No 5 Mountain Battery transferred to F Group 6th Div Arty.

8th: Preparations for Operations on 9th.

Army Form C. 2118.

WAR DIARY
or
INTELLIGENCE SUMMARY.
(Erase heading not required.)

23rd Brigade R.F.A.

AUGUST

Instructions regarding War Diaries and Intelligence Summaries are contained in F. S. Regs., Part II. and the Staff Manual respectively. Title pages will be prepared in manuscript.

Hour, Date, Place	Summary of Events and Information	Remarks and References to Appendices
Aug 9th	At 2.45 am the Artillery Bombardment commenced. 107 and 109 Batteries forming a "barrage" on right of attack by 6th Division; and remaining Batteries keeping up a steady fire in their own front. The Operation continued throughout the day. All communications perfectly satisfactory. The Army Commander and others expressed their approval of the work of the Artillery and the C.R.A. 6th Div thanked the 107 and 109 Batteries for their very able accomplishment of their tasks.	
10th	A quiet day	
11th	107 and 109 Batteries reverted to Left Group H6th Div Arty.	

Army Form C. 2118.

WAR DIARY
or
INTELLIGENCE SUMMARY.
(Erase heading not required.)

23rd Brigade R.F.A.

AUGUST

Instructions regarding War Diaries and Intelligence Summaries are contained in F.S. Regs., Part II. and the Staff Manual respectively. Title pages will be prepared in manuscript.

Hour, Date, Place	Summary of Events and Information	Remarks and references to Appendices
Aug 12th to 17th	Nothing of importance. German Artillery very active, our Batteries and Brigade H.Q. coming in for their full share of the shelling.	
Aug 18th	Heavy battery in rear of Bde H.Q. heavily shelled about 6 pm. 2 Brigade R.F.A. 6 Div. gave us an S.O.S. call, which proved to be a phantom. Nearly a bombardment by the Germans.	
Aug 19th to 20th	Quiet day. 139 I. B. relieved by 71 I.B. 107 Battery heavily shelled in morning with "Crumps". Result - Two guns blown up, 1 gun slightly damaged, two men wounded. 10 pm. 6th Staff's Battery I.O. came to group - enemy trenches A4 - A7.	
21st 22nd	Quiet again except for slight shelling of 107 - position. No damage done.	

Army Form C. 2118.

WAR DIARY
or
INTELLIGENCE SUMMARY. *AUGUST* 23rd Brigade R.F.A.
(Erase heading not required.)

Instructions regarding War Diaries and Intelligence Summaries are contained in F. S. Regs., Part II. and the Staff Manual respectively. Title pages will be prepared in manuscript.

Hour, Date, Place	Summary of Events and Information	Remarks and References to Appendices
August 25th	German artillery again active. KRUISTRAAT shelled.	
" 24th	107 Battery moved to new position about 500 North.	
" 25th	KRUISTRAAT again shelled. No damage.	
" 26th	Much quieter. Major Carey hospital to 28th Div Amm.	
" 27th	Major Mallock joins 108 Battery. A quiet day	
" 28th	129 Battery returns to 35th Bde RFA.	
" 29th	Very quiet.	
" 30th	Brigade Commander visited wagon lines. Wet.	
" 30th	Quiet day. Capt Rice to 1st Indian from 35th Div	
	attached for 2 days.	
" 31st	Weather bad. Everything very quiet.	

W. Wright —
Adjt —
23rd Bde R.F.A.
3/9/15.

3rd Division

121/7050

CONFIDENTIAL.

WAR DIARY
of

23rd Brigade R.F.A.

from September 1st to September 30th

1915.

Vol XII

WAR DIARY
INTELLIGENCE SUMMARY

Army Form C. 2118.

23rd Brigade R.F.A.

Hour, Date, Place	Summary of Events and Information	Remarks and References to Appendices
September Brigade in position ½ mile S.E. of YPRES. Bde HQ at RUISTRAAT	Under orders of 3rd Div Arty Right group $\{$ 107, 108 & 109 Batteries $\{$ 5th & 6th Staffs Batteries	
September 1st	All batteries bgds had in small preliminary bombardment at 4. a.m on trenches S of MENIN ROAD. At this spirit wound above Maj Cadwick (5th Staffs)	
" 2d	Bombarded again from 4 a.m to 5.30 a.m. Germans retaliated heavily on our fire and communication trenches, evidently meanengett.	
" 3d	Another small bombardment. Very little retaliation	
" 4th 5th	Much enemy bombardment. KRUISTRAAT shelled.	
" 6th	Bombardment cancelled. Much aeroplane activity.	
" 7th " 8 & 9	YPRES shelled heavily with 17". Capt-Smith reported.	
" 10th	Nothing of importance. Capt Pinsen joined.	
" 11th	YPRES again heavily shelled.	
" 12th	Very quiet day. Bde Staff heavily shelled. Telephone pit hit and 3 men killed. Right Group handed over to Lt Col Stevenson - given 3rd N.M. Bde to Bde Staff went into rest.	

Army Form C. 2118.

WAR DIARY
or
INTELLIGENCE SUMMARY.
(Erase heading not required.)

September 23rd Brigade R.F.A.

Hour, Date, Place	Summary of Events and Information	Remarks and References to Appendices
September 13th & morning	108 & 109 Batteries to 40th Bde. Very quiet	
" 14th – 17th	Nothing of importance	
" 18th	Trenches round HOOGE heavily bombarded, also KRUISTRAAT. Our bombardments recommenced.	
" 19th	108, 109 Batteries return to Right Group. Batteries again bombarded German fire trenches and approaches according to prearranged programme.	
" 20th	Bombardment according to programme.	
" 21st	HQ 23rd Bde assumed command of Right Group in old 9th I.B. dug outs near KRUISTRAAT. Bombardment at 4 am. Right Group consists of 23rd Bde & 5th & 6th Staff's Btys.	
" 22nd	Guns of Brigade fired a great deal during the day. Gun of 108 damaged by shell fire. Bombardment at 4 pm.	
" 23rd	Bombardment midday. Lt J.A.E. Friend joined the Brigade.	
" 24th	Bombardment 4 am. A good deal of hostile shelling during the day.	
" 25th	Bombardment of enemy's front line at 3.50 am. Attack & left to second line & beyond, to form barrage at 4.20 am. Brigade worked from in front of B4 & FORT inclusive. Suffered Royal Scots Fusiliers – Royal Scots & 48th gardins. Objective gained without much trouble. assault on our Left	

(9 29 6) W 3332—1107 100,000 10/13 H W V Forms/C. 2118/10.

Army Form C. 2118.

WAR DIARY
or
INTELLIGENCE SUMMARY.
(Erase heading not required.)

23rd Brigade R.F.A.

September 1915

Hour, Date, Place	Summary of Events and Information	Remarks and References to Appendices
September 26th (contr.)	held up by wire at HOOGE CHATEAU. Enemy's counter attack came due South from MENIN ROAD & forced our infantry to retire. They gradually fell back & finally occupied our original line about 4pm. During the whole operation the Brigade formed a barrage in front of the infantry. Casualties 2 Lt Humfield Jones & Carlo killed in the trenches also one telephonist.	
26th	A quiet day. About 10.30pm S.O.S call from B4 & C1. All batteries fired but it proved to be only a scare, & everything became quiet again.	
27th	Quiet day. Lt Carson joined.	
28th	All quiet on our front.	
29th	Quiet morning. S.O.S B4 about 4.30pm - Huns blew up a mine and occupied crater, also B4 trench. Situation became all quiet.	
30th	Counter attack finally took place at 3pm. H.A.G. re occupied most of lost trench. Brigade formed a barrage on enemys old front line and approaches. 109 By had 3 wagons damaged by shell fire, & two men slightly wounded.	

4/10/15.

[signature]
23rd Bde RFA

3rd Division

121/7468

CONFIDENTIAL.

War Diary
of
23rd Brigade R.F.A.

from October 1st to October 31st

Vol XIII

WAR DIARY
INTELLIGENCE SUMMARY.
(Erase heading not required.) 23rd Brigade R.F.A.

Army Form C. 2118.

Hour, Date, Place	Summary of Events and Information	Remarks and References to Appendices
Brigade in position ½ mile S.E of YPRES. Bde HQ - KRUISSTRAAT		
October 1st	Situation still obscure, but we do not hear of B 4.	
" 2nd	Quiet day. Infantry decide not to attack again.	
" 3rd	Quiet day. 6th Belgian Battery of 7th Regiment joined Group. In action just N. of Belgian Garden. 108 Battery put in forward Section. Special Order of the day from Sir John French.	
" 4th & 5th	All quiet on 3rd Div front. We still cover 2nd Bde.	
" 6th	Quiet day.	
" 7th	Very quiet. Enemy's transport shelled in the evening.	
" 8th	All quiet. B50 Battery of 9th Div joined the group. Heavy firing heard to the SOUTH.	
" 9th	A quiet day.	
" 10th	About 11am Huns bombed down towards B3 and made some ground, but caused little anxiety.	
" 11th	All quiet. Much aeroplane activity.	
" 12th	Again quiet. Huns shelled our transport at night.	

WAR DIARY
or
INTELLIGENCE SUMMARY.
(Erase heading not required.)

October   23rd Brigade R.F.A.

Army Form C. 2118.

Hour, Date, Place	Summary of Events and Information	Remarks and References to Appendices
October 13th	Huns attacked B7 about 5.30am bombing our people out. Brigade retaliated but a good portion of B7 was lost. At 1.15pm Middlesex bombed up trench. Brigade co-operated, & artillery fire was much appreciated by 8th Bde.	
14th & 15th	All quiet.	
16th	A slight disturbance about 5.30am, Huns bombing B4. 107 Battery fired at working party.	
17th & 18th	Quiet days.	
19th	Brigade, less 108 Battery went to wagon lines to rest.	
20th	In rest.	
21st	CO. inspected the Bde Ammn Column.	
22nd-23rd	In rest.	
24th	Moved to new rest billets near STEENVOORDE, being relieved by 17th Division.	
25th & 26th	In rest.	
27th	H.M. The King inspected details of 5th Corps. Brigade sent a party of 20 under command of Capt. F.B. Benham R.F.A. Capt. R.T. Hammick posted to command 29th Battery.	
28th & 29th	In rest.	
30th & 31st	Church Parade.	

4.11.15.

[signature]
23rd Bde R.F.A.

3rd Division

CONFIDENTIAL

WAR DIARY
OF
23rd BRIGADE R.F.A.

FROM: November 1st TO: November 30th

1915.

Army Form C. 2118.

WAR DIARY
or
INTELLIGENCE SUMMARY.
(Erase heading not required.)

November 1915.   23rd Brigade R.F.A.

Instructions regarding War Diaries and Intelligence Summaries are contained in F.S. Regs., Part II. and the Staff Manual respectively. Title pages will be prepared in manuscript.

Hour, Date, Place	Summary of Events and Information	Remarks and references to Appendices
Brigade in rest 1 mile S.E of STEENVOORDE.		
November 1st to 3rd	In rest. Weather very bad.	
" 4th	Brigade sports.	
" 5th	Col. DELAFORCE went to do Corps advises (temporary). Major HAMILTON in command.	
" 6th	Lt PENNA joined the Brigade.	
" 7th	Church Parade. C.R.A. attended.	
" 8th to 9th & 10th	Nothing of importance.	
" 11th	Inspection (dismounted) by G.O.C. 2nd Army (Gen Plumer)	
" 12th to 14th	Nothing of interest.	
" 15th	Route march of whole Divisional artillery, & inspection by G.O.C. 2nd Army.	
" 16th	Colonel DELAFORCE returned.	
" 17th	In rest.	
" 18th	Seven German aeroplanes dropped bombs near ABEELE & POPERINGHE, doing very slight damage.	
" 19th & 20th & 21st	3rd Division is to return to the line. Church Parade.	

Army Form C. 2118.

WAR DIARY
or
INTELLIGENCE SUMMARY.

November 1915 23rd Bde R.F.A.

(Erase heading not required.)

Instructions regarding War Diaries and Intelligence Summaries are contained in F.S. Regs., Part II. and the Staff Manual respectively. Title pages will be prepared in manuscript.

Hour, Date, Place	Summary of Events and Information	Remarks and references to Appendices
November 22nd & 23rd	Nothing of importance.	
24th	3rd Division returns to the line. 23rd Brigade in reserve.	
25th	Marched via GODESWAERVELDE & BOESCHEPE to new billets, 1 mile E of BOESCHEPE. Division covers front from BOIS QUARANTE to just N of CANAL.	
26th to 30th	In reserve. Nothing of importance to report.	

Walter
Capt. 23rd Bde R.F.A.
3.12.15.

23 Bde R.F.A
Dec
Vol XV

Army Form C. 2118.

WAR DIARY
or
INTELLIGENCE SUMMARY.
(Erase heading not required.)

December 1915

23rd Brigade R.F.A.

Instructions regarding War Diaries and Intelligence Summaries are contained in F.S. Regs., Part II. and the Staff Manual respectively. Title pages will be prepared in manuscript.

Hour, Date, Place	Summary of Events and Information	Remarks and references to Appendices
December 1st	Brigade in rest near BOESCHEPE. Batteries started making reinforcing positions E. of DICKEBUSCH LAKE. Capt EELES posted home.	
2nd		
3rd 4th		
5th	Major-General 'X' visited 107th and 108th in rest. (HALDANE Cmdg 3rd Div.)	
6th	Lt. THOMSON joined 109th	
7th to 12th	In rest. Capt. BENHAM posted to 17th Division	
16th – 18th		
19th 5.30 am 10. am	A lot of firing about 5.30am and strong smell of gas. Bde ordered to "STAND BY." Cancelled about 10 a.m. as gas attack proved to be N. of 6th Corps: Germans did not leave their trenches. 6th Corps again gassed about 9 pm, but all quiet on our front. All quiet.	
20th to 23rd	Bde. Cmdr. and Bty. Cmdrs carry out reconnaissance of 40th Bde. position	
24th	DICKEBUSCH.	
25th 26th	One section per Bty. returns one section from each Bty. of 40th Bde. taking over their guns (which they had taken over from 24th Bde.) Relief of 40th Bde. completed. One section of 130th Bty. attd. to form RIGHT GROUP.	
27th		
28th	Some hostile shelling in the afternoon, but not directed against any Bty. position.	
29th	Wind very favourable for hostile gas attack. Every precaution being taken.	
30 – 31st	VOORMEZEELE shelled on both days : direct hit on 108th O.P. did no damage.	

W. Mogg Major Adjt.
23rd Bde R.F.A.

NEUVE-ÉGLISE — BELGIUM

SCALE 1:20,000

SITUATION

Poperinghe

● = Batty   X = Observing Station
● = Billets Red = Bde (carried with Inf (18 Pdrs))
            Blue = Bde 18 pdrs under Bde

Green = Howitzer Bde
X = Observing Station

N.B.
1. Reserve Bde
2. Bde Ammn Col
   Div Amn Col
   Billeted at BERTHEN
   and between that place
5. and WESTOUTRE.
   Mtn Bty S. of MONT VIDAIGNE

G.S.G.S. 2742

INSTRUCTIONS AS TO THE USE OF THE SQUARES

1. The map is divided into large squares, lettered "A," "B," "C," etc., the sides of which are 6000 yards in length.
2. The large squares are sub-divided into 30 smaller squares, numbered 1 to 30, the sides of which are 1000 yards in length.
3. The small squares are again sub-divided into 4 minor squares, the sides of which are 500 yards in length.
   These minor squares are to be considered as lettered a, b, c, d, but the letters are only printed on one small square in each large square to avoid confusing the map.

4. A point can thus be described as lying in square A.1.a., D.5.c., etc. If the position of a point can be identified more closely the further description N., S., E. or W., or again N.W., N.E., S.W., S.E., may be added.
5. If only the description of one small square is given, e.g. A.2., the position indicated will be taken to be the centre of A.2. Similarly A.2.d. will be understood as meaning the centre of the minor square A.2.d. unless a further description N., S., is added.
6. The description A.2.c.d. can be used if uncertainty exists as to whether c. or d. is the correct minor square.

Scale 1:20000

Yards 1000 500 0   1000   2000   3000   4000   5000   6000   7000   8000   9000

Contours at One Metre interval.

TRANSPARENT DRAWING - OVERLAY ON MAP
SHEET 2 (Position located on map)
[BOX 1399]

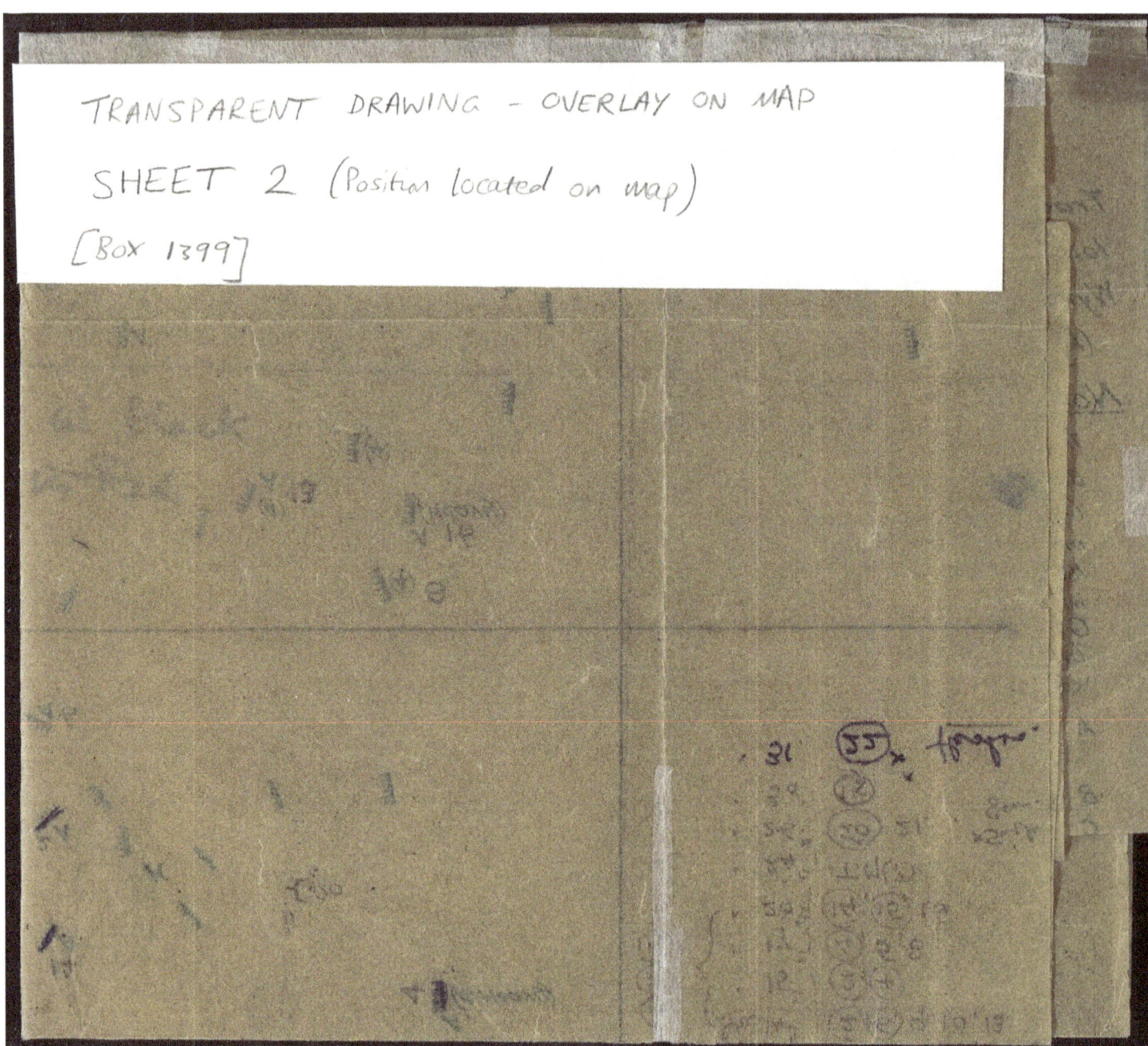

TRACING shows 3rd Div Trenches in black
and position of 5th Div & French in Red

TRANSPARENT DRAWING — OVERLAY ON MAP

SHEET 1 (Position located on map)

[BOX 1399]

1	2	3	4	1
5	6 Night	7 ○ 107	8 ○ 109 ✗109	5
9 Div HQ ✗	10 ●45 HB	11 ●108 108 4●45	12 2 Guns ✗ 48 H.B. 130	9 3 Siege ✗107
13 Div Ark HQ At	14 HQ At 12q 12q	15 20✗ 12q	16 HQ	13
1 2●○	2	3 HQ	4	1
5	6	7	8 1 Gun 5 H.B.	5

3RD DIVISION
DIVL. ARTILLERY

23RD BRIGADE R.F.A.

JAN - DEC 1916.

Became Army Brigade Jan 1917

2. ARMY

3rd Divisional Artillery.

23RD BRIGADE R. F. A.

JANUARY 1916.

WAR DIARY or INTELLIGENCE SUMMARY

Army Form C. 2118.

JANUARY 1916

23rd Bde R.F.A

Hour, Date, Place	Summary of Events and Information	Remarks and references to Appendices
January 1st / 2nd	VOORMEZEELE and ELZENWALLE heavily shelled. 108th and 109th had a combined shoot on some German Communication trenches where much work had been done — A large proportion of H.E. was used, and considerable damage done —	
3rd / 4th	9th Brigade relieved 8th Brigade during night — 3/4 Colonel Mifford (Gen. R.A.A.) joins from England for two days attachment — Mobile Artillery active round Inf. Bde. H.Q. and 2nd Siege Battery.	
5th	Three officers join from England for about a fortnights instruction — The Brigade carried out a small shoot on enemy's transport roads at 8.30 p.m.	
6th / 7th	Our Heavy Artillery (6", 8" & 9.2") bombed the left sector heavily with excellent results.	
8th	Enemy shelled T1 trench blowing down about 80 yards of parapet. This caused postponement of an enterprise intended for the night of the 8/9th.	
9th	Much movement on our left, reported to be the 50th Div. bombarding Hill 60.	
10th	Enterprise by 9th Bde. Bns. from R3 and T1 respectively, to much two points in Enemy lines to the enemy. 3.45 am began to capture prisoners, a canal behind points of assault and stop flanks shooting to form barrage. Front trenches after Infantry had returned, later dropping to trenches crowded with Germans, and were not able to Capture any live prisoners — It is thought that our fire must have caused many losses. (continued)	

WAR DIARY
or
INTELLIGENCE SUMMARY.

(Erase heading not required.)

Army Form C. 2118.

Hour, Date, Place	Summary of Events and Information	Remarks and references to Appendices
10ᵗʰ continued.	In the afternoon the enemy began to bombard our trenches in this sector (P's and Q's) heavily – Preparations had been made for this, and a "special brand" of retaliation was immediately carried out. Later in the evening the enemy again started to bombard these trenches, but stopped very quickly, so no action was taken.	
11ᵗʰ 12ᵗʰ 13ᵗʰ	Enemy shelled VOORMEZEELE, ELZENWALLE, and SCOTTISH WOOD. Our support and communication trenches heavily shelled. Retaliation by 3ʳᵈ Div Rty in similar points in enemy line. 2/Lt TYACKE, posted to 11th Brigade from D.A.C., is attached to 109ᵗʰ.	
14ᵗʰ	SCOTTISH WOOD received about 60 10.5cm Hr. shells, and was simultaneously searched by 15cm gun from railway mounting (silent sue). 108ᵗʰ and 109ᵗʰ fired 50 rds H.E. into a wood in rear of enemy 2ⁿᵈ line, opening fire simultaneously and employing gun fire.	
15ᵗʰ	The 109 effectively dispersed a German working party which had been worrying our trenches – 108 engaged a 7.7 Dn Bty the caught in the open, which immediately ceased firing.	
16ᵗʰ	Quiet day except for a little retaliation given for intermittent shelling of our trenches. (continued)	

WAR DIARY
or
INTELLIGENCE SUMMARY.
(Erase heading not required.)

Army Form C. 2118.

Instructions regarding War Diaries and Intelligence Summaries are contained in F.S. Regs., Part II. and the Staff Manual respectively. Title pages will be prepared in manuscript.

Hour, Date, Place	Summary of Events and Information	Remarks and references to Appendices
17/5	Quiet, wet, misty.	
18/5	Brigade Commander visits wagon lines.	
19/5 20/5 21/5 22/5	Very little artillery activity from either side	
23/5	Shooting on enemy support and C.Ts in retaliation. In the afternoon the enemy's win in front of his first line trench was "cut" opposite R3 trench Pl 4, and Pl 2. It is hoped that this induced him to fill his trenches.	
24/5	1.45 am mine was exploded but was rather too short to be really effective. Enemy occupied far side of crater.	
25/5	15 cm and 21 cm Howitzers started intermittent shelling of 107 Bty position and the RESTAURANT, with the help of Aeroplane observation. Major HAMILTON 2Lt HUDSON and Adjt. ALFRED DITTE (Interpreter) Killed - 1 Bombardier (107) Killed, 1 Gunner (109) wounded, Trumpeter (107) wounded (subsequently died).	
26/5	Capt. J de B.T. LUCAS posted to command 107 (from 40th Bty 23rd Bty). 2/Lt HUDSON and Bde. HITCHCOCK were buried at DICKEBUSCH MILITARY CEMETERY at 10 a.m.	(R.A. Millne)

Army Form C. 2118.

WAR DIARY
or
INTELLIGENCE SUMMARY.
(Erase heading not required.)

Instructions regarding War Diaries and Intelligence Summaries are contained in F.S. Regs., Part II and the Staff Manual respectively. Title pages will be prepared in manuscript.

Hour, Date, Place	Summary of Events and Information	Remarks and references to Appendices
26th (continued)	A memorial service for Major HAMILTON and another for Adjutant ALFRED DITTS were conducted at RENINGHELST after which both coffins were taken to POPERINGHE and there deposited in a vault.	
27th		
28th	10.9 — See and disperse a party of huns led by an Officer, and later in the day silenced a 7.7 cm Bty.	
29th	One enemy m.g. emplacement was destroyed.	
30th	Two Btys of 7.7 cm and one single gun were shelled. Some enemy front line trench RUCKELDERE, an m.g. emplacement which had been active at nights being destroyed.	
31st		

Moyh Walker Major
23rd Brigade R.H.A.

3rd Divisional Artillery.

23RD BRIGADE R. F. A.

FEBRUARY 1916.

Army Form C. 2118.

February 1916

WAR DIARY
or
INTELLIGENCE SUMMARY.
(Erase heading not required.)

Instructions regarding War Diaries and Intelligence Summaries are contained in F.S. Regs., Part II and the Staff Manual respectively. Title pages will be prepared in manuscript.

Hour, Date, Place	Summary of Events and Information	Remarks and references to Appendices
Feb. 2nd.	Very quiet, cold and misty.	
3rd.	104th Battery registered with aeroplane observation (by means of wireless).	
4th.	Very quiet day. Some rifle shelling of VOORMEZEELE.	
5th.	Enemy shelled KRUISTRAATHOEK Roads. Zeppelin passed over lines above Cassel about 10 p.m., again heard at 11.20 p.m.	
6th.	Very quiet. Fine day. A good deal of aeroplane activity.	
7th.	Again quiet except for German Aeroplane still very much in evidence. Advance Parties of 79th Brigade arrive.	
8th.	C.O. 79th Brigade and 1st. Sections arrive.	
9th.	Finally handed over to 79th Brigade about 7 p.m. and trekked to WEEMEARS via their march to ZAEM and billets at WEEMEARS CAPPEL & ZEERMEZEELE. 109th to have the Div.	
10th.	Brigade march to training area via WATTEN, NORDAUSQUES to BONNINGUES (H.Q. 2108) AGUENY (C of E) 109th Brides transport and E.) WATTEN.	
11th.	Settling down. We are to remain a 2 Battery Brigade at present.	

Army Form C. 2118.

WAR DIARY
or
INTELLIGENCE SUMMARY.
(Erase heading not required.)

3 February 1916

Instructions regarding War Diaries and Intelligence Summaries are contained in F.S. Regs., Part II. and the Staff Manual respectively. Title pages will be prepared in manuscript.

Hour, Date, Place	Summary of Events and Information	Remarks and references to Appendices
Feb. 12d.		
13d.	All quiet. Col. Delafore C.R.A. H.Q. acting C.R.A.	
14d.	Weather bad. Heard much shelling N 17 & Dir	
16d.	76d. Bd gave called up to the line in consult of N front	
17d.	Notice at the BLUFF	
	No further news. We are not apparently required to return	
	to the line	
18d. 2 a.m.	40d. Bde ... same orders to return. Destination unknown	
	Brigade. General Powell takes over C.O. of Bd Brigade	
	Brigade Commander returned	
2dd.	Church Parade — Scout field day	
2d 21st	Brigade Commission event board, Major Michell +	
22d }	General Commission to Engineer forge South	
23d }	... running until training Brothers and cross airmen	
24d }	Turned	
25d }		
27d.	Brigade Church Church Parade in morning	
28d	Major Dunlop R.H. takes over as	
29d	Brigade march part C.R.A.	

[signature] Major R.H.A
for Adjutant 22nd Bde R.H.A

3rd Divisional Artillery.

23RD BRIGADE R. F. A.

MARCH 1916.

March 1916

3rd Div
23rd Bde
23rd Bde R.F.A.

WAR DIARY or INTELLIGENCE SUMMARY.

Army Form C. 2118.

Hour, Date, Place	Summary of Events and Information	Remarks and references to Appendices
Mar. 1st	Maj. Gen. Haldane C.B. inspects 107 & 108 at work	
2nd	Bde Commander returns	
3rd to 9th	Usual Nr. patrons observed	
10th	Relief (part of) Forward to Naves in preparation for move to trenches.	
11th	Move to North Battery 5.15 a.m. from BOHNINGUES. Billet near WERMERS CAPPEL, H.Q. at CHATEAU LE TOM	
12th	Artillery reconnaissance & DICKEBUSCH billets	
13th	Relief of 37th Bde, 17th Div in the position. Reserve (Brigade) march up to village & Relief completed about 6.30 p.m. We now have 3 4guns (Baton the 18 pdr disposed of) section 107 & 1 section Howr under command of CAPT. LOEWE.	
14th	Hostile Arty v. VOGELZANG Ca 2nd & Cad much confusion astirby. In the evening our section D/107 withdrawn and put in trench alongside Battery which now becomes 107 6 guns. The other sections take one to 108 also two have 4 guns in BUND & LAKE and 1 detached section	

Army Form C. 2118.

WAR DIARY
or
INTELLIGENCE SUMMARY.
(Erase heading not required.)

March 1916

Instructions regarding War Diaries and Intelligence Summaries are contained in F. S. Regs., Part II. and the Staff Manual respectively. Title pages will be prepared in manuscript.

Hour, Date, Place	Summary of Events and Information	Remarks and references to Appendices
March 15th.	Quiet day. Detd. Sectn. 108 gun fwd during night to a position W of BRASSERIE in NSR	
16th	15 cm. Shells DICKEBUSCH Windmill but does not do any damage	
17th.	1 Section of 129 Battery joins group in NIOC. 108 forward Section withdrawn to its former position during night, as had not fired from its forward position on account of dets obtainable from there	
18th	15cm. starts on ridge between SCOTTISH WOOD and SUICIDE COPSE at 12.30 P.M. Considerable Rifle artillery activity than first day.	
19th	At 7.30 A.M. a shell passes through roof of our house, he one hurt. Two groups of 27th Begian artillery (6 (4) gun batterys) join the Group.	
20th.	3rd Belgian Battery, Reserve Shed at Bedford House before firing. Move to position occupied by dets section 108 into region clear better.	
21st.	Quiet day	
23rd	R., Q, and P heavily shelled at about 5 P.M.	
24th	At 2.30 P.M. a combined Shrapnel wood hunya, 50 rds, per battery being fired. a little rifle fire particularly into VOORMEZEELE	

(73989) W4141-463. 400,000. 9/14. H.&J.Ltd. Forms/C. 2118/10.

March 1916

Army Form C. 2118.

WAR DIARY
or
INTELLIGENCE SUMMARY.
(Erase heading not required.)

Instructions regarding War Diaries and Intelligence Summaries are contained in F. S. Regs., Part II. and the Staff Manual respectively. Title pages will be prepared in manuscript.

Hour, Date, Place	Summary of Events and Information	Remarks and references to Appendices
March 25th	At 3 P.M. and 5 P.M. 77 pm Shelled X roads and between S.P. Bdc. HQrs. and 4th Belgian Battery.	
26th	3rd Belgian Battery Shelled. From 2½ to five and 2 Canadian wounded. 16R, 17th, (18 pr) and 23rd (How) Canadian Batteries from the 4 pm through hail [?] fire up to 5.0 harassed [?] till tomorrow 4.15 a.m. upon Taj.	
Operation at St. Eloi on 27th March and following days	In the present operation the RIGHT GROUP under the Brigade Commander consists of the following:-	
	107, 108, 1 section 130, 1 section 129, 4th C.F.A. Bde = 16th, 17th, 18 Pr. and 23rd Hows (4 gun batteries), 1st Belgian Group (3 4 gun batteries) and 2nd Belgian Group (3 4 gun batteries Every section)	
	Total $\begin{cases} 20 & 18 \text{ pr.} \\ 23 & 7.7 \text{ pr. Belgian Guns} \\ 8 & 4.5" \text{ Hows.} \end{cases}$	
March 27th	Intention "I and J Company Salient at St. Eloi. 1Pl. 9 N.F. and 1Bt. 1 R.F. to assault	

March 1916

WAR DIARY
or
INTELLIGENCE SUMMARY.
(Erase heading not required.)

Army Form C. 2118.

Hour, Date, Place	Summary of Events and Information	Remarks and references to Appendices
March 27th. 4.15 am.	6 mins fired under Germans position and intense bombardment which proved to be a preliminary to an assault from flanks 30 seconds after explosion 7 mines	
4.45 am	Bombardment slowed to Ref war	
6.10 am	F.O.O. with Right Bn. reports position taken on right with few casualties	
7.40 am	Inf. Bgd. Reserve Officer reports Right and Centre read objective and in touch with Left.	
11 am.	Situation on Right stationary. Garrison on Right and Centre Bns. are short of ammunition. Stop fire but in touch with Gtte.	
1.10 p.m.	Hostile fire on captured trenches and our own trenches became very intense. Can always report enemy ammunition for counter attack. Apparently only a bombing party.	
	During the evening all Battns. replenished to 400 rounds per gun. 2nd E.R. Battn. & 50th. Divn. relieve the Battery. Belgians trying own to shake off their ammunition. Ammunition pre regt up who fire the night	
28th	Situation in morning appears to be the same. Situation in shooting with occasional intense bombardment carried out all the morning.	
3.25 pm.	Rapid trench mortar stated as enemy reported very few mins, Machines	
4.30 p.m.	M.Gun bit from again at 4.30 p.m. in retaliation	

March 1916

Army Form C. 2118.

WAR DIARY
or
INTELLIGENCE SUMMARY.
(Erase heading not required.)

Hour, Date, Place	Summary of Events and Information	Remarks and references to Appendices
March 29th	During the evening and night 28/29 we continued intermittent shooting unnecessary rate at 10 p.m. and 11.40 p.m. for retaliation	
12.20 a.m.	R.G. got Sgt. Ryde with fire from all guns to cease in enemy shooting	
3.13 a.m.	Q and R trenches being heavily shelled ordered groups turned on to 5 min. rapid, when slacken fire. During the night 5/L Potter, 7 R.W.2 Ralph Coy. withdrew small stream way and making portion unteneble. 2 posts were considerable guns down the rifle by continuing down patrols of signature that had no personnel keep them. On the left the front signature have not yet been attained. Throughout the day the enemy trenches were bombarded with a freedom at no intervals, according to the enemy's actions.	
30th. 11 a.m.	Periodic bursts of fire were first throughout the night. From this time a desultory barrage until 6.15 p.m. and 2 hours was kept up opposite left & objective. Snipers very hard pressed.	

March 1916

Army Form C. 2118.

WAR DIARY
or
INTELLIGENCE SUMMARY.
(Erase heading not required.)

Instructions regarding War Diaries and Intelligence Summaries are contained in F.S. Regs., Part II and the Staff Manual respectively. Title pages will be prepared in manuscript.

Hour, Date, Place	Summary of Events and Information	Remarks and references to Appendices
March 30th. (contd.)	Enemy Artillery showing much more activity against Batteries. 13a being heavily shelled with 15cm and 2 E.R. until 10.5am. No casualties. Some Intermittent Fire and Barrage maintained throughout the night.	
31st.	A most quiet day. No counter battery work done by enemy. Trenches and Gap heavily shelled. Barrage maintained and crater occupied by enemy shelled.	

E. Willson
2 Lt. R. Fa.
for Captain 22nd Bgde. R. Fa.

3rd Divisional Artillery.

23RD BRIGADE R. F. A.

APRIL 1916.

April 1916

23 Bde
R.F.A.

WAR DIARY
or
INTELLIGENCE SUMMARY.
(Erase heading not required.)

Army Form C. 2118.

Hour, Date, Place	Summary of Events and Information	Remarks and references to Appendices
April 1st. 1am	S.O.S. received from B3. Opened a fire momentarily without fire from all guns and howrs. The group of S.O.S. was cancelled. A bombing attack by the enemy had been attempted and defeated.	
	Ranges:- Retaliation fire over Ptarmigan and Cambrin Right. Remainder of our registered subjected to intense fire for rest of am.	
	9. In the afternoon 10E was heavily shelled with 15 cm & 10.5 cm Rounds and 10 cm Gun (Weichselmann Rifle and mortar) and left Section (Red Learn Battery) also its approach when a battery of Cossa Group was also to get them ranged and rammed. 10E Rd. were withdrawn at 2pm. They resumed direct R.A. on their elephant pit 2 signallers, Bombardier Berry killed throughout the night	
5.15 pm	3 guns 10E opened fire again and continued on Barry	
2nd	Quite peaceful morning though some from trenches visible after heavily shelled. Barry continued without cessation "Judge Z" Bombarded. The enemy thought she right, night 2/3.	

April 1916

WAR DIARY
or
INTELLIGENCE SUMMARY.
(Erase heading not required.)

Army Form C. 2118.

Instructions regarding War Diaries and Intelligence Summaries are contained in F.S. Regs., Part II. and the Staff Manual respectively. Title pages will be prepared in manuscript.

Hour, Date, Place	Summary of Events and Information	Remarks and references to Appendices
April 3rd 1.33 am	Bombardment became intense till	
2 am	10 am. Infantry assault. Artillery lifting then for to a safe range which was continued until assault was received that objective had been obtained. About 70 or 80 prisoners taken.	
	Ammunition expended by Group since beginning of operation until 12 noon 3rd. —	
	H.E. Shrap. Rgtl. } Rounds	
	17,526 15,719 5,923 } 39,168	
2.30 P.M.	Barrage commenced again and continued for an hour	
4.50 P.M.	on Hun Shell H3SA	✱ Sheet 28
5 P.M.	Barrage commenced again and continued with varying intensity until first evening	
	During evening and night reported 10 cm. gun Shelled H29 a & c & H266 at intervals. Quiet night no firing on our part. Our infantry relieved by Canadian Infantry.	
4th.		
	During afternoon 2 S.O.S. calls reported from T7, on trench being heavily shelled but no attack being attempted by Hun.	
6.25 P.M.	S.O.S. call, 2nd verbale reported from mound. Heavy Hun shelling of trenches but no infantry attack	

WAR DIARY or INTELLIGENCE SUMMARY

Army Form C. 2118.

April 1916

Hour, Date, Place	Summary of Events and Information	Remarks and references to Appendices
4th (contd) 6.15 P.M.	Bgde. Recon. Officer reports that Crater No. 5 is in hands of Huns again. Reparation effort to fire and barrage with our own intended put on to a time	
5th	1 Section each of 1st & 2nd Scott. Return.? Batteries are being relieved by Sections of Batteries of 1st Canadian Div. Last night's report that Crater was in hands of Huns turns out to be incorrect. Few firing during the day than on previous days. Relief of 1st & 2nd S.R. Batteries by 2nd & 1st Canadian Batteries completed.	
10.36 P.M.	Huns shell our front line heavily and intense rifle fire from for about 20 min.	
6th	Huns counter attacked after a heavy bombardment of our rear front line trenches, following their attack on support trenches was heavily shelled and an intense barrage, shell fire was put along the Scottish Wood Ridge. All communication between infantry and trenches broken up and message going through us with difficulty. We kept up fire with our 17th Canadian Battery. DICKEBUSCH and the batteries on the BUND were shelled at intervals during the day from 6 A.M. onwards. 15th el Batter had a direct hit on No 2 gun but only slight damage done.	
6.45 a.m.	It appears that Huns hold all the Salient (including Craters) with the exception of 7.3, 7.4 & 9.2	(Ref. Special 1/5000 map)

WAR DIARY or INTELLIGENCE SUMMARY

Army Form C. 2118.

April 1916

Hour, Date, Place	Summary of Events and Information	Remarks and references to Appendices
April 6th (contd) 12.30 P.M.	Commenced to shell craters 2&3, bombardment to cease at 1.30 P.M. when Bombers will attack. No adversary found however.	
1.30 P.M.		
12.45 P.M.	Report from Brd. D.A. that we hold Crater 5	
1.30 P.M.	107th Battery heavily shelled and put out of action, Capt. L. LOEWE, 2nd Lieut. H.M.S. BARNET and 1 man killed.	
	Very little definite information about the situation received during the day.	
	Barrage alternating with bursts of fire kept up throughout night	
7th 10.30 A.M.	107 & 158 Batteries each ran out 2 guns out of action	
11.20 A.M.	Situation — we hold craters 4 & 5.	
11.40 A.M.	Batteries ordered to register craters 2&3 and other points	
	During afternoon 107th & 130th Batteries and BUND shelled with "tear" shells.	
	Intermittent bombardment of points registered during the morning carried out at intervals from 4.20 to 7.10 P.M.	
	During the night a 10 c.m. gun was shelling round about our HQrs. 1 round scored a direct hit on one of the bedrooms. No damage done to our communications.	
	No1. Belgian Group was attached to 40th Bgde. R.F.A. which then came under our Group commander.	
8th 11.35 A.M.	A comparatively quiet day. 17th & 23rd Canadian Batteries ordered to cut wire in front of Hun front line from O2c7.2 to O2c9.6	Special map 1/5000

WAR DIARY or INTELLIGENCE SUMMARY

Army Form C. 2118.

April 1916

Hour, Date, Place	Summary of Events and Information	Remarks and references to Appendices
April 8th. 5.10 P.M.	Very intense bombardment of Q & R Support trenches which did not slacken off until 5.50 P.M. In spite of its severity it did not cause a single casualty.	
12 m.n.	Canadians made an attack on lost trenches without Artillery Support.	
9th. 2.25 A.M.	Reported that attacking party met with strong resistance and were compelled to return.	
3.25 A.M.	Intense bombardment of Cu. O2c 7.3 – 9.6 ordered	
3.30 A.M.	Fire lifted and a second attack launched but without success.	
9.30 A.M.	Reported from Infantry Rifle that we have established ourselves on the W. side of Gate 3	
1 P.M.	Enemy shelled old P trenches and we retaliated with 5 mm intense.	
9.30 P.M.	Barrage opened at moderate rate and Infantry made another attack	
10th. 2 – A.M.	Mtr rate was increased and Infantry made another attack on Gates 1, 2 & 3	
2.10 A.M.	Between 2 & 2.30 the Huns sent up many Green and red lights	
2.20 A.M.	S.O.S. from T.7	
2.30 A.M.	Heavy barrage from MOATED GRANGE to VOORMEZEELE	
2.55 A.M.	Enemy fire began to slacken	
	Enemy again opened fire on C.T.s, and wood E. of VOORMEZEELE We continued to fire wind ranging intervals throughout the rest of yesterday evening the relief of this Brigade by 4th Canadian I.A. Bgde. 69 subsections commenced.	

April 1916

WAR DIARY
or
INTELLIGENCE SUMMARY.
(Erase heading not required.)

Army Form C. 2118.

Instructions regarding War Diaries and Intelligence Summaries are contained in F.S. Regs., Part II and the Staff Manual respectively. Title pages will be prepared in manuscript.

Hour, Date, Place	Summary of Events and Information	Remarks and references to Appendices
April 10d. (contd.)	Situation: Last night our Infantry captured crater 2. We now hold Craters 2, 4 & 5 and the near side of crater 3.	
12 - noon	10th and 1st C.A. Battns. carried 10th d. cleared than pits. No casualties. D.S.O. In the afternoon we hear that Capt. A.W. Eaton T.M.C. 7 eld. Bgd. Div. who had his leg broken a month ago on Mess was killed that morning. He was up in one of our planes which was shot down by Jets Manor.	
11d.	Fairly quiet day. Huns put in a heavy barrage South of DICKEBUSCH LAKE in the afternoon and damaged the communications considerably.	
12d.	Round all day and thing quiet in consequence. Relief of the Brigade by 6th C.F.A. Brigade complete about 7.30 P.M.	
13d - 15d.	Remainder of Brigade went out to rest in EECKE (Hqrs.) & area round about there and St. Sylvestre Cappel (10), 102 & Q.C. Nothing to report.	
16d.	Church Parade in Cinema Hall at EECKE	
17d - 18d.	Preparations for Divisive Sports in Review.	
19d.	Preliminaries of Divisive Sports held.	
20d.	Annual for men of H. Qr. Staff. in the evening. Very tiring afterwards. Finals of Divisive Sports. A good day for it.	
21st - 22nd	Nothing to report.	

Army Form C. 2118.

April 1916

WAR DIARY
or
INTELLIGENCE SUMMARY.

(Erase heading not required.)

Hour, Date, Place	Summary of Events and Information	Remarks and references to Appendices
April 23rd	Lt. S.M. de H. WHATTON, the Adjutant, awarded Military Cross for his good work during recent operations at St. ELOI. Easter Sunday; church parade at CINEMA HALL.	
24th	Maj. Gen. Haldane Cmdg. IIIrd. Div. presented ribbons of decorations awarded for services in recent operations. 107th. Battery temporarily detached from Brigade and sent to STEENVOORDE to become the Northern Artillery School. In the afternoon 4 2nd. Brigade R.F.A. Ten Sports.	
25th - 26th	Nothing to report.	
27th	Brigade Ammn. Column have a route march and are inspected by Brigade Cmmander.	
28th	102d. Battery have a route march and are also inspected	
29th	Nothing to report.	
30th.	108th. Battery are attached to Col. Man D.S.O., commanding XXX d. Bde., for tactical purposes and goes into rest near VIERSTRAAT ROAD in Nq6.	Sheet 28

E Morgan
2Lt. R.F.A.
for Adjutant 22nd Bgde. R.F.A.

3rd Divisional Artillery.

23RD BRIGADE R. F. A.

M A Y 1 9 1 6.

May 1916

WAR DIARY
or
INTELLIGENCE SUMMARY. 23 Bde R.F.A.

Army Form C. 2118.

(Erase heading not required.)

Hour, Date, Place	Summary of Events and Information	Remarks and references to Appendices
May 1st	Our H.Qrs. Coast rest area at EECKE and moved into BURGRAVE FARM in Nigs between LOCRE and KEMMEL. We came into action on 107th. Battery in steel cotry to Northern Artillery Scheme and 108th. Battery to work the command of it. Centre Group for tactical purposes.	
2nd to 5th. 6th. 7th to 9th. 10th.	Nothing to report. H.Qr. moved to new Wag. Rm. in M16d.0.7 Nothing to report. Accident at 108th. Battery. A fuse No. 8 and Sig. How. Shell exploded wounding two men one of whom died shortly afterwards.	Sheet 28
11th.	Reorganisation of Divisional Artillery taken place. A new 4 gun 4.5 How. Battery, D23, is formed and becomes part of our Brigade. It is made up as follows:- 1 section each of 129 & 13 Batteries, Battery Staff from 30th. Bde. H.Qrs. and Establishment of horses made up from 3rd. Bde. Ammn. Column. Officers: C.O. Capt. Marsh, 2nd. Lt. O'Sgood late of 130th. Battery, 2nd Lt. Bennett late of 129th. Battery, 2nd. Lt. Koop late of 107th. Battery, 2nd. Lt. Collard. We are rough first a Brigade Ammn. Column.	
12th to 13th. 14th.	Nothing to report. Our H.Qr. got into action (in N26 near MILLEKRUSSE) taken over the command of the Centre Group (D23, 49th & 108th. Batteries) from the 3rd. Bde. R.F.A. which has ceased to exist.	Sheet 28

Army Form C. 2118.

WAR DIARY
or
INTELLIGENCE SUMMARY.
(Erase heading not required.)

May 1916

Instructions regarding War Diaries and Intelligence Summaries are contained in F. S. Regs., Part II. and the Staff Manual respectively. Title pages will be prepared in manuscript.

Hour, Date, Place	Summary of Events and Information	Remarks and references to Appendices
May 15th. 16th.	Gas quiet. The General reconnoitred 4 proposed Battery positions. Hun Trench Mortars very active. Capt. N.W.W. Free posted to command 1/D23 Battery.	
17th.	The General visits 23 T.M.B. which is now affiliated to the Brigade for tactical purposes. Hun T. Mortars are again very active. We did a certain amount of retaliation.	
18th. 19th.	Quiet. 158th Battery badly crumped once at about 1.30 P.M. and again at about 4 P.M. They vacated their gun pits each time and had no casualties. Their No. 3 was destroyed.	
20th.	158th are to move to one of the positions reconnoitred on the 16th. Hun shelled near HALLEBAST CORNER and Wippely Beans in the morning.	
21st.	Quiet. A Hun plane was shot down near LA CLYTE.	
22nd	Nothing of importance to report.	

Army Form C. 2118.

WAR DIARY
or
INTELLIGENCE SUMMARY.
(Erase heading not required.)

May 1916

Hour, Date, Place	Summary of Events and Information	Remarks and references to Appendices
May 23rd.	Quiet. Relief of 9th Infantry Bgde. by 149th Inf. Bgde. commenced	
24th.	About 12.25 P.M. No 4 gun of D23 Battery had a Premature. Two men were singed. Some set. charges were set on fire and where in turn set alight the gun pit on fire. There were 81 rounds of ammn. in the pit and about half an hour later these exploded. Only a mangled piece of scrap iron was left of the gun and the pit was completely destroyed. 149th Inf. Bgde. takes over 9th Bgde. Sectn.	
25th.	The J, K and L received a bad hammering from Russian guns, howitzers and trench mortars commencing at about 2.40 P.M. and continuing for over 2 hours. The Battery in the full sub sector had 4 & casualties. We retaliated and fired 6" and 8" howr. were turned on.	
26th 27th.	Nothing to report. Today is the 200th Anniversary of the Founding of the Royal Warrant to the Royal Regiment of Artillery. About mid day D23 had another Premature, just outside the muzzle. The gun was damaged and three men were wounded.	
28th.	Nothing to report.	

Army Form C. 2118.

WAR DIARY
or
INTELLIGENCE SUMMARY.
(Erase heading not required.)

May 1916

Instructions regarding War Diaries and Intelligence Summaries are contained in F.S. Regs., Part II. and the Staff Manual respectively. Title pages will be prepared in manuscript.

Hour, Date, Place	Summary of Events and Information	Remarks and references to Appendices
May 29ch.	About 12.45am. 149th Bgde. Sent a bombing patrol to examine crater caused by explosion of German Mine in no mans land. Spotted by trench. Our Brigade "Stood to" but were not required to shoot. Noise section of our group relieved on night 29/30 by 250th Bgd R.E.	
30th.	Command of Group passes to O.C. 250th Bgde R.E. Remainder of Group relieved after dark and marched to rest area at EECKE	
31st.	Setting in	

E. Winston 2 Lt. R.E.
for Adjutant 23rd Brigade R.E.

3rd Divisional Artillery.

23rd Brigade R. F. A.

J U N E 1 9 1 6.

I. D.A.G. IIIrd Echelon   3

Herewith War Diary for June
1916

E.L. Morgan 2Lt R.F.A.
for Lt. Col. Cmdg 23RD BRIGADE, R.F.A.

Vol 20

Army Form C. 2118.

WAR DIARY
or
INTELLIGENCE SUMMARY.
(Erase heading not required.)

June 1916

Hour, Date, Place	Summary of Events and Information	Remarks and references to Appendices
June 1st 2nd	Capt. N.W.W. FREER in command of the Brigade	
2nd 6 a.m.	of evening orders received to "Stand to" Brigade and Battery commanders & up to reconnoitre positions to cover G.H.Q. 2nd line swing to Canadian Railway cutting from W Salient Lt. Burden awarded Military Cross	
h/f 3rd/4th	108 Battery go into position at H21d11 near DICKEBUSCH and D/23 close to them. Both attached to 42nd Brigade (Right Group)	(Sheet 28)
SW	107 Battery re-form and go into position near ASYLUM, YPRES under 40th Bde. (Left Group) High Prussell receives from Hospital and takes over command	
6 u.	of lot again. 107 shelled.	
h/f 6/7 u.	107 Pr. S. now wounded, 3 horses killed and several wounded. They move to a position N.W. of ASYLUM	
W 7 u.	D/23 & forward into action in LAUNDRY KRUISSTRAAT	
8u. to 12 u.	Artillery to re-park	

Army Form C. 2118.

WAR DIARY
or
INTELLIGENCE SUMMARY.

(Erase heading not required.)

Instructions regarding War Diaries and Intelligence Summaries are contained in F.S. Regs., Part II. and the Staff Manual respectively. Title pages will be prepared in manuscript.

Hour, Date, Place	Summary of Events and Information	Remarks and references to Appendices
June 13th. 2.30 AM	Cambrais attacked and rescued nearly all the ground which had been lost. D/23 took part in the forward movement	
14th.	Lt. Col. Delafora takes over command of Right Group	
15th 16th 17th	Further report entitled Belgian German Army C.R.A. Brigade leaves Sailly for 2nd ARMY TRAINING area and stands by at RENESCURE	
18th.	Brigade marches to NIELLES - LES - BLEQUIN where to 5 miles from training area.	
19th 20th.	ACQUIN reconnoitred. Brigade moves to ACQUIN which is now our training area. Brigade commander returns from HQ 2nd RA	
21st to 30th.	Training at ACQUIN. Battery Gun Drill and Signalling Schemes.	

E. Munro M. 28. R.9.
for Adjutant 23rd Brigade R.F.A.

3rd Divisional Artillery.

23RD BRIGADE R.F.A.

JULY 1916.

July 1916

Army Form C. 2118.

23rd Bde RFA

Vol 21

WAR DIARY
or
INTELLIGENCE SUMMARY
(Erase heading not required.)

Hour, Date, Place	Summary of Events and Information	Remarks and references to Appendices
July 1st 1916 ACQUIN	Received orders to march to AUDRUICQ the following day.	Ref: MAPS HAZEBROUCK 5A
" 2nd July 3rd	11:30 am left ACQUIN for AUDRUICQ 3:30 pm Arrived AUDRUICQ and entrained 4am Arrived DOULLENS, detrained and marched to HEM. 6:30am Arrived HEM, and billeted. 9:30am Received orders to march at NOON to VIGNACOURT 11:30am marched from HEM 2:30 pm Arrived CANAPLES, watered and feed. After 2 hrs a delay on road were ordered to billet for night in CANAPLES	← MAP AMIENS 17 & LENS 11
July 4th	1:30 pm Recd orders to move to DAOURS 9:20 pm marched from CANAPLES	
July 5th	5:30 am Arrived DAOURS after 8 hours march. Spent night here.	
	12 n.o.nt. Received orders for Bde and Bty Commanders to reconnoitre Battery Positions near CARNOY.	
July 6th	Bde and Bty Commanders reconnoitre Positions Divisional Artillery to cut wire opposite BAZENTIN-LE-GRAND. 10 am Div: Arty: moved from DAOURS to march into Action.	

23rd Brigade, R.F.A.   Army Form C. 2118.

WAR DIARY
or
INTELLIGENCE SUMMARY.
(Erase heading not required.)

Hour, Date, Place	Summary of Events and Information	Remarks and references to Appendices
July 6. 1916 (Cont.)	9.30 p.m. Reached wagon lines – watered and fed – and marched on to CARNOY (1x for Battery). H.Q. behind LA GUERRE WOOD – Battery positions between old German Front and 2nd line.	
July 7th.	Remaining sections moved into action. Registration and wire-cutting began.	
July 8"	Wire cutting	
" 9"	Wire cutting	
" 10"	2Lt I.N.F. FUTTYCKE wounded (107 Battery) 1 gunner 108 wounded	–12". 1 Gunner killed 107 Bty 1 Sergeant wounded [?]
" 11"	H.Q. move to old British Front line. Wire cutting	
" 12"	Wire cutting.	
" 13"	Wire cutting	

Army Form C. 2118.

23rd Brigade R.F.A.

Summary of Operations commencing July 14th : 1916.

WAR DIARY
or
INTELLIGENCE SUMMARY.
(Erase heading not required.)

Hour, Date, Place	Summary of Events and Information	Remarks and references to Appendices
July 14th 1916 3.25am	Intense bombardment of enemy front line and wire by all guns.	Ref: MAPS $\frac{1}{10,000}$ LONGUEVAL $\frac{1}{20,000}$ MARTIN PUICH (combined)
3.30am	Infantry assault front line - Fire lifted to support line.	
3.35am	Infantry assault and capture support line.	
4.20am	Infantry of 9th Brigade have taken and consolidated enemy front and support line. 8th Bde on right hung up by thick wire.	
4.25am	Infantry advance on to crest N.Nua BAZENTIN-LE-GRAND WOOD	
6.30am	Village of BAZENTIN-LE-GRAND assaulted and taken.	
12.30am	Small enemy counter-attack on BAZENTIN-LE-GRAND repulsed.	
1 pm	Strong enemy counter-attack on BAZENTIN-LE-GRAND. Attack crushed by Field ARTILLERY; enemy do not reach our front line or the VILLAGE.	

Army Form C. 2118

23 Brigade, R.F.A.

Summary of Operations
Commencing July 14, 1916.

WAR DIARY
or
INTELLIGENCE SUMMARY
(Erase heading not required.)

Instructions regarding War Diaries and Intelligence Summaries are contained in F. S. Regs., Part II. and the Staff Manual respectively. Title pages will be prepared in manuscript.

Hour, Date, Place	Summary of Events and Information	Remarks and References to Appendices
		Ref: MAPS 1/10,000 LONGUEVAL 1/20,000 MARTINPUICH (Contoured)
July 14th 1916. 5 p.m.	Village of LONGUEVAL reported to be in our hands.	
6.15 p.m.	7th Div'n on our left advance to the assault of HIGH WOOD – 2 reg'ts of 2nd Indian Cavalry Division advance to attack DELVILLE WOOD from N.W.	
7.15 p.m.	Enemy counterattacks and forced a temporary footing in BAZENTIN-LE-PETIT but was driven out again.	
8.20 p.m.	Infantry of 7th Div'n. enter HIGH WOOD.	
July 15th 1916. 12.5 am	Line of outposts formed in front of HIGH WOOD — consolidated line runs along road N. of BAZENTIN-LE-GRAND	

5

Army Form C. 2118

23rd Brigade R.F.A.
Summary of Operations
Commencing 14th July 1916.

WAR DIARY
or
INTELLIGENCE SUMMARY
(Erase heading not required.)

Instructions regarding War Diaries and Intelligence Summaries are contained in F. S. Regs., Part II. and the Staff Manual respectively. Title pages will be prepared in manuscript.

Hour, Date, Place	Summary of Events and Information	Remarks and References to Appendices
July 15th 1916.	Except for heavy bombardments on both sides, day uneventful.	Ref. MAPS LONGUEVAL 1/10,000 MARTINPUICH 1/20,000 (confused)
July 16th 1916.	3rd Divisional Artillery moved forward - 23rd Bde into CATERPILLAR VALLEY. Heavy bombardments.	
July 17th 1916.	Uneventful day. Heavy bombardments.	
July 18th 1916.	Heavy bombardments - Enemy very active shelling all points. At 6 p.m. after an intense bombardment enemy attacked and recaptured DELVILLE WOOD and part of LONGUEVAL. From 10.30 pm till 6 am July 18 enemy shelled MONTAUBAN with men and of GAS SHELL. 1 Telephonist gassed at H.Q. 1 GAS SHELL.	
July 19th.	During day, Enemy artillery very active - paying particular attention to CATERPILLAR VALLEY and the batteries in it. 2/Lieut T.W. OSGOOD killed 2/23 battery. 108: had 1 gunner killed and 2 wounded. 107 2 gunners wounded. H.Q. 1 telephonist wounded.	

Army Form C. 2118
23rd Bgde. RFA.
Summary B Operations
Commencing July 14th 1916.

WAR DIARY
or
INTELLIGENCE SUMMARY
(Erase heading not required.)

Hour, Date, Place	Summary of Events and Information	Remarks and References to Appendices
July 19th 1916.	Enemy's artillery very active all day. During night after our intense bombardment he retook DELVILLE WOOD and part of HIGH WOOD – Infantry established themselves along ridge from HIGH WOOD to LONGUEVAL.	Ref. MAPS. LONGUEVAL 1/20000 MARTIN PUICH (combined).
July 20th 1916.	Batteries moved to positions covering DELVILLE WOOD Position near MONTAUBAN – MARICOURT road.	
July 21st	H.Q. moved to position near TRAIN ALLEY in old German 2nd line. After a heavy bombardment, the enemy attacked LONGUEVAL but was repulsed. Capt. G. L. KEYNES R.A.M.C. to No. 38 C.C.S. Capt. H. L. MANN RAMC to H.Q.	
–22nd	Hostile Artillery very active – 9.50 p.m. 5th Divn attacked HIGH WOOD. At same moment Enemy attacked LONGUEVAL but was again repulsed.	

23rd Brigade. R.F.A.

Army Form C. 2118.

WAR DIARY
or
INTELLIGENCE SUMMARY.
(Erase heading not required.)

Hour, Date, Place	Summary of Events and Information	Remarks and references to Appendices
July 23rd 3.40 a.m.	Attacks by part of 3rd Divn. on LONGUEVAL (9th Brigade) DELVILLE WOOD and GUILLEMONT (8th Brigade) in conjunction with 5th Divn. Objective was not gained.	
July 24 -	Enemy artillery very active – shelling roads and batteries with 21 cm and downwards. Enemy also shelled MONTAUBAN with 11" and 15". Another Counter attack on LONGUEVAL repulsed.	
July 25th.	Enemy artillery again very active. H.Q. Conkelles to move to dug.outs in old German front line.	
July 26th.	A quiet day. Enemy began small shooting with about 7 p.m. Enemy heavy howitzers. Direct hit on 108 Bty Sergeants mess – 3 Sergeants killed.	108 3 sergeants killed 107 {1 gunner killed / 1" wounded} D/13 1 gunner killed.
July 27th.	Attack by 2nd Division on LONGUEVAL and DELVILLE WOOD. 23rd Bde R.F.A. barraging in support. Objective gained. 107 Battery withdrawn with only 2 guns in action 108 lost over 107 guns and fires with 5 guns in action	

WAR DIARY
or
INTELLIGENCE SUMMARY.

23rd Brigade R.F.A.   Army Form C. 2118.

(Erase heading not required.)

Hour, Date, Place	Summary of Events and Information	Remarks and references to Appendices
July 27 (cont)	2nd Division took 4 Officers and 157 O.R. in attack on DELVILLE WOOD. Ground gained was consolidated in spite of heavy Counter-attacks.	
— 28.	H.Q. again shelled from 11.30am till 1.0pm. German counter-attack on LONGUEVAL repulsed.	1 for H.Q. wounded.
— 29.	Quiet day.	
— 30.	4.45am. Attack of GUILLEMONT by 30th Divn - XIIIth Corps. 23rd Bde. remaining in support. XXth French Corps and other French troops attacking on our right. After 10 am., a quiet day. 107 - 2nd Lieut E. FARBROTHER wounded by premature from 4.7's.	
— 31	A very hot and quiet day.	

[signature] Major Bhatar A/ Capt-Col
Cmdg. 23RD BRIGADE, R.F.A.

3rd Divisional Artillery

23rd BRIGADE

ROYAL FIELD ARTILLERY

AUGUST 1916

SECRET 50/10

SECRET

To B.M. 3rd D.A.

Herewith War Diary for
August 1916.

E. Morgan 2nd R.F.A.
for Lt. Col Comdt
23RD BRIGADE, R.F.A.

H.Q. 23rd BRIGADE
1 SEP. 1916
ROYAL FIELD ARTILLERY

SECRET

23 Bde R.F.A. Vol 22

23rd Bde. R.F.A.

WAR DIARY
or
INTELLIGENCE SUMMARY
(Erase heading not required.)

Army Form C. 2118.

August 1916

Hour, Date, Place	Summary of Events and Information	Remarks and references to Appendices
August 1st.	Talus Boise Valley. Camped at midday. H.Q. Shrapnelled during afternoon. Further news of relief.	
2nd.	Vacated position about midday and marched to rest area at TREUX. 55th. D.A. took our place in the line although they did not take over till positions of the Brigade	
3rd to 13th.	Rest at TREUX	
4th.	IIIrd Div. team Red Lion & jumping competitions. 102th Battery won team competition. Lt. HEG, Burdon (102nd) was 3rd in jumping competition.	
6th.	C.R.A. visited Batteries with A.D.V.S.	
7th.	Major Gen. Haldane C.B., D.S.O. posted to command of VII A. Corps	
14th.	Bde & Battery Commanders reconnoitred positions E of MARICOURT.	
15th.	No action open	
	Bde. HQ. in deep dugout at A23.a.S.O. Battery all very close. We relieved a Brigade of 35th Div. Arty.	

WAR DIARY
or
INTELLIGENCE SUMMARY.
(Erase heading not required.)

Army Form C. 2118.

August 1916

Instructions regarding War Diaries and Intelligence Summaries are contained in F.S. Regs., Part II and the Staff Manual respectively. Title pages will be prepared in manuscript.

Hour, Date, Place	Summary of Events and Information	Remarks and references to Appendices
August 16th	Attack by IIIrd Dis., 153rd French Dis. and 24th Div. on German line S. of GUILLEMONT Zero at 5.40 P.M. Bombardment started at 5.10 P.M. All objectives gained in front, not quite as by S of L.	
17th	Persons were sheered in morning and Valley * in afternoon. Y wood shelled in evening and D/23 Officers mess hit. Capt Frier scraped on the head by splinter.	* Main road thro MARICOURT + from Y wood down to SOMME
18th		
1.30 A.M.	107th Battery had 2 telephonists killed and 1 wounded (due subsequently) by stray shell	
10.30 A.M.	Direct hit by S.9" shell on No.1 gun D/23. 2 gunners killed & 2 wounded.	
2.45 P.M.	Attack by 24th, IIIrd & 153rd (FRENCH) Division on German trenches between GUILLEMONT and ANGLE WOOD. 4 Phases. D/23 fire S.K. shell at LEUZE WOOD. A further report to have reached objective	
6.30 P.M.	Stray enemy counter attack from directions of GUILLEMONT. 3rd & 4th Phases of operation cancelled.	

WAR DIARY
or
INTELLIGENCE SUMMARY.

(Erase heading not required.)

Army Form C. 2118.

August 1916

Hour, Date, Place	Summary of Events and Information	Remarks and references to Appendices
August 19th.	Barrage on line in front of our Infantry all day.	
9 P.M.	Ammunition dump of 6" French Howitzer was seen up in hostile fire.	
20th. 1.30 A.M.	Cordite charge of 6" Siege Battery close to the HQ set on fire. 4 men severely burnt.	
9.3 A.M.	Divnl. Service held at H.Q.	
	IIIrd Div. Infantry relieved by 25th Div. 94.	× LONGUEVAL SHEET
	Strong point S2b6 7.2 bombarded for 2 hrs. by Corps Heavy Artillery and afterwards assaulted by our Infantry. North lobe ANGLE WOOD again during the night.	
21st.	Star Barrage all day.	
22nd	A good deal of hostile fire during the day.	
5.32 P.M.	108th Battery had 4 Officers Servants killed and 1 wounded severely by a stray bump.	
24th.	Further advance by XIV th Corps and French on our right. 20th Div attached to N of GUILLEMONT. 35th Div. bombed up to S.E. corner of FALFEMONT FARM. French got well into SAVERNAKE WOOD	

Army Form C. 2118.

August 1916

WAR DIARY
or
INTELLIGENCE SUMMARY.
(Erase heading not required.)

Instructions regarding War Diaries and Intelligence Summaries are contained in F.S. Regs., Part II. and the Staff Manual respectively. Title pages will be prepared in manuscript.

Hour, Date, Place	Summary of Events and Information	Remarks and references to Appendices
August 24th	D/23 fired 600 THERMITE at LEUZE WOOD with the object of igniting Hun Gallery Strongpoint. The THERMITE did not come quite up to expectations as LEUZE WOOD was not burnt down.	
25th	Appreciation of III rd Div. Gaps received from G.O.C. IV th Army on the transference of III rd Div. to another army.	
27th 9.30 A.M.	Divine Service. Very wet. 9th Brigade is not covered. 13th Lt. Bde. IV th Div. has field in their a gap [N.E.] of ANGLE WOOD.	
29th	Preliminary bombardment for further Minor Commences.	
3.30 P.M.	Operations postponed.	
30th	Twelfth Offensive of the Fourth Army postponed for 48 hours on account of very wet weather. Bar. 28.90	
31st	Weather much improved. Brigade and Battery Commanders of 16th Div. C of some up to reconnoitre our positions preparatory to relieving us.	

E.D. Mewgarge R.F.E.
for Adjutant 23rd Brigade R.F.A.

(73989) W4141—463. 400,000. 9/14. H.&J.Ltd. Forms/C. 2118/10.

3rd Divisional Artillery.

23RD BRIGADE R. F. A.

SEPTEMBER 1916.

SECRET   S0/12

To Brigade Major 3rd DA

Herewith War Diary for September 1916.

1/10/1916

E.L. Morgan
Lt-R?A
for Lt. Col. Comdg. 23rd Brigade RFA

23rd Brigade R.F.A. 3rd Divn

1st – 30th September 1916

Army Form C. 2118

Instructions regarding War Diaries and Intelligence Summaries are contained in F. S. Regs., Part II. and the Staff Manual respectively. Title pages will be prepared in manuscript.

WAR DIARY
or
INTELLIGENCE SUMMARY
(Erase heading not required.)

Vol 23

Hour, Date, Place	Summary of Events and Information	Remarks and References to Appendices
September 1st.	During early morning we were much annoyed by gas and tear shells.	
2nd.	Preliminary Bombardment for renewed offensive commences in earnest.	
3rd.	The Day! XV th Corps to take GINCHY and French XIV th Corps to reach the line T20 a 6.5. W. edge of LEUZE WOOD, joining tank with French about SAVERNAKE WOOD. French troops immediately S. of XIV th Corps attacking trenches W. of SAVERNAKE WOOD.	(GUILLEMONT SHEET)
9 A.M.	ZERO ers 3 Bde. FALFEMONT FARM attacked by 13d. Inf. Bde. 5th Divn. as a separate operation. Unsuccessful. Our troops got into the FARM but by nightfall were back again on their original line N.E. of ANGLE WOOD	

Army Form C. 2118.

WAR DIARY
or
INTELLIGENCE SUMMARY

(Erase heading not required.)

September 1916.

Instructions regarding War Diaries and Intelligence Summaries are contained in F.S. Regs., Part II. and the Staff Manual respectively. Title pages will be prepared in manuscript.

Hour, Date, Place		Summary of Events and Information	Remarks and References to Appendices
September 3rd.	12 NOON	ZERO HOUR. General attack. Further N. the XIV C. Corps did much better. 20th. Div. on left captured GUILLEMONT and reached cross roads E. N. of the place. No news of French. The XV C. Corps reached the outskirts of GINCHY	
	Evening	D/23 had a Premature, 1 man killed	
September 4th.	3.10 P.M.	Further attack on FALFEMONT FARM by 5 d. Div. Not very Successful at first but during the night the FARM was entirely captured. Further N. we reached N.W. corner of LEUZE WOOD.	During the whole of the period 2nd to 4th inclusive the Brigade was shooting according to the time table laid down, chiefly Barrage works.
September 5th.	7 A.M.	Relief of our 1st. Sections by 1st. Sections 77th. 7 A.B 164 Div. arty. carried out. During the day our the right 5th/6d. our Infantry advanced into LEUZE WOOD. On the Right they were checked by M.G. fire and got out of touch with the troops on their right, on the left however they kept in touch.	

September 1916

Army Form C. 2118

WAR DIARY
or
INTELLIGENCE SUMMARY
(Erase heading not required.)

Instructions regarding War Diaries and Intelligence Summaries are contained in F. S. Regs., Part II. and the Staff Manual respectively. Title pages will be prepared in manuscript.

Hour, Date, Place	Summary of Events and Information	Remarks and References to Appendices
September 6th 7.30 A.M.	Relief by 2nd Sections 77th F.A.B. cancelled.	
6 P.M.	Handed over command to 77th F.A.B. and got away safely. Turn of the incoming batteries went into new positions and found ours being by them reach at 9 range of the Huns. We spent the night in the Wagon line at BRAY	
September 7th	Brigade marched to AGNICOURT where we bivouacked	} AMIENS SHEET
" 8th	" " " " HEM, night spent in billets	
" 9th	" " " " MONCHEL	
" 10th	" " " " BERGUENEUSE	} LENS SHEET
" 11th	" " " " LAPUGNOY where we	} HAZEBROUCK SA SHEET
September 12th 7 A.M.	Settled down to remain for a few days. Inspected on firm by C.I.O.M. I Corps. Our Doctor Capt H.L. MANN R.A.M.C. went back to 142nd F.A. his place being taken by Capt. B.B. MORGAN R.A.M.C.	
September 13th	Cleaning up.	

Army Form C. 2118

WAR DIARY
or
INTELLIGENCE SUMMARY
(Erase heading not required.)

Instructions regarding War Diaries and Intelligence Summaries are contained in F. S. Regs., Part II. and the Staff Manual respectively. Title pages will be prepared in manuscript.

Hour, Date, Place	Summary of Events and Information	Remarks and References to Appendices
September 14th. 6.30 A.M.	Brigade and Battery Commanders took Buses from LAPUGNOY to PHILOSOPHE and MAZINGARBE to reconnoitre positions to be taken over. 107th. Battery to relieve C/164 at G.20.b.2.9. which forward gun at G.28.c.15. and to come under HULLUCH GROUP Lt. Col. T. G. West 105th. & D/23 Batteries to relieve C/178 and D/178 at G.26 & 7½.5 and G.27.c.8.6. and to come under 14 BDE GROUP, Lt. Col. G. T. Mair D.S.O. Buses for Rec. HQ. which will be temporarily out of action reconnoitred in LES BREBIS. All wagon lines to be at NOEUX-LES-MINES	All Map References for Sheet 36C N.W.
September 15th. Evening	107th. & D/23 moved up to W.L. at NOEUX-LES-MINES 1st Echelon went in.	
September 16th. Evening	105th. & H.Q. moved up to new W.L. 105th. and remainder of 107th. & D/23 went into action. H.Q. moved into Billet in LES BREBIS, L.36.a.1.9 (Sheet 36B) D/23 had direct hit on a gun pit, no one wounded and gun not damaged.	

September 1916

Army Form C. 2118

WAR DIARY
or
INTELLIGENCE SUMMARY
(Erase heading not required.)

Instructions regarding War Diaries and Intelligence Summaries are contained in F. S. Regs., Part II. and the Staff Manual respectively. Title pages will be prepared in manuscript.

Hour, Date, Place	Summary of Events and Information	Remarks and References to Appendices
September 17th to September 21st incl.	The batteries had a very quiet time firing very slow. 107th fired about 60 rds 108th fired 70 rds and D fired 58 rounds.	
September 20th.	CRA went on leave. Brigade Commander went to 2nd D.A. on acting CRA. Orders for relief of 2nd Div. A.A. by E.A. and 40th Div. Arty. received	
September 21st/22nd.	1st Section 107th Battery came out.	
September 22nd.	H.Q. moved down to W.H. at NOEUX-LES-MINES	
September 22nd/23rd.	Remainder of 107th came out and whole battery marched to old Billets at LAPUGNOY	
September 23rd.	1st Section 108th & D/23 came out. H.Q. marched to LAPUGNOY	
September 23rd/24th.	Remainder D/23 & 108th came out, the latter marched to LAPUGNOY	
September 24th.	D/23 marched to LAPUGNOY	
September 25th.	Brigade marched to First Army Training Area (MAMETZ) Watered and fed at ESTREE BLANCHE 107th, 108th & 149. & billets at MAMETZ, D/23 at CRECQUES.	

WAR DIARY
or
INTELLIGENCE SUMMARY

(Erase heading not required.)

September 1916

Army Form C. 2118

Hour, Date, Place	Summary of Events and Information	Remarks and References to Appendices
September 26th.	Settling in. Weather Splendid. Notice received that Pte. E. Wheeler, R.A.M.C. has been awarded Military Medal	
September 27th.	Gunnery Commenced	
September 28th.	Notice received that Capt N.W.W. FREER has been awarded Military Cross	
September 29th.	Brigade Commander rejoined on C.R.A's return from leave	
September 30th.	Nothing of importance.	

E. W. Logan
2nd Lieut.
for Adjutant 23rd Bde. R.O.A.

3rd Divisional Artillery.

23RD BRIGADE R. F. A.

OCTOBER 1916.

SECRET.   SO/23

To Bde. Major 3rd D.A.

Herewith War Diary
for October 1916.

E.L. Morgan
2Lt R.F.A.
2/11/16   for Major Cmdg. 23rd Bde. R.F.A.

WAR DIARY
or
INTELLIGENCE SUMMARY

Army Form C. 2118

Vol 24
23rd Bde R.F.A

October 1916

Hour, Date, Place	Summary of Events and Information	Remarks and References to Appendices
October 1st.	Church Parade at 11.15 A.M.	
2nd 3rd	nothing to report	
4th 5th 6th 7th 8th	Division to be transferred to VII Corps, Reserve Army. Brigade marched off at 6.40 A.M. Night spent at ANVIN. March to REBREUVIETTE. March to wagon lines at ACHEUX. Bivouac for night. Battery positions reconnoitred at WHITE CITY in Q.4.A.	
9th.	Bde HQ at MAILLY - MAILLET	BEAUMONT HAMEL Sheet.
10th & 11th.	Bde. HQ. moves up from Wagon line. Batteries commence work on positions at WHITE CITY.	
12th.	107th & 108th. Batteries have 5 men wounded	
13th.	D/23 have 2 Sergeants killed, 1 Sergeant & 2 men wounded. 108th Battery position practically completed. Detachments go back to Wagon line.	
14th.	Commence building a Bde Battle HQ. at Q.2.d.0.2.	
15th to 17th.	nothing to report.	do
18th.	D/23 position practically complete. Their working parties return to Wagon line.	do
19th.	Everything altered. Battery positions at WHITE CITY and Bde Battle HQ. to be handed over to 155th Bde. RFA 32nd Divn.	

October 1916   23rd Wk RFA Army Form C. 2118.

WAR DIARY
INTELLIGENCE SUMMARY
(Erase heading not required.)

Hour, Date, Place	Summary of Events and Information	Remarks and References to Appendices
October 19th (continued)	Positions recently vacated by A, B & C/317th Bde. RGA. 63rd Div., in the Left Sector of the Division Front, to be occupied instead. Bde. H.Q. in COLINCAMPS	HEBUTERNE SHEET 107 at K27a.1½.4 108 K27a.3.7 D/23 K26b.3.6
19th/20th	2 Sections each 107 & 108 Ea.in.	
20th	Carton amount of registration done.	
20th/21st	D/23 and remainder 107 & 108 Ea.in.	
21st	23rd Bde. R.Ja. to work with 76th Inf. Bde. Zone: from a line E. & W. through the S. point of JOHN COPSE to a line E. & W. through the S. point of MARK COPSE. Gaps made in 2nd, 3rd, & 4th lines to be cut.	
22nd	Good visibility. Progress made with wire cutting.	
23rd	Very misty. Wire cutting almost entirely held up.	
24th	Mist and fine drizzle. Observation impossible.	
25th	The Bde. Commander Lt. Col. E.F. DELAFORCE C.M.G. records on promotion to the command of R.A. 6th Div. Major ALLSOP, 49th Battery RGA. takes over the command of the Brigade, temporarily.	

Army Form C. 2118

WAR DIARY
or
INTELLIGENCE SUMMARY
(Erase heading not required.)

October 1916   Sheet 3

Instructions regarding War Diaries and Intelligence
Summaries are contained in F. S. Regs., Part II.
and the Staff Manual respectively. Title pages
will be prepared in manuscript.

Hour, Date, Place	Summary of Events and Information	Remarks and References to Appendices
October 26th.	2 Lt. S. WILLIAMS 107 Battery wounded. Raid by 1st ~~Gordons~~ unsuccessful.	
27th	Weather still very bad.	
28th	Nothing of importance	
29th	~~...~~	
30th	Weather still bad. ~~...~~	
31st	Raid carried out by 2nd Lt Rees in the evening. Unsuccessful.	

11/11/16.

E. Williams
2nd. Lt. R.A.
for Adjutant 23rd Brigade R.F.A.

3rd Divisional Artillery.

23RD BRIGADE R. F. A.

NOVEMBER 1916.

SECRET. 50/55

To Brigade Major 3rd D.A.

Herewith War Diary
for November 1916.

E.H. Morgan 2/Lt R.F.A.
1 12/1916. for Lt. Col. Cmdg. 23rd Brigade
R.F.A.

3rd Div

Army Form C. 2118

23rd Bde. R.F.A

Vol 25

WAR DIARY
or
INTELLIGENCE SUMMARY
(Erase heading not required.)

1st to 30th November 1916

Place	Date	Hour	Summary of Events and Information	Remarks and references to Appendices
Brigade H.Qrs at COLINCAMPS	1st Nov. to 7th Nov. inclusive		Very wet, stormy weather on account of which the projected new offensive by the Fifth Army was put off from day to day. Wire cutting on German 2nd and 3rd Lines whenever visibility was good enough. Very little hostile retaliation.	
	8th	11.45 A.M.	10 Bde. Battery. Red one man killed and one wounded	
	10th		Barometer started to rise rapidly and the weather to improve greatly. It was decided that the 13th Should be "the day". Construction of dug outs for a Brigade Battle HQ just E of COLINCAMPS begun. Preliminary bombardment commenced. Steady improvement in the weather	
	11th		Very little reply to our bombardment.	
	12th	3.0 Pm	All Battle HQrs. manned.	
	13th	5.45 A.M.	Zero hour! Combined attack by V L. Corps on Left (N. of ANCRE) and II nd Corps on Right (S. of ANCRE) assisted by 31st Div. (XIII L. Corps) on the Left of the 3rd Div. The capture of SERRE was the task of the 3rd. Div. This Brigade covered the 76th Inf. Brigade, the left Sector, 8th Inf. Brigade had right sector, 9th Inf. Bde. were in reserve. Two Battalions of the 76th Inf Bde attached, 2nd Suffolks and 1st/1st Royal Welch Fusiliers.	

Army Form C. 2118

WAR DIARY
or
INTELLIGENCE SUMMARY
(Erase heading not required.)

NOVEMBER 1916

Instructions regarding War Diaries and Intelligence Summaries are contained in F. S. Regs., Part II. and the Staff Manual respectively. Title Pages will be prepared in manuscript.

Place	Date	Hour	Summary of Events and Information	Remarks and references to Appendices
	November 13th		The Suffolks on the left never reached their objective. The 10th. R.W.F. got to the 1st. and 2nd. lines but withdrew and the 1st. Grenadiers who were in support reached WALTER TRENCH. At the end of the day however the whole Division was back on its original line. The centre and right of the attack was met successful. BEAUCOURT BEAUMONT HAMEL and PIERRE DIVION fell. The V.th. Corps took nearly 4000 prisoners. 76th. S.F. Bde. took over defence of 3rd Div front.	
	14th	Evening	A quiet day. Occasional surprise bombardments by us. The 31st. Div. who captured their objective yesterday withdrew to their original line.	
	15th	5.30 P.M.	Hun bombarded our front and support lines very heavily until about 6.30 P.M. We retaliated.	
	16th		During the afternoon the area round 107th. & 108th. Batteries was shelled but no damage done.	
	18th		It transpired that the 3rd Div. attack failed owing to weather conditions impossible mud etc. The Division transferred to XIII th. Corps.	

Army Form C. 2118

WAR DIARY
or
INTELLIGENCE SUMMARY
(Erase heading not required.)

NOVEMBER 1916

Instructions regarding War Diaries and Intelligence Summaries are contained in F.S. Regs., Part II. and the Staff Manual respectively. Title Pages will be prepared in manuscript.

Place	Date	Hour	Summary of Events and Information	Remarks and references to Appendices
	November 20th.		Officers of a new Howitzer Battery which was about to join the Brigade arrived and were attached to batteries for instruction.	
	21st.		D/124 Battery position inspected with a view to occupation by D/23	
	22nd.		Major T.W. Robinson of 130th Battery attached temporarily to command the Brigade.	
	23rd.		Major E.S. Allsup returned to 49th Battery. The new Howitzer Battery to be 534th. Henceforth it will be known as C/23	
	24th 3.30 P.M.		32nd Div. on the right had an attack with the object of recovering some men cut off in MUNICH TRENCH. We put up a heavy bombardment. COLINCAMPS Sheet.	
	25th.		10 5th Battery commenced work on a new position to take 4 guns.	
	26th		a position chosen for C/23	
	27th.		D/124 position to be taken by D/23. Work of improving gun pits begun	
	28th.		Lt. Col. Bellingfeld posted to the command of the Brigade via Col. Clover.	
	30th.		2nd Lts. BARNETT and BAXTER attached to the Brigade. A. PEAKE went away sick.	

E. Morgan, 2Lt R.A.
for Adjutant 23rd Brigade RFA

3rd Divisional Artillery.

23RD BRIGADE R. F. A.

DECEMBER 1916.

To Brigade Major 3rd D.A.

Herewith War Diary for
December 1916

E.H. Morgan
2Lt RGA

1/1/917   for Lt. Col. Cmdg 23rd Bde RGA

Army Form C. 2118

23rd Bde R.F.A.

Vol 26

1st to 31st December 1916

WAR DIARY
or
INTELLIGENCE SUMMARY
(Erase heading not required.)

Instructions regarding War Diaries and Intelligence Summaries are contained in F. S. Regs., Part II. and the Staff Manual respectively. Title Pages will be prepared in manuscript.

Place	Date	Hour	Summary of Events and Information	Remarks and references to Appendices
December	1st		Huns shelled our Posts and support between 1 p.m. and 2 p.m. Major Robinson left.	Map Ref. HEBUTERNE 57d N.E. 3 & 4 1/10,000
	2nd		Very little firing. Infantry had mining parties out.	
	3rd		C/23 went into action in an old position at K20d08 close to new position in course of construction	
	4th			
	5th		108 & D/23 moved 1 section each into field positions	
	6th		Another section each of 108 & D/23 moved into new positions	
	7th		Reconnaissance for an O.P. made in MONK and CAMPION trenches without success	
	8th		108 whizzbanged in evening, all telephone wires broken for a short time	
	9th	10 p.m	The Brigade took over the Zone 1 of the 169 Brigade on the left, the POINT to S. of JOHN COPSE	
			D/23 had a man killed	
	11th		Brigade H.Q. moved to huts at COURCELLES	
	14th		During the night of the 14th/15th the 31st and 3rd Divisions had a lot of SOS work repeated.	
	16th		C/23 put out of action for 2 days to give them extra time to get their new position completed. D/23 fired their allotment of ammunition	
	17th 18th to 23rd		Rapid Command Shells on wagon lines at BOS LES-ARTOIS. Work continued on new gun positions, railways & improvements.	

WAR DIARY or INTELLIGENCE SUMMARY

Army Form C. 2118

December 1916

Place	Date	Hour	Summary of Events and Information	Remarks and references to Appendices
December	24th		Brigade Scouts in conjunction with 31st. Div. made a night raid.	
	25th.		A very quiet day, Christmas celebrations.	
	27th.		The Brigade Commander recommended wire cutting patrols	

E Mulligan 2nd Lt.
for Adjutant 23rd Brigade R.S.R.

1/1/1917

3RD DIVISION
DIVL ARTILLERY

30TH BRIGADE R.F.A.

AUG - DEC 1914

3rd Divisional Artillery.

30th BRIGADE R. F. A.

AUGUST 1914.

War Diary 12/1096

30th Brigade R.F.A.

3rd Division

4.8.14 – 31.8.14

30th Brigade RFA

Army Form C. 2118

WAR DIARY
or
INTELLIGENCE SUMMARY.

(Erase heading not required.)

Instructions regarding War Diaries and Intelligence Summaries are contained in F.S. Regs., Part II. and the Staff Manual respectively. Title pages will be prepared in manuscript.

Hour, Date, Place	Summary of Events and Information	Remarks and references to Appendices
1914		
8 pm August 4th — Bulford	Order to Mobilise received	
August 5th to August 9th — Bulford	Mobilization normal	
August 10th	Reported ready mobilized	
6.30 am. Aug. 18th Amesbury	Entrained for Southampton	
8.30 a.m. Southampton	Arrived at Docks	
7.30 pm Southampton	Honours arrived – loading horses & vehicles of 128 & 142 Bys.	
	all night – 129 Embarked in another boat.	
10 a.m. Aug 19th Southampton	Bde Embarked on COLLEEN BAWN in afternoon.	
12 midnight Havre	Sailed - Havre	
6 a.m. Aug. 20th Havre	Reached Havre	
3 p.m. ROUEN	Sailed up Seine for ROUEN	
11 a.m. Aug. 21st ROUEN.	arrived at ROUEN did not disembark all the same night –	
	as French workmen would not go on after 8 p.m. Struck Camp	
8.30 pm Aug 22nd ROUEN	& set tight in. Having disembarked went to rest camp at LA BRUYÈRE	
	Entrained	
10 a.m. Aug 23rd VALENCIENNES	Arrived Detrained – 130th Battery in action S of MONS.	
3 p.m. "	Started for BAVAY	
7.30 pm BAVAY	Arrived here & bivouacked.	
12.30 a.m. August 24th BAVAY	Marched off –	
4.30 a.m. CIPLY	Reached CIPLY	

30th Brigade R.F.A.

Army Form C. 2118.

WAR DIARY
or
INTELLIGENCE SUMMARY.
(Erase heading not required.)

Instructions regarding War Diaries and Intelligence Summaries are contained in F.S. Regs., Part II. and the Staff Manual respectively. Title pages will be prepared in manuscript.

Hour, Date, Place		Summary of Events and Information	Remarks and references to Appendices
9 a.m.	Aug 25th CIPLY	128 & 129 went into action — relieved further position from which all batteries retired under fire unto another position facing N. and thence retired to	1 N.C.O. & 2 men missing 2 men wounded
11 a.m.			
3 p.m.	BERMERIS	bivouack at BERMERIS via BAVAY.	
9 p.m.			
1 a.m.	Aug 26th BERMERIS	Moved with 7th Infy. Bde. in rearguard action near BERMERIS without firing. Batteries came into	
5 p.m.	SOLESMES	action near BERMERIS without firing. 130 Bty. came into action N. of town as rearguard action.	Major C.I.C. Popylka 129, killed
9 p.m.	VIESLY	reached this place	2 N.C.Os wounded & missing
10 p.m.		moved to CAUDRAY	
10 mn.	CAUDRAY	reached CAUDRAY & bivouacked in its streets	
3 a.m.	Aug 27th CAUDRAY	129 & Bde came into action in S.W. of town & 128 & Bde. fired but not fire.	
8 a.m.		All batteries moved to position East of town & took N.B railway.	
11 a.m.		129 Bty. moved to position near MONTIGNY.	
2 p.m.		130th Bty. moved to position 300 yards further N.E. came under heavy fire.	
4 p.m.		The Brigade retired through MONTIGNY — BEAUREVOIR marching all night	
6 a.m.	Aug 27th ESTREES	to ESTREES then to VILLERET where 129 & 130 came into action but did not fire.	
1 p.m.	VILLERET		
9 p.m.	VILLERET	moved to VERMAND	
unknown	VERMAND	arrived & bivouacked	
Midnight	VERMAND	moved off marching via ST. QUENTIN	

W. Farley Lt.Col.
30.F.R.A.

30th Brigade R.F.A.

WAR DIARY
or
INTELLIGENCE SUMMARY.
(Erase heading not required.)

Army Form C. 2118.

Hour, Date, Place		Summary of Events and Information	Remarks and references to Appendices
6 am	Aug. 28th HAM	Arrived & went into position south of the river.	
2 pm		Retired from position through Libermont and arrived at	
4 pm	TARLEFESSE	at TARLEFESSE where we bivouacked.	
2 pm	Aug. 29th NOYON	Moved to NOYON — 128 Bty. came into position & observation	
		East of town.	
10 pm	NOYON	Moved in direction of CUTS	
5.30 am	Aug. 30th CUTS	Moved off & marched via AUDIGNICOURT to VASSENS	
		where we halted for 2 hours.	
1 pm	VASSENS	Moved via MORSAIN, BERNY RIVIÈRE, VIC to	
6 pm	ORCAMP	ORCAMP where we bivouacked.	
10 am	Aug. 31st ORCAMP	Marched via VIVIÈRES, VILLERS-COTTERETS to	
4 pm	COYOLLES	COYOLLES where we bivouacked in a Chateau.	

3rd Divisional Artillery.

30th BRIGADE R. F. A.

SEPTEMBER 1914.

30th Brigade R.F.A.

Army Form C. 2118

WAR DIARY
or
INTELLIGENCE SUMMARY.
(Erase heading not required.)

Instructions regarding War Diaries and Intelligence Summaries are contained in F.S. Regs., Part II. and the Staff Manual respectively. Title pages will be prepared in manuscript.

Hour, Date, Place	Summary of Events and Information	Remarks and references to Appendices
7.30 a.m. Sept 1st COYOLLES.	Marched off to BOUILLANCY, and went into fighting billets	
3.30 am " 2nd BOUILLANCY	Marched off via MARCILLY, BARCY to PENCHARD	
1.0 p.m " PENCHARD	Arrived and bivouacked	
6.0 a.m " 3rd PENCHARD	Moved off via MEAUX to VILLEMAREUIL where we halted for 2 hrs.	
2.0 p.m " VILLEMAREUIL	Moved off to HAUTE MAISON & bivouacked there	
10.0 a.m " 4th HAUTE MAISON	Went to reconnoitre positions for batteries facing North	
1.30 pm " HAUTE MAISON	Moved to new bivouack at MONTANSON FARM & reconnoitred positions here	
10.30 pm " MONTANSON FM	Moved off via CRECY TIGEAUX and FÔRET DE CRECY when we halted two hours. Thence via NEUFMOUTIERS, CHATRES to LIVEROY	
6.0 a.m " 5th LIVEROY	where we arrived at 6 a.m & bivouacked	
6.0 a.m " " LIVEROY	Moved NE through CHÂTRES, halted 2 miles S. of NEUFMOUTIERS for 2 hours	
2.0 p.m " "	Moved off via LA MOUSSAYE where we halted	
4.30 pm " 2nd S. of NEUFMOUTIERS	Moved off via CRÉVECOEUR to HAUTEFEUIL where we arrived at 9 pm	
10.0 a.m " MOUSSAYE	Moved off to PAREMOUTIERS arriving at 1.30 pm & halted there	
5.15 p.m " 7th HAUTEFEUIL	Marched to ST PIERRE arriving at 9 pm & bivouacked	
5 am " PAREMOUTIERS	Moved via COULONNIERS, ST DENIS, to REBAIS, halting near BOULEVILLIERS FM. 130/8¼ towards two action N.W. of BOISSAUDRAY	Y Medical transport wounded
" 8th ST PIERRE	about noon against ORLY, fire gun to action in wood S. of C. BAITER but could not do much owing to machine gun fire.	
8 pm " REBAIS	Moved over river at ORLY to BUSSIERES where we bivouacked.	
5 a.m " 9th BUSSIERES	1.29 p.m 8¼ moved with Advance Guard	
5.30 am " "	Rear of Bty moved via LES FUCHERES to NANTEUIL and halted there	
8 am " NANTEUIL	12.9.14 AS came into action facing N near Br 199 S of CHAMP RUCHS Opened a battery - fire appeared effective, battery captured by 9 of 1st Bde.lrs	
2 pm " NANTEUIL	Battery fired at by heavy guns from to SABLONNIERE but no damage. Brigade moved into bivouack just South of BEZU	

30th Brigade R.F.A.

Army Form C. 2118.

WAR DIARY
or
INTELLIGENCE SUMMARY.
(Erase heading not required.)

Instructions regarding War Diaries and Intelligence Summaries are contained in F. S. Regs., Part II. and the Staff Manual respectively. Title pages will be prepared in manuscript.

Hour, Date, Place	Summary of Events and Information	Remarks and references to Appendices
4.00 a.m. Sept. 10th BEZU	Shoot to our forces	
5.0 a.m.	127th Bty moved with its Advanced Guard.	
7.0 a.m.	Remainder of the Bde moved via VEUILLY, VINLY, CHEZY to DANMARD where we arrived at 6pm and bivouacked.	
6 pm. DANMARD	During the day 1 section 127th Bty came into action against retreating Germans just S of P. in LA POTERIE near VEUILLY. Arrived and bivouacked.	
8 a.m. " 11th "	Marched via NEUILLY, ROZET, DULCHY LAVILLE to GRAND ROZOY arriving about 1 pm. Bivouacked with D.A./8 Bde.	
7.45 pm " 12th GRAND ROZOY	Marched via LES CROUTTES, MAAST, CUIRY-HOUSSE, CERSEUIL, LIME to BRAINE where we arrived at 5 pm. Billeted in BRAINE.	
5 a.m. " 13th BRAINE	Moved on the direction of CHASSEMY with 8th Inf Bde in the Advance Guard	
12 noon " " Nr CHASSEMY	130th went into action N E of LA RUE D EN HAUT. 129th came into action just N of LA GRANGE FARM. 128th & 129th Bivouacked near LA GRANGE FARM about 8pm. 130th Bivouacked near BRENET	Lieut H H Bacon R.F.A. joined 130th Bty from Base details
3.55pm " " LA GRANGE FARM	One Gun of 129th went forward with Advance to CHATEAU BOIS MORIN. Remainder of the Battery went into position of Observation behind ANCIENNE	
9.0 a.w. " 14th CHATEAU BOIS MORIN	129th Bty came into action near H of LA CHATEAU in the Grounds against hostile artillery.	
10.0 a.m. " "	128th Bty came into action first behind 129th Bty - 200x South of it.	
12 noon " " LA RUE D EN HAUT	130th Bty came into action just S of A in LA RUE D EN HAUT. There heavily shelled. They came into action against hostile Bty near pt 166 Yumb NE B	3 killed 2 wounded Men
4 a.m. " 15th CHATEAU LA RUE D EN HAUT	Shoot to guns all batteries remained in same position with approximately the same effective Amm. Col. between BRENELLE & BRAINE. Bivouacked in position W	
4 a.m. " 15th "	128th Bty moved to a new position on edge of 1304 just N of BRENELLE - CHASSEMY road	

30th Brigade R.F.A.

WAR DIARY
or
INTELLIGENCE SUMMARY.
(Erase heading not required.)

Army Form C. 2118.

Instructions regarding War Diaries and Intelligence Summaries are contained in F. S. Regs., Part II. and the Staff Manual respectively. Title pages will be prepared in manuscript.

Hour, Date, Place	Summary of Events and Information	Remarks and references to Appendices
9 p.m. Sept 17th CHATEAU	1section 129 & 76 Bty went into position with Middlesex Rgt facing CONDE BRIDGE just N of CHATEAU to prevent any advance over the bridge	
4:30 a.m. 18th QUARRY near LA RUE D'EN HAUT	Capt France went to VAILLY in afternoon to locate enemy's guns, could not locate much.	
	All batteries in same positions. Fire on guns at VALOREUX FM & ROUGE MAISON reported effective.	
2:30 a.m. 19th CHATEAU	180* 3ons from CHIVRES to AIZY. 128* 3ons from VERDONNE to ROUGE MAISON.	
5:0 a.m. QUARRY	(Capt Newland in afternoon at VAILLY, located gun positions.	
3:30 a.m. QUARRY near LA RUE D'EN HAUT	(section (Lt Morrison) 159 went to position near VAILLY, N of RIVR AISNE fire at approximately. Same targets as 3ons by batteries.	
	1section (Lt Archdale) 128 went to 2878ths on right of position. Observing officer went to VASSENY to observe fire on CONDE FORT. Guns shelled in afternoon.	2 N.C.O.s rank killed 1 slightly wounded.
10 p.m.	Snipers and captured 2 Germans in wood near Quarry.	
4:30 a.m. 3.8.	Batteries in same positions at approximately the same objectives	
7:30 p.m.	Attack on infantry 128 and 130 was valid with their fire which was reported.	
4:30 a.m. 22.1d	My effective. Detached section in VAILLY silenced 2 hostile guns.	
5 a.m. 23.rd	Batteries in same positions at approximately same objectives.	
5 p.m.	Batteries in Same positions at same objectives	
5 a.m.	129 at CHATEAU shelled by heavy guns. No damage to equipment	9 men slightly wounded
	Batteries in same positions	
	Zones as follows: 128th – BOIS DE VERNINS – ROUGE MAISON F.M.	
	129th – CONDE – BOIS DES LOGES.	
	130th – 4 guns CELLES – AIZY	
	2 guns CONDE BRIDGE + RIDGE – ORME pt 162.	
9.55	Batteries in same positions at same objectives approximately.	
	M.B shelled by heavy guns during the morning – moved 2 guns 150 yards further west for safety. No one wounded. One wagon broken.	

79
3298

30th Brigade R.F.A.

Army Form C. 2118

WAR DIARY or INTELLIGENCE SUMMARY

(Erase heading not required.)

Instructions regarding War Diaries and Intelligence Summaries are contained in F.S. Regs., Part II. and the Staff Manual respectively. Title pages will be prepared in manuscript.

Hour, Date, Place		Summary of Events and Information	Remarks and references to Appendices
5 a.m.	Sept. 26th QUARRY LA RUE D'EN HAUT	Batteries in same positions at same objectives. Horses from 129th and 130th sent to BRAINE to bivouack — 180th horses remained in Quarry, and 129th kept horses with them attacked section.	Major Mgr Schwabe joined 130th Battery
5 a.m.	" 27th	Batteries in same positions.	
5.30 p.m.	" "	Ordered to be ready to turn out immediately in case of a night attack — horses eased during the night.	
2 a.m.	" 28th VAILLY	Lt Morrison brought detached section 129th back from VAILLY	
5 a.m.	" " QUARRY	Section 129th bivouacked near the CHATEAU — Batteries in same positions	
5 a.m.	" 29th	Detached section 129th sent to position on hedge of wood ARGIENNE, N of the BRAINE — CHASSEMY road.	
5 a.m.	" 30th	Batteries in same positions.	
	" "	Batteries in same positions. Lt Morrison keeps observing station near Detached section 130. Order to detached section 129th to be able to fire at S edge of BOIS DE VERVINS by night if required — A new position to be reconnoitred	

W.J. Horsley, Lt Col.
Lt Col. 30 Bgde RFA
(Chargeur.)

3rd Divisional Artillery.

30th BRIGADE R. F. A.

OCTOBER 1914.

30th BRIGADE R.F.A

WAR DIARY or **INTELLIGENCE SUMMARY**

Army Form C. 2118

Hour, Date, Place		Summary of Events and Information	Remarks and references to Appendices
5 a.m.	October 1st LA RUE DEN HAUT	Batteries in same positions at same objectives.	
8 a.m.	"	Position orders to be prepared for section under Lt. MORRISON just N of the quarry.	
5.p.m.	"	Section 129 ordered to rejoin battery at CHATEAU BOIS MORIN.	
9 p.m.	"	Brigade gets orders to be ready to move to-morrow to ARCY.	
6 a.m.	2nd "	Batteries in same positions, but too foggy to shoot all day.	
8 a.m.	"	Officers from relieving Brigade came to see battery positions and information about targets.	
7 p.m.	"	Brigade moved off and marched via BRAINE to CUIRY HOUSSE and bivouacked there.	
8 p.m.	3rd CUIRY HOUSSE	In billets all day.	
"	"	Moved [via ARCY – GRAND ROZOY – LE PLESSIER HULEU – BILLY-sur-Ourcq – CHOUY] to NOROY.	
1 a.m.	4th NOROY	Arrived and got into billets – Spent the day in billets.	
7.30 p.m.	"	Moved [via TROESNES – LA FERTÉ-MILON] to COYOLLES.	
11.30 p.m.	COYOLLES	Got into bivouac in the grounds of the Chateau.	
5 a.m.	5th "	Party under Lt. Baxter & Lt. Mann sent to fetch 80 remounts.	
6 p.m.	"	Moved via CRÉPY – BETHANCOURT to LA BREVIÈRE and went into billets.	
6 a.m.	6th LA BREVIÈRE	129th Bty marched to LE MEUX and entrained here – also 1 section of Am. Col.	
7.30 a.m.	"	Br. Hd Qrs, 130 B Bty & 1 sect Am Col marched to LE MEUX and entrained all except section of Am. Col.	
9.45 a.m.	"	128 A Bty marched to COMPIÈGNE & entrained. 4 sect Am. Col.	
11 p.m.	ABBEVILLE	129th Bty arrived & started to detrain.	

30TH BRIGADE R.F.A. WAR DIARY

INTELLIGENCE SUMMARY.

(Erase heading not required.)

Army Form C. 2118.

Hour, Date, Place	Summary of Events and Information	Remarks and references to Appendices
10 a.m. October 7th ABBEVILLE	130th Bty HQrs started to detrain.	
2 p.m. "	Two batteries Hd Qrs. 1 section of Amn. Col. bivouacked near the canal.	
2 p.m. "	Bde Hqrs 128th Bty & 2 sections Amn. Col. moved to billet ½ mile N. of ABBEVILLE near THUISON.	
4 p.m. "	128th Bty arrived at billet having marched from NOYELLES, where they detrained, via LE TITRE.	
	80 remounts were given to the Brigade were distributed among batteries.	
8th "	Bde Hqrs 128th Amn. Col in billets all day.	
12.30 p.m. "	Remaining section Amn. Col. arrived from NOYELLES.	
2 a.m. 9th "	Brigade moved via CANCHY, LE BOISLE to LABROYE.	
8 a.m. " LABROYE	Bde arrived & went into billets - staying all day.	
5 p.m. "	Brigade moved via REGNAUVILLE - [BRAILLY - ST GEORGES - FRESNOY - INCOURT - ECLIMEUX - BERMICOURT - FLEURY - HESTRUS] to TANGRY.	
7 a.m. 10th TANGRY	Bde arrived & went into billets & stayed all day.	
1.20 p.m. "	Got orders to move at 8 a.m. to-morrow.	
6 a.m. "	Got orders to move tes 130th at 9.5 a.m. starting at 10 a.m. exit of TANGRY.	
7.45 a.m. "	130 F. Bty to move at 7.45 a.m. behind 40th F.A. Bde.	
9.5 a.m. "	130th moved behind 40th Bde to HINGES and billeted there.	
8.30 a.m. 12th GONNEHEM	Bde Hqrs 130th Bty moved via PERNES - FLORINGHEM - AUCHEL - LOZINGHEM - ALLOUAGNE - PONT DU REVEILLON to GONNEHEM & billeted there.	
9.30 a.m. " " PONT D'HINGES	Orders to move starting point PONT D'HINGES at 9.30 a.m. 130 A.B. ½ rejoined the Bde to La CROIX MARMEUSE.	
3 p.m. " CROIX MARMEUSE	Moved via LE CORNET MALO - FOSSE Church. 1 sect. 129 & 1 sec. 128 came auto action near CROIX MARMEUSE against	
6 p.m. "	Moved to billets at LE CORNET MALO.	

30TH BRIGADE R.F.A.

Army Form C. 2118

Instructions regarding War Diaries and Intelligence Summaries are contained in F.S. Regs., Part II. and the Staff Manual respectively. Title pages will be prepared in manuscript.

WAR DIARY or INTELLIGENCE SUMMARY

(Erase heading not required.)

Hour, Date, Place		Summary of Events and Information	Remarks and references to Appendices
October 6	13th LECORNET MAID	Moved to crossroads S. of LA CROIX MARMEUSE.	
6 a.m.	13th		
10 a.m.	" CROIX MARMEUSE	129 F.By went into action in ZELOBES against PONT DU HEM – CROIX BARBÉE road	
11 a.m.	"	4 guns 130 went into action just W. of VIEILLE CHAPELLE moved to position near LES 8 MAISONS, against PONT RIQUEUL.	
2 p.m.	VIEILLE CHAPELLE	One section withdrawn into readiness with reserve section just W. of VIEILLE CHAPELLE –	
6.30 p.m.	"	128th F.By remained in readiness all day near CROIX MARMEUSE. Brigade went into billets between ZELOBES and VIEILLE CHAPELLE. Amm. Col. at LA TOMBE WILLOT.	
6 a.m.	14th ZELOBES	Brigade in readiness	
7.30 a.m.	"	1 section 129th By sent to RUE DU PONCH but recalled immediately.	
1 p.m.	"	128th By under 9th Inf Bde – 130th under 87th Inf Bde –	
5 p.m.	"	129th went into action by RUE DU PONCH to assist FRENCH attack on RIEZ BAILLEUL – PONT ROGNON. Brigade 2 churns to same billets	
8 a.m.	" 15th	Batteries in same positions attached to same Inf. Bdes. – Brigade returned to same billets –	Major Hope (mustre Slightly wounded.
6.30 p.m.	"	128th By attached to 7th Inf Bde 130th By attached to 9th Inf Bde.	
6 a.m.	" 16th	129th By in reserve at ZELOBES.	
10 a.m.	"	Amm. Col. 9.5th cats to move to LES LOBES.	
5 p.m.	"	129th By moved to LACOUTURE + billeted there – also H.Qrs.	
1 p.m.	" 17th LACOUTURE	128th near NEUVE CHAPELLE – 130th in RUE DU BACQUEROT. H.Qrs + 129th moved to NEUVE CHAPELLE + billeted there 128th + 130th under Same Inf. Bdes. Amm Col. at CROIX BARBÉE.	

Army Form C. 2118.

30TH BRIGADE R.F.A. WAR DIARY or INTELLIGENCE SUMMARY.

(Erase heading not required.)

Instructions regarding War Diaries and Intelligence Summaries are contained in F.S. Regs., Part II. and the Staff Manual respectively. Title pages will be prepared in manuscript.

Hour, Date, Place		Summary of Events and Information	Remarks and references to Appendices
8 a.s.	October 18th NEUVE CHAPELLE	129th Bty in reserve in billets – Other Batteries with same Inf. Bde.	
12 noon	"	129th moved to road junction ½ mile S of B in BAS POMMEREAU.	
2 pm	BAS POMMEREAU	129th moved into billets at BAS POMMEREAU FARM. Bde Qrs same.	
6.30 am	19th	NEUVE CHAPELLE	
		129th Bty in readiness – Other batteries with same Infantry Bdes. Moved to position ½ mile NE of AUBERS Church to fire at trenches	
11.0 am	"	SE of HERLIES –	
6.30 pm	"	Returned to same billets	
6.30 am	20th	Batteries in same positions + same objectives	
		Returned to same billets in the evening	
6.45 am	21st	Same position + objective – 129 had observation officer forward at RIEZ.	
6.30 am	22nd	Batteries in same positions approximately – 129th places under 57th Inf. Bde.	
		Amm. Col. moved to PONT LOGY.	
9 pm	"	Orders to move to cross roads ⅓ mile S of CROIX BARBÉE.	
11 pm	"	The whole Bde bivouacked just S of CROIX BARBÉE – Town Col. near	
5 am	23rd CROIX BARBEE	VIEILLE CHAPELLE.	
		129th Bty moved to position N of RUE DU BACQUEROT were under Hr orders of 8th Inf Bde. 128th + 130th in reserve.	
3 pm	"	128th + 130th ordered into positions of observation S of CROIX BARBÉE	
6 pm	"	against AUBERS + HAUT POMMEREAU, BOIS DE BIEZ. Bde Hqrs 129 in same billets	
6 am	24th	Same Bde positions + objectives.	
6 pm	"	billets on 23rd + Oct.	
6 am	25th	Same positions of batteries – 128 under 7th Inf Bde removed in other div might. In the afternoon 130 fired on German batteries with observation from Western aeroplane.	
6 pm	"	130 the Qrs killed by D.V. VIEILLE CHAPELLE – Amm Col at same place	

30TH BRIGADE R.F.A. WAR DIARY or INTELLIGENCE SUMMARY.

Army Form C. 2118.

Instructions regarding War Diaries and Intelligence Summaries are contained in F. S. Regs., Part II. and the Staff Manual respectively. Title pages will be prepared in manuscript.

(Erase heading not required.)

Hour, Date, Place		Summary of Events and Information	Remarks and references to Appendices
6.0 a.m.	October 26th CROIX BARBÉE	Batteries in same positions – 128 F Bty but under 75 F at Bde – assist 42nd & 79th Bdes	
9.0 a.m.	" "	130 F short took nineteen aeroplane – got 4 hits on one Bty and 1 on another	
12 noon	" "	One gun 130 went into action near PONT LOGY to shell houses NE of	
5 p.m.	" "	Church in NEUVE CHAPELLE.	
	" "	Same billets for the night.	
6.30 a.m.	" 27th	Battery in same position and same objectives	
3 p.m.	" "	Returned to same billet but remained harnessed up all night.	
6.30 a.m.	" 28th	Battery in same position at same objective.	
7.30 a.m.	" "	130 F ranged on NEUVE CHAPELLE ready to fire.	
11 a.m.	" "	An attack was made on NEUVE CHAPELLE after bombardment in which Bt	
6.30 p.m.	" "	Bty Bty shot part.	
	" "	Same arrangements for billets.	
6.0 a.m.	" 29th	Battery in same position – did not fire during the day.	
6.0 p.m.	" "		
	" "	130 F returned to same billets	
6.0 a.m.	" 30th	Same positions – 130 F did not fire all day.	
6.0 p.m.	" "	130 F returned to same billets	
	" "	129 F Bty again came under orders 15 16 O.E. Brigade & went for 2 days	
	" "	into billets 3/4 mile W. of PONT DU HEM.	
6.30 a.m.	" 31st	129 F Bty remained in billets all day.	
	" "	130 F Bty in same position but did not fire during the day.	
5.30 p.m.	" "	130 F returned to the same billets	

31/10/1914. Yours truly St.L.L.
Com. 25. R.B.R.F.A. (Charing 2nd)

	3rd Bn R.F.A					
	Officers			Other Ranks		
Date	Killed	Wounded	Missing	Killed	Wounded	Missing
19.10.14						
20.10.14					2	
25.10.14	Lt G.H. Pigou			1		
28.10.14		2/Lt C.R. Hutchison			1	1
1.11.14						1

38

3rd Divisional Artillery.

30th BRIGADE R. F. A.

NOVEMBER 1914.

307th BRIGADE. R.F.A. WAR DIARY or INTELLIGENCE SUMMARY.

Army Form C. 2118.

(Erase heading not required.)

Hour, Date, Place			Summary of Events and Information	Remarks and references to Appendices
6.30 am	November	1st MON BARBÉE	Batteries in same positions	Lt. AUTHION slightly wounded.
3 pm	"	"	130ᴿ fired a few shots at a horse in front of Jenfosses 1/2 mile E. of toot T	
6 pm	"	"	in ST VAAST Returned to same billets	
6.0 am	"	2nd	129ᴿ relieved 128ᴿ — came under orders of 42nd Bde R.F.A. 128ᴿ went into billets just S. of second U in RUE DU RONCQ. for 3 days rest. 130ᴿ in same positions.	
8.30 am	"	"	Tried to take on MEINEN WERFE which was reported to have annoyed 2nd Ghurkhas – unable to locate it. fired no more.	
6.0 pm	"	"	Shelled road triangle NE of NEUVE CHAPELLE to repel attack Returned to same billets, but section left in action in case of ryth attack	
6.30 am	"	3rd	130ᴿ ready to take on MEINEN WERFER but it was not located. did not fire 128ᴿ still resting in billets	
3 pm	"	"	130ᴿ fired at hostile battery with enemy aeroplane observation – result not known on guns but no direct hits reported Returned to same billets	
6 pm	"	"		
6.30 am	"	4th	Batteries in same positions – no firing all day Returned to same billets.	
6.0 pm	"	"		
6.30 am	"	5th	128ᴿ relieved 130ᴿ who went to billets in ZELOBES. for 3 days rest.	
3.0 pm	"	"	128ᴿ fired at road triangle to repel slight attack on Ghurkhas.	
6.30 am	"	6th	Batteries in same positions. Too foggy all day to observe – 128ᴿ fired a few rounds at Germans digging a trench in front of Ghurkhas under observations from forward observing officer.	

30TH BRIGADE R.F.A

WAR DIARY or INTELLIGENCE SUMMARY

(Erase heading not required.)

Army Form C. 2118.

Instructions regarding War Diaries and Intelligence Summaries are contained in F.S. Regs., Part II. and the Staff Manual respectively. Title pages will be prepared in manuscript.

Hour, Date, Place	Summary of Events and Information	Remarks and references to Appendices
6.30 a.m. Nov. 7th CROIX BARBEE	Batteries in same positions. Too foggy all day to observe. One section 128th Bty left in action for night-firing.	
6.30 a.m. " 8th "	130th Bty relieved 129th Bty who went to rest billets for 3 days first. 5. S.U in RUE DU BONCH. 130th Bty came under CRA and 128th went into position vacated by 129th Bty.	
4 pm " " "	Orders received for 1 section to go on 9th units, 42nd Bde. R.F.A. at LAVENTIE.	
6.30 a.m. " 9th "	Remainder to billets. 130th Bty in farm just S.B.J in BOUT DEVILLE. Batteries in same positions.	
8 a.m. " " "	Report received that MENNEN WERKE had fired 130th fired at supposed position.	
5 pm " " "	130th left 1 section in action for night-firing + remainder returned to billets.	
6.30 a.m. " 10th "	Batteries in same positions.	
5 pm " " "	at 3 pm & 3.45 pm 130th Bty fired for 10 minutes at chateau in triangle NE of NEUVE CHAPELLE. 0.30 Bty in action for night-firing. 4 guns on corner SW of NEUVE CHAPELLE. 2 guns on trench to foot of Chateau.	
12 midnight " " "	CHAPELLE. 130th fired 130 rounds with 4 guns on corner, bombardment lasting till 12.45 a.m.	
10 am " 11th "	130th Bty relieved to billets, 129th Bty reliev'd the section remaining in action on trench. 130th Bty in position. 129th relieved 128th who went to rest billets for 3 days first. S. B.E in FOSSE	
6.30 a.m. " " "		
5 pm " " "	One Section 130th in action for night-firing, remainder return to billets	221 F.H. Men returned 128th Bty from the Base

307TH BRIGADE RFA

WAR DIARY or INTELLIGENCE SUMMARY

Army Form C. 2118.

Hour, Date, Place	Summary of Events and Information	Remarks and references to Appendices
Nov 12* CROIX BARBEE	130" B⁴ in position at same objectives	
6.30 am " 13* "	at 5 pm left the section in action for n/fast firing. Remainder return to billets.	
6.30 am " 13* "	130" RA in same position at approximately same objectives	
5 pm " " "	130* B⁴ returned to billets	
6.30 am " 14* "	128* B⁴ relieved 130* who sent 1 section to LAVENTIE - remainder of B⁴	
5 pm " " "	to rest billets at FOSSE	
6.30 am " 15* "	128* B⁴ 2 guns to billets just S.E. D in BOUT DEVILLE leaving 1 section	
" " " "	in action for n/fast firing	
" " " "	128* B⁴ in same position at same objectives	
5 pm " " "	stacked section, 130* returned to billets with remainder of B⁴	
" " " "	Got orders to be clear of ESTAIRES by 9 am on 16*. B⁴ receipt	
" " " "	of orders relied up all telephone wires.	
6.15 am " 16* BOUT DEVILLE	128* left section in action for n/fast firing - Remainder returned to billets	
" " " "	The Brigade moved, starting p* D.Q BOUT DEVILLE via LA GORGUE	
" " " "	NEUF BERQUIN to VIEUX BERQUIN where RHQs went into	
7 pm " " VIEUX BERQUIN	billets	
" " " "	Orders received to move to DRANOUTRE on 17* leaving at 7 am.	
" " " "	The Bde Commands. to meet CRA 5* Div at 8 am while N of NEUVE EGLISE	
7 am " 17* "	the Brigade less the Amm Col. moved via BAILLEUL to DRANOUTRE	
" " " "	arriving at 10 am.	
" " " "	128* B⁴ attached to 15* Bde RFA went to billets ¾ mile N of NEUVE EGLISE	
" " " "	129* B⁴ " " 38* Bde RFA) had 4 guns in action just by the in	
" " " "	HINDENHOEK - 2 guns in reserve at DRANOUTRE with billets in	
" " " "	DRANOUTRE.	
" " " "	130* B⁴ went to billets ¾ mile N of L in LOCRE	

30TH BRIGADE RFA

WAR DIARY or INTELLIGENCE SUMMARY

Army Form C. 2118.

Hour, Date, Place	Summary of Events and Information	Remarks and references to Appendices
Nov. 7th VIEUX BERQUIN	HQrs and Ammn Col. went to billets at CROIX POPERINGHE	
" 18th CROIX POPERINGHE	128th Bty went into action just S. of their billets	
	130th Bty went into action just S. of just N in KEMMEL with a Section in reserve near LOCRE. Batteries in same position.	10/11 2/Lt R. Wason wounded
" 19th "		
" 20th "	130th Bty ordered to take up a position near LA HUTTE Post 7, NEUVE EGLISE. Billets at INN 3/4 mile S.of just E of NEUVE EGLISE.	2/Lt RS Shave and 2/Lt McTague joined the Brigade and posted to 130th & 129th Bties respectively
	129th B.S.C. sent their reserve section into action 1/2 mile SE W in IVULVERGHEM. 128th did not go into action, remaining in billets.	
" 21st "	Batteries in same positions - 130th still in Wytschaete 1st day and digging gun positions at night.	2/Lt Winchcole joined the 128th and was posted to 130th Bty.
" 22nd "	Batteries in same positions at approximately same objective.	
" 23rd "	130th Bty got orders to move at 8am on 23rd to LA CLYTTE. A position just N.B.K. in KEMMEL was selected & prepared. The Battery went to billets just West of LA CLYTTE.	
8 am "	130th Bty went to LA CLYTTE.	
3 pm "	H.Qrs. went to billets just by G. north of LA CLYTTE. kilometre stone	2 NCO's promoted.
" 24th LA CLYTTE	LOCRE road - 128th & 129th Btys in same positions. 130th Bty in position near KEMMEL L registered various points - 130th changed to billets by M of MONT ROUGE. 128th & 129th Btys in same positions	Lt. G.H. Stanley } went to LawR Lt. G.I. M. Thwaite } 214th & 30th 2nd A. Johnston

30TH BRIGADE R.F.A.

WAR DIARY or INTELLIGENCE SUMMARY.

Army Form C. 2118.

(Erase heading not required.)

Instructions regarding War Diaries and Intelligence Summaries are contained in F. S. Regs., Part II. and the Staff Manual respectively. Title pages will be prepared in manuscript.

Hour, Date, Place	Summary of Events and Information	Remarks and references to Appendices
Nov. 25th LACLYTTE	Batteries in same positions at same objectives. Batteries returned to same billets.	Lt. M Mouchta went to Flying Corps from Pom-Pom Gun
" 26th "	Batteries in same positions at same objectives.	
" 27th "	Batteries in same positions.	
8a.m. 28th "	12.8 K By moved from NEUVE EGLISE to form 1 mile N of KEMMEL VILLAGE. 12.9 K By moved from LINDENHOEK to rear billets 1 mile E of BERTHEN. All batteries of 1/6 Brigade come under 3rd Division.	
" 29th "	Batteries in same positions. 128 K By reports points round WYTSCHAETE - Both Howitzer Brigade and 3rd Siege Bty under O.C. 30th Bde and directly under C.R.A. 3rd Div. 3rd Siege Bty have 1 section in action 1/4 W of 6 kilometre stone from ouen.	BSM Twombey } Went on leave BQMS Bourne } 29th to 5th Dec.
" 30th "	1/4 GROOTE VIERSTRAAT — KEMMEL road, with remainder in billets 1 1/4 miles E of WESTOUTRE. 12.5 K By still N.E of WYTSCHAETE and OOSTTAVERNE. 130 K R.G at same objectives.	Lt.Col Fapeley } returned Lieut H. Marsha } from 2nd. G. Mackie } leave

3rd Divisional Artillery.

30th BRIGADE R. F. A.

DECEMBER 1914.

30TH BRIGADE R.F.A.

Army Form C. 2118.

WAR DIARY
or
INTELLIGENCE SUMMARY.
(Erase heading not required.)

Hour, Date, Place	Summary of Events and Information	Remarks and references to Appendices
Janus December 1st LA CLYTTE	129/15 B.y relieved 128th By who went to rest billets near BERTHEN.	
6 p.m.	130th By in same position. Both batteries fear 1 section in action for night firing.	
Jan. " 2nd "	Orders received that no firing after 8 p.m. Batteries in same position.	2nd Lt. Strong } went on leave. Maj Karstake 2nd to 15th
4.30 pm " "	Return to billets - Sections in action for night firing.	Maj Heathcote
Jan. " 3rd "	Batteries in same position.	
1.15 pm " "	128/15 By sent party to SCHERPENBERG to inspection by H.M. netting.	
4.30 pm " "	Same arrangements for night firing.	
Jan. " 4th "	Batteries in same positions at same objectives.	
4.30 pm " "	Targets for night firing - 129/15 By - Trenches N+S of PETIT BOIS 130/15 B.y - Trench at 8 poplars G.3a NW. army map. 3rd fuze - WYTSCHAETE VILLAGE	
Jan. " 5th "	Batteries in same positions. 1 officer + gunner with TRENCH MORTAR attached to 73rd for supply purposes.	BSM Tunsley } returned from leave Bgns Bourne } B.M. Owen
Jan. " 6th "	128/15 B.y relieved 129/15 B.y who went to rest billets near BERTHEN.	BQMS Markell } went on leave Sgt Corney 6½ K.F.E.
4.30 pm " "	Batteries at usual objectives. Same arrangements for night firing.	

Army Form C. 2118.

30TH BRIGADE R.F.A.

WAR DIARY
or
INTELLIGENCE SUMMARY.

(Erase heading not required.)

Instructions regarding War Diaries and Intelligence Summaries are contained in F.S. Regs., Part II. and the Staff Manual respectively. Title pages will be prepared in manuscript.

Hour, Date, Place	Summary of Events and Information	Remarks and references to Appendices
Nov December 7th LA CLYTTE	Batteries in same positions at same objectives. Same arrangements for night firing.	BSM Hall, BQMS Mackell promoted to QMS, Cory] 2nd Lieutenant Sass] Staffs
" 11.30pm "		
" 8am "	Batteries in Same positions at same objectives.	
" 4.30pm "	Same arrangements for night firing.	
" 9am "	Batteries in Same positions ready to fire on WYTSCHAETE WOOD in Case of German counter attack. 9th How ¾ Bart went to the Base.	Lt Col Strong returned, Maj Karslake]Maj Newland] from leave. 11b Barnard & Brazier Creagh posted to the Brigade.
"	Same arrangements for night firing.	
" 10K "	Batteries in Same positions.	
"	Remaining Section of 3rd Siege B⁴y went into action with Section already in action.	Maj Karslake went to 6·⁵" Bart and B.M. R.A. Maj Prance transferred to 129 IF Lt. Mackie " " 128 IF Mr. Barnard posted " 130 IF 2Lt. Brazier Creagh " Amm. Col.
" 11K "	Same arrangements for night firing.	
"	Batteries in same positions— Nothing of importance all day.	
" 12K "	Same night arrangements as usual.	
"	128th B⁴y went into rest billets 5 of SCHERPENBERG— WESTOUTRE road.— ¼ mile W of 10 kilometrestone.	
" 13K "	1st Siege B⁴y relieved them and got 2 guns into action.	
"	3rd Siege B⁴y got another gun into action.	
"	1st Siege got their 4th gun into action & registered on points in WYTSCHAETE and PETIT BOIS.	
"	Night arrangements as usual.	

30TH BRIGADE R.F.A.

WAR DIARY or INTELLIGENCE SUMMARY

Army Form C. 2118.

Hour, Date, Place		Summary of Events and Information	Remarks and references to Appendices
6.45 am	Dec 14th LA CLYTTE	Batteries all ready in position for bombardment.	Ref. Artillery Map 1/10000
7. a.m	" " "	Preliminary Bombardment continued until 7.45am. —	
		136th Bty. — Trenches in front of pt. 73.	
		3rd Siege Bty. — 19am. Trenches by pt. 73.	
		1 sect. N edge of PETIT BOIS.	
		At 7.45 a.m. Bombardment started.	
		136th Bty. — Cross roads C.i.b.a.	
		1st Siege Bty. WYTSCHAETE BOIS and VILLAGE	
		3rd Siege Bty. WYTSCHAETE VILLAGE and HOSTILE ARTILLERY.	
		136th Bty remained in action for rifle firing and 1 sect of 1st and	
		3rd Siege.	
7am	Dec 15th " "	Bombardment started at same objectives.	
		129 R Bty came into action @ of KEMMEL – LOCRE road W of	
		Mt KEMMEL TOWER. at PETIT BOIS and pt. 73.	
		Normal rifle arrangements.	
		Nothing of importance all day.	
Dec. 16th	" "	No firing all day as 5th Div were registering various points.	
Dec. 17th	" "	Three bombardments during the day – 10.k.10.2. – 10.12 – 10.15 —	
Dec. 18th	" "	1pm 15.12 – 1.12.15 1.15 – 3.k.32 and 3.12.k. 3.15.pm. —	
		135th Bty at Trenches in front of MAEDELSTEDE FARM.	

/ 30TH BRIGADE R.F.A.

WAR DIARY or INTELLIGENCE SUMMARY

Army Form C. 2118

(Erase heading not required.)

Hour, Date, Place	Summary of Events and Information	Remarks and references to Appendices
Dec 18th LA CLYTTE	129 R.B.H. at PETIT BOIS. 1st Siege B.H. Trench S.W. of PETIT BOIS to MAEDELSTEDE. 3rd Siege B.H. PETIT BOIS 1st Siege had an officer observing from trench near S.W corner of PETIT BOIS. Normal night arrangements	
Dec 19th "	129 R.B.y relieved 13 R.B.y who are to rest billets. Howitzer kept up steady rate of fire on usual targets. Bombardment at same objectives 3pm to 3.33 and 3.12.6.3.15 pm 3rd siege B.H. fires 8 rounds each at cross roads D.13.B.4 D.13.D Normal night arrangements	2Lt Westfold to 129 B.y
4pm Dec 20th " "	Bombardments at 2pm to 2.3 and 2.17 to 2.20 at same objectives except 1st Siege and not fire owing to presence of German aeroplane Usual night arrangements.	
Dec 21st " "	Batteries in same positions. If Major went to trenches N.W. corner of PETIT BOIS to locate machine gun Night arrangements as usual	Maj Muirhead NM Pearce went on leave Capt Salter BSM Pearce TSS Peabrook went on leave Sgt Tiensley
Dec 22nd " "	Batteries in same positions - nothing all day	
Dec 23rd " "	Batteries in same positions - Nothing all day	

30th BRIGADE R.F.A.

Army Form C. 2118

WAR DIARY
or
INTELLIGENCE SUMMARY.
(Erase heading not required.)

Instructions regarding War Diaries and Intelligence Summaries are contained in F.S. Regs., Part II. and the Staff Manual respectively. Title pages will be prepared in manuscript.

Hour, Date, Place	Summary of Events and Information	Remarks and references to Appendices
Dec. 24th LA CLYTTE	Batteries in same positions. 128th Bty fired new O.P. to engage 3 mm between pt.176 G.3.a and 60 in G.9.b. New O.P. in pt.132. in F.3.c. 2nd Siege A/we able to engage same 3mm – new O.P. in F.4.a. 1st Siege got a 6 m district region 1st Corps at BETHUNE and march at 9 p.m. No shooting all day owing to fog. 13d. Try Hd. Qrs. changed to farm in G.3.a N.W. – 1/4 mile N.G./M in MONT KEMMEL	
Dec. 25th "	Batteries in same positions – nothing all day.	
Dec. 26th "	Batteries in same positions.	
Dec. 27th "	Batteries in same positions. 128th have forward officer to observe trenches by SPANBROEK MIL. Maj Mumbers, Maj France return from leave, Capt Lasler. Shot 5 of FME D'HOINE	Maj Mumbers } Maj France } return from leave Capt Lasler }
Dec 28th "	Batteries in same positions. From 1.30 till 3.10 p.m. 3rd Siege B.G. position bombarded but no damage done.	RSM Pearce " " " Pte Benbrook " " " Sgt Townsley " " "
Dec 29th "	Batteries in same positions. At 4 pm B.G.F. relieved by fires B.G.S.F. who left sector for night firing.	Capt Cochrane } on leave Capt Baxter } 2nd Lt. Brylan } A.S.S. Roots } FQMS Pris } RSM Hilton from 1st to reserve the base 2 Lt.

30TH BRIGADE R.F.A

WAR DIARY or INTELLIGENCE SUMMARY

Army Form C. 2118.

Hour, Date, Place	Summary of Events and Information	Remarks and references to Appendices
Dec. 30th LA CLYTTE	Remainder of 130th in action by 10am. 779th to reat. 131st rejoin. Trenches by SPANBROEK MILL.	
Dec. 31st "	Batteries in same positions. In the afternoon Bde shelled SPANBROEK MILL. Night arrangements as usual.	

Index

SUBJECT.

3RD DIV.

No.	Contents.	Date.
	R.F.A. 30TH BRIGADE — WAR DIARY, JAN – DEC, 1915	

12/4259

3.ze Division

30 Bde: R.J.A.

Vol IV. 1-31.1.15

Nil

Army Form C. 2118.

30th BRIGADE RFA

WAR DIARY
INTELLIGENCE SUMMARY.
(Erase heading not required.)

Instructions regarding War Diaries and Intelligence Summaries are contained in F. S. Regs., Part II. and the Staff Manual respectively. Title pages will be prepared in manuscript.

Hour, Date, Place	Summary of Events and Information	Remarks and references to Appendices
Jan 1st 1915 LA CLYTTE	Batteries in same position. Night arrangements as usual.	
Jan 2nd " "	Batteries in same position. 131st Bty have new OP on E. slopes of KEMMEL in F.4.a.	
Jan 3rd " "	Batteries in same positions. O.C. 128th Bty and 3rd S.B. reconnoitred alternative positions. Lt.Col Strong ordered to command a Bde of 2nd Division. 5th Divn Bombardment.	Major Muirhead to command 128th Bty. Capt Baxter from 129 Bty to 130 Bty. Capt Archdale from 128 Bty to command Bde Amm Column.
" 7.30 - 8.30 AM		
Jan 4th LA CLYTTE	Batteries in same positions. One battery of 30th Bde to join 29th Divn. 130th Bty selected. 3rd Divn firing line extended up to VIERSTRAAT-NYTSCHAETE road	Capt Almack to 128. Lt Lyon Smith to Bde Staff. Lt Austin to 128.
Jan 5th "	Majors 129 + 3rd S.B. in same positions. 128 Bty from reck took up new position near Bde Day H.Q. 130th Bty went to billets in Mt ROUGE. OC 30th Bde reconnoitred artillery positions in area to be taken over from French 32nd Divn (General Bucher). Enemy shelled KEMMEL village during afternoon, and our infantry trenches N.W. of PETIT BOIS	
10 p.m. " "	Orders to move 30th Bde H.Q's night billet tomorrow.	

30th BRIGADE R.F.A

Army Form C. 2118.

WAR DIARY

INTELLIGENCE SUMMARY.

(Erase heading not required.)

Instructions regarding War Diaries and Intelligence Summaries are contained in F.S. Regs., Part II. and the Staff Manual respectively. Title pages will be prepared in manuscript.

Hour, Date, Place	Summary of Events and Information	Remarks and references to Appendices
Jan 6th LA CLYTTE	Bde H.Q's moved to billet vacated by 42nd Bde.H.Q's situated just N of letter V of BURGRAVE F.me N19 c.W. Weather misty and some rain.	2/Lt Thynne Smith joined from 3rd DAC posted as ad Officer to R & 5 Staff Capt Almack joined 128th By 2/Lt Austin " " " Major Muirhead " " " Capt Archdale " Bde A.C.
Jan 7th KEMMEL	OC 130th Bty (Major Muirhead) gave details of new gun positions. 3rd S.B fire on SPANBROEK reported effective by infantry.	
Jan 8th	Bombardment by 129th & 3rd S.B of HOLLANDSCHESHUUR FARM. Very effective firing.	130th By joined 24th Div.
" "	OC 128th Bty shelled SPAN BROEK MOLEN trenches and along to NYRVISTRAAT Capt. Also registered EIGHT POPLARS and Ken Registered trenches on extreme right of zone	
11.20am "		
Jan 9th "	Batteries in same positions. Enemy's guns reported (by infantry) just SE of HOLLANDSCHHUUR FARM. 129th By + 3rd S.B took these guns on by G.O.C's orders	

WAR DIARY

INTELLIGENCE SUMMARY

30th BRIGADE RFA

Army Form C. 2118.

Hour, Date, Place	Summary of Events and Information	Remarks and references to Appendices
Jan 10th KEMMEL	129th & 3rd S.B. bombarded enemy's guns reported by aeroplane reconnaissance (same guns as reported yesterday.)	2/Lt Archer ordered to proceed to Central flying school at UPAVON.
Jan 11th "	130th By crumped, detachments withdrawn	
" "	129th By did good shooting on trenches near HOLLANDSCHESCHUUR FARM.	2/Lt Archer left for UPAVON
" "	One 6 rounds fired by heavy German Battery from near MESSINES	
" "	12 rounds " " German field " from about 11° R of WYTSCHAETE TOWER.	
Jan 12th "	128th By fired on MAEDELSTEDE and SPANBROEK.	
" "	129th By fired on guns located in Square D.13.c.	Capt Athack left 128 By to join 5th Div.
9.30 am "	3rd S.B. fired 6 rounds at PE 14.	
10.45 am "	" " 18 " N.30.C. SPANBROEK MOLEN	Capt Colfox joined 128th By vice Capt Athack
12.0 pm "	" " 34 " on working party on N.24.C.	
2.30 pm "	" " 12 " at N.24.C.E (Trenches)	
3.8 pm "	" " 16 " D.13.C (guns)	
Jan 13th "	Enemy shelled VIERSTRAAT - KEMMEL road. 6" Howitzers did good firing between WYTSCHAETE WOOD and MAEDELSTEDE FARM	2/Lt BAYLY joined and posted to 128th By.

30th BRIGADE RFA

Army Form C. 2118.

WAR DIARY
~~INTELLIGENCE~~ SUMMARY.
(Erase heading not required.)

Instructions regarding War Diaries and Intelligence Summaries are contained in F. S. Regs., Part II. and the Staff Manual respectively. Title pages will be prepared in manuscript.

Hour, Date, Place	Summary of Events and Information	Remarks and references to Appendices
Jan 14th KEMMEL	3rd S.B. did damage to trenches in N 24 d. E, assisted by 128th By.	
" "	Enemy shelled Mt KEMMEL from between MESSINES + WYTSCHAETE.	
" "	129th By fired. Conference at 9th J/Bde H.Q, and foll. arrangements made:- Infantry "Tomasha".	
Jan 15th 6.40 am "		
" 6.55 am "	Fired on named targets by 30th Bde, 42nd Bde, and 3rd S.B.	
Jan 16th "	Result of Bombardment reported as very effective	
" "	Batteries in same positions	
" "	3rd S.B. fired at PECKHAM, and trenches in N 24 d.	
" 12 noon "	KEMMEL shelled by German guns.	
Jan 17th "	3rd S B + 128th By fired from PECKHAM nalware to VERTICAL Row	
Jan 18th "	KEMMEL shelled by field guns.	
" "	Batteries in same positions.	
" 6.50 am "	3rd S.B. fired on SPANBROEK.	Dr Goodwyn (129th By) was refused leave to visit his sick wife
" 9 pm "	Enemy shelled VIERSTRAAT	Cloxton (129th) made "B" for period of leave to visit sick wife

WAR DIARY

INTELLIGENCE SUMMARY.

(Erase heading not required.)

30th BRIGADE R.F.A.

Army Form C. 2118.

Hour, Date, Place	Summary of Events and Information	Remarks and references to Appendices
12.30 pm Jan 19th KEMMEL	3rd S.B. fired on SPANBROEK Trenches	
12.43 pm " "	" " " at O.P. in houses in O.19.d.	
2.15 " " "	" " " Trenches in N.24.b+d	
10.30 am – 2.30 pm " "	Enemy shelled KEMMEL.	
Jan 20th "	Batteries in same positions.	Capt Colfox (128th By) } staff 2/Lt Hecht (129th By) } on leave.
" "	Enemy's guns did damage 15th Middlesex	
" "	2 guns located near Pt 79 L'ENFER.	
Jan 21st "	Batteries in same positions.	
11.30 am " "	128th By fired on SPARNBROEK trenches	
4 pm " "	129th By " " MAEDELSTEDE "	
Jan 22nd "	Enemy shelled KEMMEL and PETIT BOIS trenches.	
" "	128th and 129th Bys fired on same positions as day before	
" "	3rd S.B. fired on K2, drew fire from 2 German field batteries.	
Jan 23rd "	3rd S.B. " " " (range reported correct.)	
2.30 pm " "	128 By fired on SPANBROEK trenches	

30th BRIGADE R.F.A.

WAR DIARY
INTELLIGENCE SUMMARY.

Army Form C. 2118.

Hour, Date, Place	Summary of Events and Information	Remarks and references to Appendices
Jan 23rd KEMMEL	Enemy shelled KEMMEL, and KEMMEL-LOCRE road.	
8.15 AM Jan 24th "	3rd S.B. fired on PECKHAM.	
" "	129th By " " MAEDELSTEDE.	
" "	128th By fired on trench opposite F5.	
Jan 25th "	Batteries in same positions.	S.M. Pearce (128#) wounded 2nd W. and proceeded to the base.
" "	No firing owing to mist.	
10AM Jan 26th "	128th By fired on Communication trench near MAEDELSTEDE	
" "	129th By " " same target.	
10.40 AM " "	3rd S.B. fired into trench opposite H2.	
5.14 PM " "	" " " " PETIT BOIS	
12noon Jan 27th "	128th, 129th and 3rd S.B. fired on WYTSCHAETE WOOD	
" "	Misty day; some snow.	
Jan 28th "	Batteries in same positions.	
11 AM " "	3rd S.B. fired on MAEDELSTEDE; helped by 129th By	2nd/Lt Brazier Creagh 30th A/Left " Lyon Smith 30th AQ on leave
" "	128th By " " SPANBROEK	

Army Form C. 2118.

30th BRIGADE R.F.A.

WAR DIARY
INTELLIGENCE SUMMARY.
(Erase heading not required.)

Instructions regarding War Diaries and Intelligence Summaries are contained in F.S. Regs., Part II. and the Staff Manual respectively. Title pages will be prepared in manuscript.

Hour, Date, Place	Summary of Events and Information	Remarks and references to Appendices
Jan 29th KEMMEL	Firing by 128th & 129th By on trenches.	
" "	3rd S.B. also at trenches.	
Jan 30th "	3rd S.B fired on WYTSCHAETE TOWER (10 hits out of 15.)	
" "	128th By fired on house near ".	G. King's Chauffeur hit by shrapnel on KEMMEL hill as he was driving over the ridge.
Jan 31st "	Enemy's guns very active; also fired on KEMMEL Batteries in same positions.	
" "	128th By shelled house beyond PECKHAM.	
" "	3rd S.B. fired on trenches opposite K2.	
" "	Enemy searched for 3rd S.B; no result.	H.F. Stanley Lt-Col. Comdg. 30th Bde. R.F.A. Am.dg 30th Howitzer R.F.A.

3rd Division

30th Bde R.F.A.

Orders 1.2 — 31.3.15

30th BRIGADE R.F.A.

Army Form C. 2118.

WAR DIARY
INTELLIGENCE SUMMARY.

Hour, Date, Place	Summary of Events and Information	Remarks and references to Appendices
Feb. 1st KEMMEL	128th By fired on SPANBROEK.	Gen Wing proceeded to BOULOGNE to have his leg X-rayed.
" "	129th By " houses at S end of WYTSCHAETE.	
" "	3rd S.B. fired on trenches opp hole F2 and R2	Major Newland (130) wounded, lyddite by shell exploding in a dug out caused by brazier being upset.
Feb 2nd "	3rd S.B. silenced enemy's guns ?	19 gunner killed.
" "	Enemy shelled KEMMEL-LOCRE road.	Major Robinson RFA joined, and took over 130th Battery.
Feb. 3rd "	Batteries in same positions.	2nd Lt Marshall joined Bde AC
Feb. 4th "	128th By fired on MAEDELSTEDE	
" "	129th " " HOSPICE	
" "	3rd S.B. " " PECKHAM	
" "	KEMMEL heavily shelled.	
Feb. 5th "	Batteries in same positions.	2nd Lt Lydjon Smith returned from leave
Feb. 6th "	Batteries fired on WYTSCHAETE and MAEDELSTEDE.	2nd Lt Brasier-Creagh joined 130th By from Bde A.C.
" "	KEMMEL-LOCRE road shelled.	2nd Lt Boylan left 130th By to join R.H.A.
Feb. 7th "	3rd S.B. shelled trenches S. of PETIT BOIS	
" "	128 and 129 Bs fired at houses S end of WYTSCHAETE	

30th BRIGADE. R.F.A.

Instructions regarding War Diaries and Intelligence Summaries are contained in F.S. Regs., Part II. and the Staff Manual respectively. Title pages will be prepared in manuscript.

Army Form C. 2118.

WAR DIARY
INTELLIGENCE SUMMARY.
(Erase heading not required.)

Hour, Date, Place	Summary of Events and Information	Remarks and references to Appendices
Feb 8th KEMMEL	3rd S.B. shelled trenches near HOLLANDSCHESHUUR FARM.	
" 1.45 pm "	4.5" Howitzers fired daily allowance.	
" "	KEMMEL-KOERE road shelled.	
Feb 9th "	Batteries in same positions.	
" "	3rd S.B. on HOLLANDSCHESHUUR FARM Trenches.	
Feb 10th "	3rd S.B. shelled opposite R2.	
" "	KEMMEL-KOERE road shelled.	
Feb 11th "	No firing by 4.5" Howitzers owing to bad light.	Lieut. Barnard (04130) died at Vincneux.
" "	KEMMEL again shelled by 15cm guns	
Feb 12th "	hit many their hugdens.	
" "	KEMMEL-KOERE road shelled	
" "	Batteries in same positions.	
Feb 13th "	128" Bat on S. end of WYTSCHAETE	
" "	3rd S.B. on MAEDELSTEDE Trenches.	2nd Lt SCOTT ⎱ joined
" "	Enemy shelled KEMMEL CHATEAU and KEMMEL-KOERE road	" " Wilkins ⎰ 30th Bde.

30th BRIGADE R.F.A.

WAR DIARY / INTELLIGENCE SUMMARY

Army Form C. 2118.

Hour, Date, Place	Summary of Events and Information	Remarks and references to Appendices
Feb 14th KEMMEL	Batteries in same positions.	
Feb 15th "	128th, 129th + 3rd S.B. fired on enemy's trenches	
" "	KEMMEL - LOCRE road shelled.	
Feb 16th "	3rd S.B. shelled WYTSCHAETE TOWER.	
" "	128th + 129th on trenches	
Feb 17th "	128th and 129th did not fire.	
" 2.35 pm "	3rd S.B. 4 H.L. on WYTSCHAETE TOWER	
" 2.40 pm "	" 12 L.L. at road in O.9.	
Feb 18th "	128th + 129th did not fire.	
11.35 am "	3rd S.B. fired 4 H.L. at O.19.d.2.8.	
3 pm "	" " 12 J.H.L. at redoubt S.W. of PECKHAM	
4.35 pm "	" " 4 J.H.L. at HOSPICE	
" "	KEMMEL - LOCRE road shelled	
" "	Windy day, but fine.	

30th BRIGADE R.F.A

WAR DIARY
or
INTELLIGENCE SUMMARY.
(Erase heading not required.)

Army Form C. 2118.

Instructions regarding War Diaries and Intelligence Summaries are contained in F. S. Regs., Part II. and the Staff Manual respectively. Title pages will be prepared in manuscript.

Hour, Date, Place	Summary of Events and Information	Remarks and references to Appendices
Feb 19th KEMMEL	128th & 129th did not fire	
" "	3rd S.B. fired 2 H.L. at O.20.c.	
Feb 20th "	128th & 129th did not fire	
3.5 pm " "	3rd S.B. fired 14 H.L. at HOLLANDSCHESCHUUR FARM	
4.17 pm " "	" " 2 H.L. at WYTSCHAETE TOWER	
" "	Weather fine & warm.	
Feb 21st "	Batteries in the same positions.	130th Battery from 27th to 5th Division
" "	128th and 129th did not fire	
2.30 pm "	3rd S.B. fired 14 H.L. at Targets 44, 45, and 46 by aeroplane registration.	
5.19 pm "	" " 4 L.L. on cross roads at O.15.a.3.1.	
3 pm – 4 pm "	Mt KEMMEL and KEMMEL – LOCRE road shelled.	
Feb 22nd "	128th & 129th did not fire	
" "	3rd S.B. 4 L.L. at TORRENKEN FARM. O.20.d.2.3.	
Feb 23rd "	128th and 129th did not fire	
" "	3rd S.B. 4 L.L. at O.19.6.1.6.	Reinforcements
Feb 24th "	3rd S.B. 4 L.L. at house in O.25.a.9.9.	129 { N.A. Hunter } joined for a
	128th and 129th did not fire.	{ W.H. Pyman } fortnight's
		128 H.H. Maverty } course from England.

Army Form C. 2118.

30th BRIGADE R.F.A.

Instructions regarding War Diaries and Intelligence Summaries are contained in F.S. Regs., Part II. and the Staff Manual respectively. Title pages will be prepared in manuscript.

WAR DIARY
or
INTELLIGENCE SUMMARY.
(Erase heading not required.)

Hour, Date, Place	Summary of Events and Information	Remarks and references to Appendices
Feb 25th KEMMEL	128th +129th did not fire.	
" "	3rd S.B. 4 hh on Observation Posts on WYTSCHAETE RIDGE.	
Feb 26th "	128th +129th did not fire	
2.15 pm "	3rd S.B. 20 hh on target 44 by air registration.	Capt Scaife went on leave.
3.50 pm "	" 11 hh. at WYTSCHAETE TOWER.	Major Prance (129) " " .
Feb 27th "	128th + 129th did not fire.	
12.5 pm "	3rd S.B. 16 hh. at WYTSCHAETE TOWER.	
12.30 pm "	KEMMEL - LOCRE road shelled.	
Feb 28th "	128th 12 shrapnel on trenches between PECKHAM and EIGHT POPLARS.	
" "	129th 12 " " " behind PECKHAM.	
" "	3rd S.B 16 H.t. on PECKHAM FARM.	
" "	KEMMEL VILLAGE shelled.	
March 1st "	128th + 129th did not fire.	Col Stanley went on leave.
" "	KEMMEL VILLAGE shelled.	
March 2nd "	128th +129th did not fire.	Stanley Lt.Col. 2m 30 Hy Bde
" "	3rd S.B 4 hh on WYTSCHAETE TOWER.	28.2.1916.

30th BRIGADE R.F.A.

WAR DIARY

INTELLIGENCE SUMMARY

Army Form C. 2118.

Hour, Date, Place	Summary of Events and Information	Remarks and references to Appendices
March 3rd KEMMEL	Batteries in same positions.	
3 pm " "	128th & 129th did not fire.	
2.30 March 4th "	3rd S.B. 50 H.L. at HOLLAND FARM Trenches.	
12.50 pm " "	129th fired 11 hyddite to register trenches N of PECKHAM.	
3 pm " "	128th " 3 " & 8 Shrapnel " S " " .	
March 5th "	3rd S.B. 16 H.L. on SPANBROEK MOLEN.	
" "	Hostile fire on HINDENMOCK and KEMMEL HILL.	
" "	128th & 129th registered their allotted targets on SPANBROEK RIDGE.	
March 6th "	Left Section of 3rd S.B. proceeded to DICKEBUSH to assist 24th Division.	
" "	128th, 129th and right section of 3rd S.B. did not fire.	
" "	Left Section of 3rd S.B. fired 130 H.L. on St ELOI Trenches.	
" "	Slow Hostile shrapnel (15cm guns) and H.E. on KEMMEL HILL.	
4 March 7th "	3rd S.B. fired 30 H.L. on HOLLANDSCHESCHUUR FARM.	Col Stanley } Returned from leave. Capt Scaife }
3.15 pm "	128th fired 15 L and 15 Shrapnel on MAEDELSTEDE Trenches.	Major Prance (129) returned from leave.
3.15 pm "	129th " " " " " HOSPICE.	
5.30 pm "	KEMMEL — LOCRE shelled.	

Army Form C. 2118.

50th BRIGADE R.F.A.

WAR DIARY

INTELLIGENCE SUMMARY.

(Erase heading not required.)

Hour, Date, Place	Summary of Events and Information	Remarks and references to Appendices
March 8th KEMMEL	Batteries in same positions	2/Lt Taylor joined for instruction from England
3.5 p.m. "	128th fired 20L and 20S on trenches in N.30.C.	2/Lt Hunter } left for England after course of instruction
" "	129th " " " " " " "	2/Lt Pyman } left for England after course of instruction
" "	3rd S.B. fired 20 H.L. on SPANBROEK MOLEN and to KEEP.	Marrak }
10.5 A.M. "	15 cm gun fired 10 S on Mt KEMMEL	
8 A.M. March 9th	3rd S.B. fired 20H on MAEDELSTEDE KEEP.	
8.5 A.M. "	128th & 129th fired 35 rounds (½L + ½S) on trenches N & SW of PECKHAM	
1.58 A.M. March 10th to 4.50	128th fired 58L at trenches in front of SPANBROEK MOLEN & CABARET.	
" "	129th " 81L " northern portion of trench Md " " "	
" "	3rd S.B. " 30 H.L. on SPANBROEK KEEP.	
7.54 A.M. to 8.23 A.M.	3rd S.B. " 35 " " MAEDELSTEDE FARM.	
" "	" " 15 H.L. (to 3 guns) on PECKHAM.	
1.30 p.m. March 11th to 3.30 p.m.	3rd S.B. fired 80 H.L. on HOLLANDSCHESCHUR FARM.	RSM J.A. Baker joined from England.
2.50 p.m "	129th fired 48L on trenches S of " "	
4.05 p.m to 4.5 p.m	128th fired 19S and 33L on HOSPICE RIDGE	

30th BRIGADE R.F.A

WAR DIARY

~~INTELLIGENCE SUMMARY~~

(Erase heading not required.)

Army Form C. 2118.

Instructions regarding War Diaries and Intelligence Summaries are contained in F.S. Regs., Part II. and the Staff Manual respectively. Title pages will be prepared in manuscript.

Hour, Date, Place	Summary of Events and Information	Remarks and references to Appendices
2.30pm March 12th KEMMEL to 1pm	128th fired 268L and 23S on SPANBROEK RIDGE	
" "	129th " 280L on SPAN BROEK RIDGE.	
3.30pm "	3rd S.B. " 64HL at SPANBROEK KEEP	
4.11pm "	" " 15HL at MAEDELSTEDE (1gun at Section)	
" "	" " 23HL at PECKHAM (Left Section)	
4.55pm "	" " 62HL at "machine gun emplacement" SPANBROEK MOLEN	
	Attack on the SPANBROER MOLEN was held up.	
March 13th "	128th & 129th covered lines on SPAN BROEK MOLEN	
3.50pm "	129th fired 12S. at PECKHAM.	
2.43pm "		
to 4.45pm "	3rd S.B. " 40 H.L. at SPAN BROEK MOLEN.	
5.30pm March 14th "	128th fired 109L at HOSPICE, PETIT BOIS and 5mns E of WYTSCHAETE.	2/Lt Wilkins sent to Base
to 6.35pm	129th " 28S and 8L on trenches West of GRAND BOIS.	sick from 130th By.
5.30pm "	3rd S.B. fired 58 H.L at HOLLANDSCHE SCHUUR FARM trenches.	
5.20pm "		
March 15th "	128th & 129th did not fire	2/Lt Scott posted to 130th By
3.50pm "	3rd S.B. fired 28L Lat trench at St ELOI.	from 128th By.
4.55pm "	" " 21LL " " "	

WAR DIARY

INTELLIGENCE SUMMARY

30th BRIGADE R.F.A.

Army Form C. 2118.

Hour, Date, Place	Summary of Events and Information	Remarks and references to Appendices
March 16th KEMMEL	Batteries in same positions	
" "	128th + 129th did not fire	
" "	3rd S.B. fired 3LL at ST ELOI.	
" "	all reported 'not observed', so firing ceased.	
March 17th "	foggy all day	
2.30 pm "	128th fired 13 Shrapnel at 0.25 c 99 at small field gun.	
3.20 pm - 3.45 pm		
3 pm "	3rd S.B. fired 6 HL at PECKHAM.	
" "	KEMMEL- LOCRE shelled.	
March 18th "	129th and 3rd SB did not fire	
" "	128th fired 4S at 025 c 79	
" "	Thick fog all day.	
March 19th "	128th and 5th S.B. did not fire	
" "	129th fired 6 rounds on trenches opposite K2	
March 20th "	129th 4S at suspected OP on WYTSCHAETE RIDGE.	One section of 128th By moved to position (about) N.W. of KEMMEL CHATEAU
5 pm "	3rd S.B. fired 6S at O20 L and O20 C.	

WAR DIARY

30th BRIGADE R.F.A.

Army Form C. 2118.

Hour, Date, Place	Summary of Events and Information	Remarks and references to Appendices
March 21st KEMMEL	3rd S.B. did not fire.	
" 22nd "	128 Detached Section fired 185 to register	
" " "	129th fired 76 at PECKHAM trench mortar	
" 23rd "	Batteries on same positions: did not fire	2Lt Taylor & Keane left for England Gunnery Competition 14 days round. 2Lt Bernal joined from England 2Lt Roberts " " Longan Byrne for 2 weeks course.
" " "	128th fired M.S. to register	
" " "	129 " 45 at O.P. on WYTSCHAETE RIDGE	
" " "	3rd S.B. did not fire	
March 24th "	129th Battery attached to 23rd Bde 5th Div.	
" " "	48th Heavy Battery under O.C. 30th R.F.A.	
" " "	128th fired 115 at guns behind SPANBROEK MOLEN	
" " "	3rd S.B. did not fire	
March 25th "	128th fired 138 at guns behind SPANBROEK	
" " "	" " 68 on trenches North of the line	
" " "	Rainy day	
March 26th "	128th By did not fire	Lt Cook joined 128th By.
" " "	48th Heavy fired at registered targets	

30th BRIGADE R.F.A.   Army Form C. 2118.

WAR DIARY
or
INTELLIGENCE SUMMARY.
(Erase heading not required.)

Instructions regarding War Diaries and Intelligence Summaries are contained in F.S. Regs., Part II. and the Staff Manual respectively. Title pages will be prepared in manuscript.

Hour, Date, Place	Summary of Events and Information	Remarks and references to Appendices
March 27th KEMMEL	3rd S.B. + 128th By did not fire	
" "	48th Heavy By registered O.B. D.61 and O.20.a.41.	
March 28th "	3rd S.B. + 128th By did not fire.	
" "	48th Heavy By fired with airman.	
March 29th "	3rd S.B. and 48th & 128th By did not fire	Lt Sneyd AVC. left for England, proceeding to Aldershot.
" "	48th H.B. fired on registered targets.	Lt Collet AVC. joined 30th Bde.
March 30th "	128th By fired 18 S to register new zone.	
" "	3rd S.B. did not fire.	
" "	48th H.B. on registered targets.	
March 31st "	128 Detached Section and 3rd S.B. did not fire.	
" "	128 HQ guns fired 95 at trenches near SPANBROEK MOLEN	
6.30 pm "	128 H.Q guns moved to new position, just S. of VIERSTRAAT DICKEBUSH ROAD.	

Stanley Clark
Bn. Ad. 30 Bde R.F.A
31. 3. 1915.

121/5320

3rd Division

8th Brigade R.F.A.

Jnl Vol 1 — 30.4.15

30th BRIGADE RFA

Army Form C. 2118.

WAR DIARY
INTELLIGENCE SUMMARY.
(Erase heading not required.)

Instructions regarding War Diaries and Intelligence Summaries are contained in F.S. Regs., Part II. and the Staff Manual respectively. Title pages will be prepared in manuscript.

Hour, Date, Place	Summary of Events and Information	Remarks and references to Appendices
April 1st KEMMEL	3rd SB did not fire	Capt Scarfe RAMC left for England.
" "	128th fired 14 shrapnel and 10 hostile to register	Temp/Lt. Real RAMC joined 30th
" "	48th HB fired at registered targets.	Brigade vice Capt Scarfe.
April 3rd "	128th fired 22 shrapnel + 7 hostile to register.	Rev Lieut Archer
April 4th "	128th fired 5 shrapnel and 11 hostile at ST ELOI mound	Interment auth by SA RAMC 10 BLI26
" "	3rd SB fired 15 LL to register redoubt at O7898.	
April 5th "	48th HB fired on registered targets.	4/A Brind.
3.35–4pm "	128th fired 11 shrapnel at ST ELOI mound.	2/Lt Roberts left for England for completion of "Lawson Byrne's" tonight's course.
April 6th "	128th fired 16 shrapnel at ST ELOI mound	
April 7th "	48th HB fired on registered targets	2/Lt (Temp) Whitridge joined and
" "	128th fired on ST ELOI mound	posted to 128th Battery.
April 8th "	128th fired 11 shrapnel at BRICKSTACK (near ST ELOI mound)	2 sections of 130th Battery moved
4.5 " "	" 7 and 10L at trenches near PICCADILLY FARM.	by night to new position
5.30 " "	48th HB fired on registered targets.	north of DICKEBUSCHE

30th BRIGADE R.F.A.

WAR DIARY

INTELLIGENCE SUMMARY.

(Erase heading not required.)

Army Form C. 2118.

Hour, Date, Place	Summary of Events and Information	Remarks and references to Appendices
April 9th KEMMEL	128th fired 6 shrapnel at HOLLANDSCHESCHUUR FARM.	Remaining section 130th Battery moved up to new position by night.
3.30pm " "	" 1 shrapnel and 10 lyddite at Salient in O7C 4.7.	
4 am " "	129th 6 shrapnel at HOSPICE.	129th Bty under 30th Brigade from 12 midday.
" " "	48th H.B. fired on registered targets.	
April 10th "	" " " " "	
" " "	" " " " "	
12.30pm "	128 fired 15 shrapnel to register.	
4pm " "	" 10 lyddite at BRICKSTACK (near ST ELOI)	
" " "	" Batteries in Sown positions	
April 11th "	" " " " "	
" 12th "	129th + 3rd S.B. did not fire.	
" " "	128th fired 5 shrapnel at two also N of PICCADILLY FARM.	
" " "	48th H.B. engaged registered targets	
" 13th "	129 + 3rd S.B. did not fire.	H.Q. Section 48th H.B. moved back
" " "	128 fired 14 shrapnel at BRICKSTACK near ST ELOI.	
3pm " "	48th H.B. fired 61 rounds on registered targets	

Army Form C. 2118.

50th BRIGADE R.F.A.

WAR DIARY
INTELLIGENCE SUMMARY.
(Erase heading not required.)

Hour, Date, Place	Summary of Events and Information	Remarks and references to Appendices
April 14th KEMMEL	129th and 3rd S.B. did not fire.	2/Austin rejoined 128th Battery after course of Trench Howitzer.
6.15 pm " "	128th fired 5 shrapnel + 4 HyddIte at S.V.E.101 Murmd.	
7.30 pm " "	" " " " HOLLANDSCHESHUUR trench mortar	
April 15th "	48th H.B. on registered targets.	
" " "	Hostile artillery active; DEMEBUSCH – LA CYTTE road shelled.	
" " "	48th H.B. engaged registered targets.	
" " "	128th, 129th and 3rd S.B. did not fire.	Lt. Cook transferred from 128th to 129th Battery. 3rd S.B. moved out by night destination secret? 48th H.B. left.
April 16th "	129th did not fire.	
6.15 pm " "	128th fired 6 shrapnel at trench junction S.V.E.101 Murmd.	
" " "	48th H.B. on registered targets.	
5–7 pm April 17th "	128th fired 15 shrapnel.	
" " "	129th did not fire.	Left Section 110th Battery (Capt. ——) came into position left by 48th H.B. under command of Lt.Col LAYARD.

30th BRIGADE RFA

Army Form C. 2118.

WAR DIARY
or
INTELLIGENCE SUMMARY.

(Erase heading not required.)

Instructions regarding War Diaries and Intelligence Summaries are contained in F.S. Regs., Part II. and the Staff Manual respectively. Title pages will be prepared in manuscript.

Hour, Date, Place	Summary of Events and Information	Remarks and references to Appendices
3.45pm April 18th KEMMEL	128th fired 15 Shrapnel at St. ELOI and trenches	
-4.20pm	129th did not fire.	
"	110th Battery registered.	
April 19th "	128th fired 12 Shrapnel on gun targets.	129th Battery moved to position
"	110th Battery own registered points	3/4 mile S. of DICKEBUSCHE LAKE.
"	Hostile artillery very active from DICKEBUSCHE.	
April 20th LACLYTTE	129th registered.	30th Bde HQ moved to
5.50pm	128th fired 4 Shrapnel at St ELOI. Round	LA CLYTTE.
"	110th on registered points	Lt GA Mortimer y Coma 128 for
12pm April 21st	128th registered HOLLANDSCHESCHUUR FARM	instruction
	fired 32 bdds on " "	2Lt White joined 129 for instruction 20th
10.30pm Bish-kukden	" " " " " "	
"	129th fired 32 bdds on trenches West of HOLLANDSCHESCHUUR FARM	Lt Cook (129th) left for rocket gun course at BERTHEN
"	110th on registered targets.	
5pm	Section of 129th moved to 5th Division.	5th Division mine and rush
8pm	Remainder of 129th moved to 5th Division, near YPRES.	HILL 60 during night 17/18th

Army Form C. 2118.

WAR DIARY
INTELLIGENCE SUMMARY.
(Erase heading not required.)

30th BRIGADE RFA

Instructions regarding War Diaries and Intelligence Summaries are contained in F.S. Regs, Part II. and the Staff Manual respectively. Title pages will be prepared in manuscript.

Hour, Date, Place	Summary of Events and Information	Remarks and references to Appendices
4.35 pm April 22nd J.A. CLYTTE	128th fired 12 Shrapnel between STEDI Wood + PICCADILLY FARM.	Battle of YPRES Again
"	110th Battery on registered points	
2.45 pm April 23rd	128th fired 15 shrapnel to register	
"	110th Battery fired on registered points	
"	Hostile artillery active on ELZENWALLE	
7.0 AM April 24th	128th fired 12 hydite on trenches in O7A and O7B.	
9.35 AM	" 19 Shrapnel " " in BOIS QUARANTE	
5.15 pm	" 4 L + 4 Shrapnel on PICCADILLY FARM trenches.	
"	110th on registered targets	
3.20 pm April 25th	128th registered points	
"	110th fired 33 rounds on registered points	
2.55 – 3.45 pm April 26th	128th fired 11 shrapnel and 8 hydite at N end of WYTSCHAETE	
"	110th on registered points	
5.40 pm April 27th	128th fired 6 Shrapnel and 6 hydite at HOSPICE	
"	110th fired at registered positions	

WAR DIARY of INTELLIGENCE SUMMARY

30th BRIGADE R.F.A

Army Form C. 2118.

Hour, Date, Place	Summary of Events and Information	Remarks and references to Appendices
9am April 28th LA CLYTTE	128th fired 3 shrapnel at O.P. in WYTSCHAETE	Lt Read RAMC to 7th Field Ambulance
12.15pm "	128th fired 3 shrapnel at O.P. in WYTSCHAETE	Lt McLay to 30th Brigade vice Lt Read
" "	110th on registered targets	McLAY. S.M. [signatures]
9.30am April 29th	128th fired 6 shrapnel at WYTSCHAETE	
2.40pm "	" " and Lyddite to verify BOIS QUARANTE trenches	
5.35pm "	" 2 Lyddite at M.G. emplacement in PICCADILLY FARM	
" "	110th on registered points	30th Day of Artillery YPRES
2.30pm April 30th	128th fired 10 Lyddite at junction O.15.A	
~3pm "	110th "	
" "	Hostile artillery active on DICKE BUSCH - LA CLYTTE road	

[signature] Stanley, Lt Col.
Cmdg 30 H? 4? Bdg
30/4/18
Field Corps

121/6062

3rd Division

30th Bde: R.F.A.

Vol VII 1 — 31.5.15.

a2
al6

Army Form C. 2118.

30th BRIGADE R.F.A.

WAR DIARY
INTELLIGENCE SUMMARY.
(Erase heading not required.)

Instructions regarding War Diaries and Intelligence Summaries are contained in F.S. Regs., Part II. and the Staff Manual respectively. Title pages will be prepared in manuscript.

129th Battery

- May 1st Shelled HILL 60 during evening
- " " Billet hit by Whizz bangs.
- " 2nd 76 rounds fired by midday
- " 3rd 30 rounds lyddite fired into a Sap — several direct hits
- " " Quiet afternoon.
- " 4th Heavy shelling by Germans near the battery
- " " 50 rounds fired by mah into wood in front of 27th Div. — result v. good

Lts Mortimer (128) Returned to
" Pearce (129) England after
Lt White (129) Senior of instruction.

Hour, Date, Place		Summary of Events and Information
11.30am May 1st	LA CLYTTE	128th fired 6 shrapnel to register PETIT BOIS
3.30pm "	"	" " 12 lyddite — registration by aeroplane.
"	"	110th fired at registered targets
"	"	Hostile artillery active on DICKEBUSCH and road to
11am May 2nd	"	128th fired 11 shrapnel at trenches from ST ELOI —
4.35pm "	"	" " 4 " and 6 lyddite at SNIPERS H
9am "	"	110th fired 5 shrapnel at HOSPICE
"	"	" " on registered points
10AM-12pm "	"	16 Hostile H.E. on DICKEBUSCH - LACLYTTE road.
12.35pm May 3rd	"	128th fired on trenches opposite N3 & N4.
5pm "	"	" " 4 shrapnel and 6 lyddite near ST ELOI mound.
10.50am "	"	110th fired 6 lyddite at battery in DIB. (flashes seen).
" "	"	" also " on registered targets
4.45pm May 4th	"	128th fired 17 shrapnel on working party
6.40 "	"	" " 4 " on PETIT BOIS trenches
"	"	110th on hostile artillery.

WAR DIARY
INTELLIGENCE SUMMARY

30th BRIGADE R.F.A.

Hour, Date, Place	Summary of Events and Information	Remarks and references to Appendices
11.30am May 1st LA CLYTTE	128th fired 6 shrapnel to register PETIT BOIS.	10th day of Boddy YPRES
3.30pm " "	" 12 lyddite - registration by aeroplane.	
" " "	110th fired at registered targets	
" " "	Hostile artillery active on DICKEBUSCH and road to LA CLYTTE.	
11am May 2nd "	128th fired 11 shrapnel at trenches from ST ELOI - PICCADILLY FARM.	
4.35pm " "	" 4 " " " " " " at SNIPERS HOUSE.	
9am " "	110th fired 5 shrapnel at HOSPICE	
" " "	" " " on registered points	
10am - 12pm " "	18 Hostile H.E. on DICKEBUSCH - LA CLYTTE road.	
12.30pm May 3rd "	128th fired on trenches opposite N3 & N4.	
5pm " "	" 4 shrapnel and 6 lyddite near ST ELOI mound.	Lt Mortimer (/128) Returned to France after
10.50am " "	110th fired 6 lyddite at battery in D16.(flashes seen).	" Pearce (/128) England after
" " "	" also " on registered targets.	Lt White (129) January of instruction
4.05pm May 4th "	128th fired 17 shrapnel on working party.	
6.40 " "	" 4 " on PETIT BOIS trenches	
" " "	110th saw hostile artillery.	

30th BRIGADE R.F.A.

WAR DIARY / INTELLIGENCE SUMMARY

Army Form C. 2118.

Hour, Date, Place	Summary of Events and Information
May 5th LA CLYTTE	Batteries in same positions
10.40 AM "	128th fired 4 Shrapnel at working party. O2 c
6.50 pm "	" 5 hyddite at O2 c 7.2.
May 6th " (6"Siv) 110th fired at hostile batteries
" "	128th Battery fired 40 hyddite at emplacements
" "	" " 11 Shrapnel at St ELOI
" "	110th H.B. fired at registered targets.
" "	Hostile artillery active, DICKEBUSCH shelled.
5 pm May 7th "	128th fired 12 Shrapnel on trenches
" "	110th on same registered targets.
11 AM May 8th "	128th fired 14 hyddite at redoubt S. of St ELOI
9 pm "	" 8 " HOLLANDSCHESCHUUR FARM.
11.30 pm "	" 8 " East end of WYTSCHAETE.
" "	110th fired on registered targets
" "	Hostile artillery active

May 5th. Fired all day on wood in front of 27th Div
" " Germans gassed & attacked HILL 60.
" " Machine gun emplacement hit.
" " Shelled HILL 60 all night
May 6th Fired all day on HILL 60.
" " 1186 rounds fired during last 48 hrs.
" " Fired all night - slow rate
May 7th. Still fired on HILL 60 till 2 pm, when fire ceased after 2 days + 2 nights continual firing

Capt Baxter (130 By) all
1/Lt Shone (") } wounded,
2/Lt Brazier-Creagh (") } May 7th
2/Lt Scott (")
2/Lt E.K. Crosse from 129th to 130th By.
Capt Colfox (Bd A.C.) "
2/Lt M.L. Johnston (42nd Bde) "
2/Lt D.S. Morrison (5th D.A.C.) " "
2/Lt Hurst Brown (40 Rgda) to 129 By.
Capt Beerbohm RFA SR 4 Canada joined 30th Bd. Hy vice Capt Colfox

WAR DIARY or INTELLIGENCE SUMMARY

30th BRIGADE R.F.A.

Hour, Date, Place	Summary of Events and Information	Remarks and references to Appendices
May 5th LA CLYTTE	Batteries in same positions	May 6th 680L and 250 shrapnel supplied to 129th Battn from Bde AC. 192 L and 96 S to 130th from same.
10.40 am	128th fired 4 shrapnel at working party O2 c 7 2	
6.50 pm	" 5 lyddite at O2 c 7 2.	
May 6th	(6 Siv) 110th fired at hostile batteries	Capt Archdale left 30th Bde RFA to join 1/4 N. Midland Howitzer Bde.
"	128th Battery fired 40 lyddite at emplacements of hostile Ky.	Capt Colfox (128) to 30th Bde A Column.
"	110th " 11 shrapnel at St ELOI	
"	110 H.B. fired at registered targets	Capt Baxter (130 By) all
"	Hostile artillery active, DICKEBUSCH shelled	2/Lt Shone (") wounded
5pm May 7th	128th fired 12 shrapnel on trenches	2/Lt Brazier-Creagh (") May 7
"	110 on same registered targets	2/Lt Scott (") J
11 am May 8th	128th fired 14 lyddite at redoubt S. of St ELOI.	2/Lt E.K. Grosse from 129th to 130th By.
9 pm	" 8 " " HOLLANDSCHESCHUUR FARM.	Capt Colfox (Bde AC) joins 130 By.
11.30 pm	" 8 " " East end of WYTSCHAETE	2/Lt M.L. Johnston (42nd Bde) " "
"	110th fired on registered targets	2/Lt D.S. Morrison (5th DAC) " "
"	Hostile artillery active	2/Lt Hirst Brown (40 Bde) to 129 By.
		Capt Beerbohm RFA S R 12 Lancers joins 30 Bde A vice Capt Colfox.

30th BRIGADE RFA

Army Form C. 2118.

WAR DIARY
or
INTELLIGENCE SUMMARY
(Erase heading not required.)

Instructions regarding War Diaries and Intelligence Summaries are contained in F. S. Regs., Part II. and the Staff Manual respectively. Title pages will be prepared in manuscript.

Hour, Date, Place		Summary of Events and Information
May 9th	LA CLYTTE	Batteries in same positions
		110th H.B. on registered points
11.30am May 10th	"	128th fired 20 Lyddite at SNIPER'S HOUSE.
		9 Shrapnel at PICCADILLY FARM.
3.0pm "	"	110th fired 2 Lyddite at HOSPICE.
4.5pm "	"	128th fired 12 rounds beyond PICCADILLY FARM.
thro'day May 11th	"	110th on registered targets
		Hostile artillery active
3pm May 12th	"	128th By fired 13 Shrapnel at PICCADILLY FARM.
5pm "	"	" " " 19 Lyddite "
		110th on hostile batteries
		Weather conditions bad — 128th did not fire
		110th fired at hostile batteries
7.20pm "	"	Heavy Shelling of H trenches for 5 minutes

May 8th. Fired on HILL 60 at 3am
May 9th. Fired at + blew up a Sniper's post and M.G emplacement.
" " Orders to be ready to retire. Teams brought up close
" " Teams sent back at 10pm
May 10th Shelled German working party
" " Otherwise very quiet
May 11th YPRES still blazing.
" " V. quiet day.
May 12th Shelled HILL 60 from middday to 6pm — appeared v. effective

30th BRIGADE RFA

WAR DIARY
or
INTELLIGENCE SUMMARY.
(Erase heading not required.)

Instructions regarding War Diaries and Intelligence Summaries are contained in F. S. Regs., Part II. and the Staff Manual respectively. Title pages will be prepared in manuscript.

Hour, Date, Place	Summary of Events and Information	Remarks and references to Appendices
May 9th LA CLYTTE.	Batteries in same positions	
" "	110th H.B. on registered points	
11.30AM May 10th	128th fired 20 lyddite at SNIPER'S HOUSE.	
3.40 pm "	" 9 shrapnel at PICCADILLY FARM.	
4.5 pm "	110th fired 2 lyddite at HOSPICE.	
(from May 11th	128th fired 12 rounds beyond PICCADILLY FARM.	
" "	110th on registered targets	
" "	Hostile artillery active	
3 pm May 12th	128th By fired 13 shrapnel at PICCADILLY FARM.	
3 pm "	" " 19 lyddite " "	
" "	110th on hostile batteries	
May 13th "	heather conditions bad — 128th did not fire	
" "	110th fired at hostile batteries	
12.0 pm "	Heavy shelling of "H" trenches for 5 minutes.	

30th BRIGADE RFA

Army Form C. 2118.

WAR DIARY

INTELLIGENCE SUMMARY

(Erase heading not required.)

May 13th Quieter all round.
"   "   6th gun arrived from BAILLEUL, after being overhauled.
May 14th Cold wet day
"   "   Orders not to fire unless urgent
" 15th Quiet day.
" 16th Two whizz bangs into left half battery — no damage done.
"   "   No firing.
" 17th No firing. V. quiet day.
" 18th   "   "
" 19th   "   "

Hour, Date, Place	Summary of Events and Information	
May 14th "A CLYTTE."	128th did not fire.	
" "	110th H.B. on registered targets	2Lt Collet A/Vet joined 30th Bde from 40th Bde
May 15th	110th H.B. on same targets.	
May 16th	Batteries in same positions	
2.35/am "	110th fired 2 lyddite at Hospice E.	2/Lt C A Caskin (129th) attached N.9. Bain (128th) Instruction.
	Hostile artillery active, 15cm gun fired 9 shrapnel at LA...	
May 17th "	110th H.B. fired 3 lyddite at O.15.c.3.8.	
" "	Hostile artillery active	
May 18th "	Batteries in same positions	
" "	110th H.B. fired 6 lyddite at O.15 Bard C.	
" "	110th H.B. on registered targets	
May 19th "	128th did not fire	
" "	Hostile artillery active	

30th BRIGADE R.F.A

WAR DIARY
INTELLIGENCE SUMMARY.
(Erase heading not required.)

Instructions regarding War Diaries and Intelligence Summaries are contained in F. S. Regs., Part II. and the Staff Manual respectively. Title pages will be prepared in manuscript.

Hour, Date, Place	Summary of Events and Information	Remarks and references to Appendices
May 14th LA CLYTTE	128th did not fire.	
" " "	110th H.B. on registered targets.	
May 15th "	110th H.B on same targets.	
May 16th "	Batteries in same positions.	
" "	110th fired 2 lyddite at HOSPICE.	
2.35/am "	Hostile artillery active, 15cm gun fired 9 shrapnel at LA CLYTTE.	
May 17th "	110th H.B. fired 3 lyddite at O.15 c 3.8.	Lt Collet A.V.C joined 30th Bde from 40th Bde.
" "	Hostile artillery active.	
May 18th "	Batteries in same positions.	
" "	110th H.B. fired 6 lyddite at O.15 B and C.	2/Lts C A Laslow (129th) attached " W.G. Brain (128th) for 2 weeks Instruction.
May 19th "	110th H.B. on registered targets.	
" "	128th did not fire.	
" "	Hostile artillery active.	

Army Form C. 2118.

30th BRIGADE RFA.

WAR DIARY
INTELLIGENCE SUMMARY.
(Erase heading not required.)

Instructions regarding War Diaries and Intelligence Summaries are contained in F.S. Regs., Part II. and the Staff Manual respectively. Title pages will be prepared in manuscript.

Note (pasted slip):

May 20th Ammunition all'd 3 rds per gun one of which may be HE
" 21st Quiet day.
" 22nd 26 rds (13 L & 13 S) fired opposite 41 trench near ZWARTELEN WOOD.
" 23rd 30 S. fired on HILL 60
" " 23 lyddite on trenches opposite 50 trench — Germans bolted.
" " Incendiary shells into YPRES

Hour, Date, Place	Summary of Events and Information
May 20th LA CLYTTE.	Batteries in Same positions — did not shoot.
12 noon May 21st	Hostile artillery active on VIERSTRAAT RIDGE
4 pm "	128th fired 14 shrapnel between MOUND & S'FL'OI and ZWARTELEN MOUND.
" "	10 " " " "
" "	110th H.B. fired 10 rounds on registered points
" "	Hostile artillery active on our trenches
4.35 pm May 22nd	128th fired 18 lyddite at SNIPER'S POST on S'FL'OI — 5.10 pm direct hits on SNIPER'S POST [?] all rounds on MOUND.
" "	110th H.B. on registered points
May 23rd	12.8th did not fire.
"	110th H.B. on registered targets
"	12 g'lt fired 2 lyddite + 4 shrapnel at O.2.1.C.1.3 as ordered by CRA
6 pm May 24th	10 shrapnel at trenches near SVFKOI BRICKSTACK.
6.55 pm	110th H.B. fired 35 L + S on registered points. Hostile artillery active. DICKEBVSCHE LA CLYTTE road shelled.

(Right margin notes):

to Command 41st Battery 42nd Bde
Capt L Roe to 30th Bde — Adjutant vice Capt Sadler — from 3rd D.T.C.
2/Lt Brazier Creagh struck off 130th Battery
Scott
May 22nd
Capt H Baxter struck off 130th Battery
2/Lt R.S. Shone 130th Battery
May 24th
9th Bde

30th BRIGADE R.F.A.

WAR DIARY
INTELLIGENCE SUMMARY

(Erase heading not required.)

Hour, Date, Place	Summary of Events and Information	Remarks and references to Appendices
May 20th LA CLYTTE	Batteries in same positions — did not shoot.	
" " "	Hostile artillery active on VIERSTRAAT RIDGE	
12 noon May 21st "	128th fired 14 shrapnel when MOUND of St ELOI and PICCADILLY FARM	
4 pm " "	" " 10 " " " " " "	
" " "	110th H.B. fired 10 rounds on registered points	
" " "	Hostile artillery active on our trenches.	
4.35 pm – 5.10 pm May 22nd "	128th fired 18 lyddite & 4 shrapnel at SNIPER'S POST on St ELOI MOUND — traced hits on SNIPER'S POST but all rounds on MOUND.	Capt H K Sadler left 30th Bde to Command 41st/V Battery 42nd Bde
" "	110th H.B. on registered points	Capt L Roe to 30th Bde — adjutant vice Capt Sadler — from 3rd D.T.C.
May 23rd "	128th did not fire.	2/Lt Brazier Creagh } struck off Scott } 130 IF Battery
" "	110th H.B. on registered targets	May 22nd
6 am May 24th "	128th fired 2 lyddite + 4 shrapnel at O.2.L.C.1.3 as ordered by CRA	
6.55 am "	" 10 shrapnel at trenches near St ELOI BRICKSTACK.	Capt H Baxter } struck off 2/Lt R.S. Shove } 130 IF Battery May 24th
" "	110th H.B. fired 35 L+S on registered points	
" "	Hostile artillery active. DICKEBUSCHE LA CLYTTE road shelled.	

Army Form C. 2118.

WAR DIARY
or
INTELLIGENCE SUMMARY.

30th BRIGADE RFA

(Erase heading not required.)

Instructions regarding War Diaries and Intelligence Summaries are contained in F.S. Regs., Part II. and the Staff Manual respectively. Title pages will be prepared in manuscript.

May 24th. German attack E of YPRES, preceded by gas at 3 a.m.
" " Respirators used at battery, & kept on till 5 A.M.
" " Billet shelled at night
May 25th Horse line shelled, 5 shells, 4 of which were "blind"
" " 16 Shrapnel at HILL 60
May 26th }
" 27th } very quiet
" 28th }

Hour, Date, Place	Summary of Events and Information
May 25th LA CLYTTE	128th did not fire.
8 p.m. "	110th fired 6 lyddite at O.17.d.4.1 in answer
" "	Hostile artillery active on WIERSTRAAT ridge
2.30 p.m. May 26th "	110th fired 7 lyddite at O.17.d.4.1. (JQ signal)
7.45 p.m. "	" " 6 " " " (" " : hostile)
" "	128th did not fire
3.40 p.m. May 27th "	110th N.B. fired 3 lyddite at O.22.a.5.9.
" "	128th did not fire.
May 28th "	Batteries in same positions
" "	128th did not fire.
12 noon "	110th H.B. fired 1 lyddite at O.22.B.
" "	Movement of enemy seen in O.15.d and O.17.c. working parties
May 29th "	128th did not fire
5.45 p.m. "	110th fired 3 lyddite at O.17.B.

WAR DIARY or INTELLIGENCE SUMMARY

30th BRIGADE RFA

2118.

(Erase heading not required.)

Instructions regarding War Diaries and Intelligence Summaries are contained in F.S. Regs., Part II. and the Staff Manual respectively. Title pages will be prepared in manuscript.

Hour, Date, Place	Summary of Events and Information	Remarks and references to Appendices
May 25th LA CLYTTE	128th did not fire.	
8 pm " "	110th fired 6 lyddite at O.17.d.4.1 in answer to "JQ" signal.	
" " "	Hostile artillery active on VIERSTRAAT ridge SE of 128 guns.	
23pm May 26th " "	110th fired 7 lyddite at O.17.d.41. (JQ signal)	
7.45 pm " "	" 6 " " " (" " : hostile battery active)	
" " "	128th did not fire	
3.40pm May 27th " "	110th H.B fired 3 lyddite at O.22.a.5.9.	
" " "	128th did not fire.	
" " "	Batteries in same positions.	
May 28th " "	128th did not fire	
" " "	110th H.B fired 1 lyddite at 0.22 B.	
12 noon " "	Movement of enemy seen in O.15.d and O.17.c. working parties	
May 29th " "	128th did not fire.	
5.45 pm " "	110th fired 3 lyddite at O.17.B.	

30th BRIGADE R.F.A.

Army Form C. 2118

WAR DIARY
INTELLIGENCE SUMMARY
(Erase heading not required.)

Instructions regarding War Diaries and Intelligence Summaries are contained in F. S. Regs., Part II. and the Staff Manual respectively. Title pages will be prepared in manuscript.

Hour, Date, Place	Summary of Events and Information
May 30th LA CLYTTE	110th fired 2 Shrapnel at HOSPICE.
"	Hostile artillery active on YPRES.
May 31st DICKEBUSCH	128th did not fire
"	Artillery group of 47th Brigade (14th Div.), 12?, 119th Battery (27th Bde) formed under O.C. 30th affiliated to 13th Inf. Bde, 5th Division.

May 29th. Blew up dugout opposite trench 50.

" 30th. Very quiet.

" 31st. Shot at dug outs by aeroplane observation — results good.

H. Stanley Stoll.
Cm'd'g 30th Bde R.F.A.
1-6-1915.

30th BRIGADE R.F.A.

WAR DIARY / INTELLIGENCE SUMMARY

(Erase heading not required.)

Instructions regarding War Diaries and Intelligence Summaries are contained in F.S. Regs., Part II. and the Staff Manual respectively. Title pages will be prepared in manuscript.

Hour, Date, Place		Summary of Events and Information	Remarks and references to Appendices
May 30th	LA CLYTTE	110th fired 2 Shrapnel at HOSPICE.	
"	"	Hostile artillery active on YPRES.	
May 31st	DICKEBUSCH	128th did not fire	30th Brigade H.Q. moved to DICKEBUSCH, and changed from 3rd Division to 5th Division.
"	"	Artillery group of 47th Brigade (14th Div.), 128th Battery, and 119th Battery (27th Bde) formed under O.C. 30th Brigade, affiliated to 13th Inf. Bde., 5th Division.	2/Lt Carlton (128) returned to " Bain (119) England after 2 weeks instruction.

Stanley, Lt.Col.
C/m 29, 28, 119 & 30Bde
1st 1915

3rd Division

30th Bde R.F.A.

1st VIII 1 — 30.6.15.

15/6065

Army Form C. 2118.

WAR DIARY
INTELLIGENCE SUMMARY.
(Erase heading not required.)

Instructions regarding War Diaries and Intelligence Summaries are contained in F.S. Regs., Part II. and the Staff Manual respectively. Title pages will be prepared in manuscript.

Hour, Date, Place	Summary of Events and Information	Remarks and references to Appendices
June 1st DICKEBUSCH.	129th did not fire	
" "	129th did not fire	
" "	Very quiet day.	
June 2nd "	130th fired 20 rounds at HILL 60.	
" "	129th fired 20 rounds at HILL 60.	
" "	Heavy bombardment of YPRES.	
June 3rd "	129th fired 20 rounds at HILL 60	
" "	130th " 12 rounds at new trench opposite 46.	
June 4th "	129th on HILL 60 again.	
" "	128th Battery moved to position just NE of DICKEBUSCH POND.	
June 5th "	128th registered new targets.	
" "	129th fired usual 20 shrapnel at HILL 60.	
June 6th "	130th fired 20 rounds at HILL 60.	
" "	129th very quiet	
June 7th "	130th fired 40 hyclilite at German work opposite 41.	Horses: Protean (Shepherds living with 129) broke his collar bone.
" "	Germans crumped the battery, but no damage done.	

Army Form C. 2118.

Instructions regarding War Diaries and Intelligence
Summaries are contained in F. S. Regs., Part II.
and the Staff Manual respectively. Title pages
will be prepared in manuscript.

WAR DIARY
or
INTELLIGENCE SUMMARY.
(Erase heading not required.)

Hour, Date, Place	Summary of Events and Information	Remarks and references to Appendices
June 8th - DICKEBUSCH	128th fired 17 shrapnel registering	
" 9th - "	130th fired 20 "	
" " - "	128th fired 23 shrapnel	
" " - "	129th did not fire	
" 10th - "	130th fired 20 shrapnel	No 13775 - Q.M.S. J. BOURNE
" " - "	128th fired 23 shrapnel re-registering point in 1st zone	promoted 2nd Lieut dated 25.3.15
" 11th - "	" " " 20 " at Hill 60	
" " - "	" " " "	
" " - "	128th fired 14 shrapnel registering at Hill 60	
" " - "	129th " 20 "	
" 12th - "	130th - did not fire	
" " - "	128th fired 18 shrapnel	
" 13th - "	129th " 40 lyddite & a German work in ZWARTELEN salient	2/Lt N. Whittaker sent to 6/Bde RFA 3rd DIV
" " - "	128th " fired 11 lyddite & 9 shrapnel registering with aeroplane observation	2/Lt D. Heart - Brown wounded on Je 13- died 15-
" " - "	129th fired 11 shrapnel	
	Every shower of Red Very Lights from PETIT BOIS from 9 to 10 PM as signal "We are attacked"	

Forms/C. 2118/10

Army Form C. 2118.

WAR DIARY
or
INTELLIGENCE SUMMARY.
(Erase heading not required.)

Hour, Date, Place	Summary of Events and Information	Remarks and references to Appendices
June 14th DICKEBUSCH	12.8" fuseS 14 shrapnel	
" "	12.9" fuseS 20 shrapnel at 'Caterpillar'	
" 15th "	13.0" in rest.	
" "	12.8" fuseS 9 lyddite and 35 shrapnel	
" "	12.9" " 10 " at Caterpillar, 16 lyddite and 15 shrapnel at	Lt. D. Hurst-Brown (29th) SieS. ※
	house opposite 34 French. 6 lyddite 10-10.15 p.m.	Cd. Sherry acting for Cd.
" 16th "	13.0" in rest.	Somrys on leave. 1 Lyd Sh
" "	12.8" fuseS 3 lyddite, 2 shrapnel.	10-10.15 p.m. specially pullous
" "	12.9" " 2 " 15" " at Caterpillar & Hill 60.	2 Cd. Sherry as someone absent
	to give impression of registration before attack. Fuse	13 or 27# Hunt-Brown.
	20 lyddite and 15 shrapnel at German Rly. behind	Ration of 130 rounds
	Caterpillar.	one hurt fullest. 1 gunner
" "	13.0" in rest.	wounded.
" 17th "	12.8" fuseS 21 shrapnel.	
" "	12.9" " 20 " at Hill 60.	※ Babies in DICKEBUSCH
" "	13.0" in rest.	inhabits country. — on
		detailed description
		from Sgt. Lee Jui
		Bde Records & Officers
		Ch. L. O. Shenum [signature]

Army Form C. 2118.

WAR DIARY
or
INTELLIGENCE SUMMARY.
(Erase heading not required.)

Instructions regarding War Diaries and Intelligence Summaries are contained in F. S. Regs., Part II. and the Staff Manual respectively. Title pages will be prepared in manuscript.

Hour, Date, Place		Summary of Events and Information	Remarks and references to Appendices
June 18" Dickebusch	12.8"	fires 30 shrapnel.	
" "	12.9"	" in rear.	
" "	1.30" – 13	shrapnel fires W. of Hill 60 and 15 of Lyssit at 2 hostile Batteries registered by means of aeroplane and wireless.	
" 19"	12.8"	fires 30 Shrapnel	
" "	12.9"	" in rear.	
" "	13.0"	fires 20 shrapnel at Hill 60 and 40 Lyssit at unknown stores in the "Bahnt" trenches.	
" 20"	12.8"	fires 18 shrapnel	
" "	12.9"	Ghost shell near Zillebeke Railway Station for one station & guns	2.Lt. Montague(129") Lft for 5 days leave.
" "		5 pairs of aeroplanes.	2.Lt. Whitney rejoins 12.8" from 1st Rly BA Brigade.
" "	13.0"	fires 6 shrapnel and 15 Lyssit at new Barricade in Railway cutting 70 yards south of farm 37.	
" 21"	12.8"	do not fire.	
" "	12.9"	fires 8 shrapnel at hostile aeroplane - good ranging(?) of guns) but shell bursts anneeks needed.	2.Lt.A.C. Crombly joins 12.9"(?) 2.Lt. T. Spear Smith " 12.8" 2.Lt. A. Etheridge joins Barford Hope(?) for twenty(?)
" "	13.0"	do not fire.	

Attacks complimentary message upon 6 129½ and
130½ Batteries during the Arras (9½ April – 23rd June)
When they were attached to 5½ Division.

C. R. A., 3rd Division.

If the guns went some to 129½ and 138½ Batteries
I should like to add my appreciation.

Signed T. M. Noland
Major General
Commanding 5½ Division

Forwarded, Staff Captain, 3rd Div. Artillery.

I should like to stay on record the excellent
work performed by the two Howitzer during the time
they have been in the "L/5th" Group.

129½ Battery from 21st April till 23rd of June
138½ " " " " 9½ " " 8 " "

D/I Sandys took venture being hard nudges and
18th Major Pearce and Major Robinson have been
of the greatest assistance to me. I know their
guns which has given much appreciation by the Infantry
I much regret the casualties they have
suffered in the "½" group. (SS) S. Sandys, Lt Col RFA
Commanding L/5th Group.

Instructions regarding War Diaries and Intelligence
Summaries are contained in F. S. Regs, Part II.
and the Staff Manual respectively. Title pages
will be prepared in manuscript.

Hour, Date, Place		
22nd DICKEBUSCH	128½	Bois inst.
"	129½	fired 4/1 sh
"	"	15 sh
23rd "	130½	fired 25
"	128½	" 26 "
"	129½	S/S and "
"	130½	fired 20 sh
24½ "	10 to m a
"	128½	closes to
"		to 4½ Div
"	129½	after 6 8
"		afternoon.
"	130½	nimies 3
25½ BUSSEBOOM	129½	S/S inst
"	130½	" "
2/7 "	129½	fired 11 sh
"	130½	in rest

Instructions regarding War Diaries and Intelligence
Summaries are contained in F.S. Regs., Part II.
and the Staff Manual respectively. Title pages
will be prepared in manuscript.

Hour, Date, Place	
22ⁿᵈ DICKIE BUSCH	12.27 Sw esti... 12.9 T fires 4.7... 15 shrap... 23 " " fires 25... 13.0 T " 26 s... 12.8 T S.S nothing 12.9 T fires 20 s... 13.0 T " " " 24 T 10 h.m a... 12.8 T ceases t... 1. 4 T Div... 12.9 T after 5 s... at noon ha... 13.0 T informes 3
25 T BusSEBOOM	12.9 T S/S and ... 13.0 T " " " 26 T 12.9 T fires 11 shr... 13.0 T in rest

H.H. & A.M.G. of 5ᵗʰ Division.

(TiernousenSeS.)

Battery) concur with the good report on the
Battalion of 30 T Brigade and include in it
my attention of Lt. Colonel Staveley, C.B.,
and the 128 T Battery R.F.A.
The work done by the 30ᵗʰ Brigade
R.F.A. while attached to 5 6ᵗʰ Division has
at all times been excellent.

(Sd) J. Gordon Ring ford
commanding R.A. 5ᵗʰ Div.

Instructions regarding War Diaries and Intelligence Summaries are contained in F. S. Regs., Part II. and the Staff Manual respectively. Title pages will be prepared in manuscript.

Hour, Date, Place		Summary of Events and Information	Remarks and references to Appendices
June 22nd DICKEBUSCH	12.87	SOS not fire	
" "	12.9 F	fires 47 lyddite at Caterpillar and rustld batteries, and 15 shrapnel at aeroplanes	
" "	13.0 F	fires 25 lyddite and 2 shrapnel at Hill 60	
" 23rd "	12.8 F	" 26 shrapnel	
" "	12.9 F	SOS not fire. Withdraws one/sand section after dark.	
" "	13.0 F	fires 20 shrapnel at Hill 60. Centre section moved 10 p m and joins 2 one section of 65 F Bty.	
" 24th "	12.8 F	ceases to form part of 30 F Bde, and is transferred to 4 F Div. at 12.01 a.m.	
" "	12.9 F	after 6 days of strenuous "rest" rejoins 3rd Div. pushing guns on some places.	
" "	13.0 F	rejoins 3rd Div. Went into bivot near Busseboom	
2.5 F BUSSEBOOM	12.9 F	SOS not fire	
" "	13.0 F	" " " "	
" 26 F "	12.9 F	fires 11 shrapnel at cutting at E. end of Sanctuary Wood	30 F Brigade returns to III Div. 5 F Corps. 2nd Army. B.Se. Hqrs. in hut near Busseboom.
" "	13.0 F	in rest	

Army Form C. 2118.

WAR DIARY
or
INTELLIGENCE SUMMARY.
(Erase heading not required.)

Instructions regarding War Diaries and Intelligence Summaries are contained in F.S. Regs., Part II. and the Staff Manual respectively. Title pages will be prepared in manuscript.

Hour, Date, Place	Summary of Events and Information	Remarks and references to Appendices
June 27 BUSSEBOON	129 B.S. ret: fire.	
" 28 "	130 B. in rest. cont. section moved up to new position 9.15 p.m	J. Tipping (129th) wounded (whilst laying wire)
" "	129 B. fires 60 L.S. SHE - 16 at Cornexye. 44 registering	
" "	130 B. " 24 " and 2 shrapnel registering.	
June 29 KRUISSTRAAT	129 B. fires 19 L.S.L. at Y19 Junction and 1 L.S.Sle at Annuyl - a sniper's hip.	Detr. Section of 3rd Siege Bty. came under command of O.C. 30th Request forming half a group
" " "	130 B. fires 16 L.S.Sle and 1 shrapnel registering.	
" 30 "	129 B. " 18 " registering at 28 L.S.Sle at Y20	130th establishes communication w/ F.O.P. by lamp.
" "	130 B. " 51 " and 1 shrapnel registering	

H.H. Tonley Lt. Col.
CO. 4.2.8. Hy. de R Bgd.
30/6/15

3rd Known

19/7018

30th Bde R.T.K.
—
Pd X
August 15

WAR DIARY
or
INTELLIGENCE SUMMARY.
(Erase heading not required.)

Army Form C. 2118.

Hour, Date, Place	Summary of Events and Information	Remarks and references to Appendices
1st August DICKEBUSCH	129th Fired 23 Lyddite at redoubts & trench mortar J132	
2nd "	130th Fired 48 Lyddite at various targets	
" "	129th Fired 25 Lyddite at redoubt	
3rd "	130th Fired 18 rounds at various targets & had two casualties whilst laying telephone cable	No 6452 Corp H. VANN No 67063 Corp W. CROSS
" "	129th Fired 14 Lyddite at same redoubt & got several hits	
" "	130th Fired 116 rounds at trench mortar, working party & crater	
4th " Sof POPERINGHE	Bde H.Q. move to farm about 2 miles S of POPERINGHE	
" "	129th Fired 6 Lyddite at a working party	
5th "	130th Fire 23 rounds at various targets	
" "	129th Fired 10 shrapnel at STRAND & FLEET ST also 36 Lyddite registering for 6th DIV	
" "	130th Fire 63 Lyddite at a crater & trench mortar also 3 shrapnel by aeroplane observation	
6th "	129th Fired 37 Lyddite registering points round HOOGE	
" "	130th Fire 24 Lyddite at MOUND & BRICKSTACK	

Army Form C. 2118.

WAR DIARY
or
INTELLIGENCE SUMMARY.
(Erase heading not required.)

Hour, Date, Place	Summary of Events and Information	Remarks and references to Appendices
7th August 15 POPERINGHE	129th - fired 42 rounds registering for 6th Div	Lt Col W. C. Staveley ordered to England to take up duty as Brig General RA of 38th Div
8th " "	130th - fired 27 Rounds at various targets	
" "	129th - fired 48 rounds registering for 6th Div	
9th " "	130th - fired 17 rounds at hostile trench & track.	
" "	The 6th Corps retakes trenches at HOOGE	
" "	129th fired 861 Lyddite & 121 Shrapnel, telephone worked well all day.	
10th " "	130th - fired 256 Lyddite & 60 Shrapnel during the day.	
" "	129th - fired 19 Lyddite & 1 Shrapnel in answer to hostile bombardment	
" "	130th - fired 63 Lyddite & 12 Shrapnel at PICCADILLY FARM	
11th " "	REDOUBT & BRICKSTACK	
" "	129th - had a quiet day & did not fire	
12th " "	130th - fired 41 Lyddite & 13 Shrapnel at crater & working party	Major F. W. Robinson rejoined from Hospital
" "	129th - another quiet day & did not fire but a friend B.y near fired a lot of poison shells.	
" "	130th - fired 14 Lyddite & 10 Shrapnel at working party & wood at 0142	

Army Form C. 2118.

WAR DIARY
or
INTELLIGENCE SUMMARY.
(Erase heading not required.)

Instructions regarding War Diaries and Intelligence Summaries are contained in F. S. Regs., Part II. and the Staff Manual respectively. Title pages will be prepared in manuscript.

Hour, Date, Place		Summary of Events and Information	Remarks and references to Appendices
13th August S. of POPERINGHE		1.29 P.M. did not fire	
14 " "		1.30 P.M. did not fire	
" "		1.29 P.M. shelled from 12.30 to 1.30 PM but no casualties located a hostile battery in evening along Boogh's Lectrial trenches & fired 45 Lyddite at it	
		1.30 P.M. fire 6 shrapnel at wood O146 & 6 Lyddite at Kruel Kruriger lty. Both moved back to DICKEBUSCH	
15 " " DICKEBUSCH			
16 " "		1.30 P.M. did not fire	
" "		1.30 P.M. fired 5 Lyddite rounds at battery	Major J.W.F. LAMONT joined from E.B4.RHA & took command of Bty.
17 " "		1.30 P.M. did not fire	
18 " "		1.30 P.M. fired 19 rounds at night at MOUND	

Army Form C. 2118.

WAR DIARY
or
INTELLIGENCE SUMMARY.
(Erase heading not required.)

Instructions regarding War Diaries and Intelligence Summaries are contained in F. S. Regs., Part II. and the Staff Manual respectively. Title pages will be prepared in manuscript.

Hour, Date, Place	Summary of Events and Information	Remarks and references to Appendices
19th August DICKEBUSCH	130th fir 30 rounds at various targets.	
20th "	130th fir 18 rounds at a battery (O16 a.9.9) 8 rounds at MOUND & 34 rounds at a curved screen which destroyed	2/Lt E. MUNT joins the 88th as orderly officer & is attached to 130th Bty for instruction.
21st "	130th did not fire. 4 leading withdrawn to wagon line & relieved by D/81 Bty.	
" "	130th Bty fire 6 shrapnel to left of mound on SOS call. The remaining two guns withdrawn to wagon line.	
22nd "	130th in rest	
23rd "	130th in rest	
24th "		

Army Form C. 2118.

WAR DIARY
or
INTELLIGENCE SUMMARY.
(Erase heading not required.)

Instructions regarding War Diaries and Intelligence Summaries are contained in F.S. Regs., Part II. and the Staff Manual respectively. Title pages will be prepared in manuscript.

Hour, Date, Place	Summary of Events and Information	Remarks and references to Appendices
25th August YPRES	30th Bde H.Q. move to CHATEAU S.T PIERRE YPRES	
26th "	130th Bty go into action West of ETANG DE ZILLIEBEKE	a section of 62 Div Bde comes under 30th Bde
" "	130th Bty 5 Lyddite registering by aeroplane	
" "	130th Bty 11 Shrapnel at plantation behind STIRLING CASTLE	
27th "	129th Field 5 Lyddite registering by aeroplane	
28th "	130th " 9 Lyddite registering by aeroplane	
" "	129th did not fire.	
" "	Hostile guns shelled our trenches about 1100 G.E. 130th Fired	
29th "	20 Lyddite by way of retaliation & 25 registering, also 11 Lyddite at retaliation.	
" "	129th Fired 10 Lyddite & 12 Shrapnel at hostile trenches J.23-a.8.3 & J.13 d.3.6	
30th "	130th did not fire	
" "	129th Fired 7 Lyddite & 6 Shrapnel at 10.15 PM at a working party J.13 d.2.7	
31st "	130th did not fire	
" "	129th did not fire	
" "	130th Fired 14 Lyddite at J.13 C.3.8 & J.13 a.2.1 Registration	

J. Williamson Col.
Comg. 30th Bde R.F.A.
31-9-15

121/7018

3rd 5 Division

30th Bde R.F.A.
Pot XL
Sept. 15.

Army Form C. 2118.

WAR DIARY
or
INTELLIGENCE SUMMARY.
(Erase heading not required.)

Instructions regarding War Diaries and Intelligence Summaries are contained in F.S. Regs., Part II. and the Staff Manual respectively. Title pages will be prepared in manuscript.

Hour, Date, Place	Summary of Events and Information	Remarks and references to Appendices
1st Sept. YPRES	129th Bty fired 120 lyddite at FORT, & got badly crumped. 3 casualties & a limber burnt out	**1st** No 39374 Sgt. DEWHURST C/81 Bty attd 129th Bty killed No 67729 Bdr. DAVIDSON 129th Bty wounded
2nd "	130th Bty fired 97 lyddite at hostile trenches J13C 3.9 to J13a 1.2 129th Bty fired 90 lyddite at Fort also fired 47 lyddite during hostile bombardment on trenches from J13a 1.2 to J13 C 6.3½ 130th Bty fired 90 lyddite at Fort & 171 lyddite during hostile bombardment on J13a 5.0 to J13a 5.5.	No 4359 Gr. PROVER 129th Bty wounded **2nd** No 75901 Bdr. H.T. BUCKELL 130th Bty killed **3rd**
3rd "	129th Bty fired 90 lyddite 31 lyddite at hmm on J.13 central, also J 13A 10·2 & J 13D 4·6 130th Bty fired 91 lyddite on J 13 C 4·7 – 3·9 Shelled with light H.E.	lyddite very unsatisfactory. Capt L Row attempted to Command 6th Bty 2/Lt E M and acting adjt 2/D-M LJOHNSTONE 130th Bty wounded

Army Form C. 2118.

WAR DIARY
or
INTELLIGENCE SUMMARY.
(Erase heading not required.)

Instructions regarding War Diaries and Intelligence Summaries are contained in F. S. Regs., Part II. and the Staff Manual respectively. Title pages will be prepared in manuscript.

Hour, Date, Place	Summary of Events and Information	Remarks and references to Appendices
4th Sept YPRES	129th Bty fired 7 Lyddite at Q.9 & Q.18	
	130 Bty " 63 " & 11 Shrapnel at J 13 a 24-06	
	129 " " 100 " " J 13 a 0.3.	
5th Sept YPRES	129th Bty " 120 " } on front line Q 22 - Q 23	
	130th " " 120. " } - Q 25.	
	130th Bty aeroplane blown up; no casualties	
6th "	129th " shelled & partially demolished house near Q32; fired 60 rounds Lyddite	
	130th " " 16 Lyddite on Q 23 & 24 registering	
7th "	129th Bty fired 12 Lyddite on Q 31, Q 12 & 20 "	
	130th " " 31 " " Q 36 "	
8th "	129th " " 3 " " Q 32 "	
9th "	130 " " 45 " " Q 88. 60.55. 62 "	
		63 & ECLUSETTE

Army Form C. 2118.

WAR DIARY
or
INTELLIGENCE SUMMARY.
(Erase heading not required.)

Instructions regarding War Diaries and Intelligence Summaries are contained in F.S. Regs., Part II. and the Staff Manual respectively. Title pages will be prepared in manuscript.

Hour, Date, Place	Summary of Events and Information	Remarks and references to Appendices
YPRES Sept 10th/15	129th Bty fired 29 Rydddls on trench junction 150 yds N of Q.31.	10 rounds fell in trench, a few up flanks etc.
	130th " " 30 " at trench Q 92 - Q 62	
	129th " also " 40 " on Houses E. of Q 32	8 direct hits, 6 in trench abreast
	130th " " 46 " on Q.7H. registering & searching for a reported heavy minenwerfer	
11th/15	129th Bty fired 39 Rydddls on an iron structure J 19 a 5.1	20 hits
	130th " " 70 " on various houses. A good shoot, over 20 hits	
12th	129th " " 14 " Wood N.W of STIRLING CASTLE	On this date the head of the CLOTH HALL was destroyed.
	O. C. of 130th 64, on OXFORD ST. were crumped. no casualties	12.30 7 3.5 p.m. B.nr G. Hanna 129 Bty, wounded in R. arm by shell fire.
	129th fired 4 rds of & 2 lydddl on J 25 d 5.5 & C 31, registering by aeroplane	
13th	129th Bty " 3 " & 2 lyd " on J 25 c 3.1 registering by aeroplane	
	130th " " 17 lyd on Q 60 registration, also 10 lyd on CLONMEL COPSE registration	
14th	130th " " 24 Rydddls on Q 41 - O 95 retaliation	

(9 29 6) W 4141—463 100,000 9/14 H W V Forms/C. 2118/10

WAR DIARY
or
INTELLIGENCE SUMMARY.
(Erase heading not required.)

Army Form C. 2118.

Hour, Date, Place		Summary of Events and Information	Remarks and references to Appendices
YPRES.	Sept 14/15	129 Bty fired 30 lyd. on Q 32 - 54 = registration	Good shot
"	"	130 " " 54 " "	"
"	15th	129 " " 20 " on fort in retaliation	
"	"	130 " " 16 " = Q36 registration	
"	"	129 " " 45 " wood nt Q54 with good results	
"	"	130 " " 8 " Q36 Destroyed hot horse I 13 b.o.4.	
"	16 -	129 " " 42 " Q17-23 front trench Good shoot	
"	"	130 " " 2 " Retaliation (2 rounds were enough)	
"	17	No firing	
"	18	129 & 130 Btys each fired 70 lyd on second-line trenches. First day of bombardment. All forward wires were cut during heavy retaliation by the Germans.	
"	19.	129th Bty fired 75 lyd & 130 Bty 70 lyd on J 13 a and c during bombardment	

WAR DIARY or INTELLIGENCE SUMMARY

Army Form C. 2118.

Hour, Date, Place	Summary of Events and Information	Remarks and references to Appendices
YPRES. Sept 19.15	129 Bty fired 20 rds on Q.30.d.32, & 20 on Q.21.c.26 in retaliation.	
1.30	— 113 Bty n.q. when French opened on C.1.a 13 Bty on Q.41, also retaliation. On trenches heavily shelled by the enemy.	
20	129 & 64 fired 25 rds at hour E of Q.3.2., 3 hits 25 " — work W of Q.5.4. Some damage but difficult to observe.	
21	129 & 130 Bty fired 90 rds each in bombardment. 129 Bty fired 40 rds + 130 Bty 57 rds ea in course of bombardment. good results.	

Army Form C. 2118.

WAR DIARY
or
INTELLIGENCE SUMMARY.
(Erase heading not required.)

Hour, Date, Place	Summary of Events and Information	Remarks and references to Appendices
YPRES Sept 22nd	129 Bty fired 75 Lyddite at Q 32.31.34.54 at work near	Good result.
	130 " " 51 Lyddite at J13a 5.0 - 4.3	
	130 " " 108 " " Q 42 - Q 48	
	129 " " 121 " " J 13a 4.3 - 2.4	
" 23.15	129 & 130 each fired 100 Lyddite at trenches S of HOOGE &	
	near STIRLING CASTLE, during daily bombardment.	
" 24.15	129 & 130 each fired 70 Lyddite at German front &	Good shoot.
	support trenches as above	1140584 Gnr BRIGGS. M.
		130 Bty died of
	130 Bty fired 83 Lyddite on J13a in retaliation	wounds.
	and 50 Lyddite Registration	24.9.15
" 25.15	130 Bty fired 1000 Lyddite & 94 Shrapnel	26430 Cpl AYLETT. A
	129 " " 1213 " " 162 "	17091 Gr RIX. J.
	After 30 minutes bombardment, III div infantry	96320 Dr WORTH S.H
	advanced along the whole front. They gained	all 129 Bty Wounded
	most of then Zijwechem but were unable to hold	25.9.15.
	& at dusk were back in original positions	

Army Form C. 2118.

WAR DIARY
or
INTELLIGENCE SUMMARY.
(Erase heading not required.)

Instructions regarding War Diaries and Intelligence Summaries are contained in F. S. Regs., Part II. and the Staff Manual respectively. Title pages will be prepared in manuscript.

Hour, Date, Place	Summary of Events and Information	Remarks and references to Appendices
YPRES 25.9.15.	2 German officers & 176 other ranks captured. C.R.A. expressed his satisfaction at shooting of the Brigade. Later about 380 Lyddite were shot away by 129 By & 120 Lyd by 130 By at various targets.	
" 26.9.15.	129 fired 202 Fyd & 130 fired 216 Lyd at FORT & B.E. in answer to S.O.S. from Infantry.	
" 27.9.15.	No firing; very good. Infantry mending trenches.	
" 28.9.15.	130 Bty fired 13 Lyddite on FORT - Ablahon	

WAR DIARY
or
INTELLIGENCE SUMMARY.

(Erase heading not required.)

Army Form C. 2118.

Hour, Date, Place	Summary of Events and Information	Remarks and references to Appendices
YPRES 29.9.15	12 g.H. fired 258 Lyddite on receipt of S.O.S. from Infantry at B4, B8 & FORT. 130 fired 150 Lyddite at Q.3.6 Registration. at 5.30 p.m. 130 Lyddite on receipt of SOS from Infantry at C.1 & C.2.	
30.9.15	12 g.H. fired 70 Lyddite during attack 5.15 – 5.30 70 Lyddite to form Barrage at J.19 – 7.9 – 9.9 to J.15 c 9.2 – 8.4. 1 section fired 147 Lyddite + 22 shrap: at T Barlow J.1.3 5.5. 2 Casualties Killed. 130 H. fired 95 Lyddite during attack + 85 Lyddite + 25 shrapnel to form Barrage J.15c 7.9 – c. 5.9 6 H. siege 9 casualties 1 killed 8 wounded	

Johnsont Lt Col.
Cmg. 30th 15th Bdes RFA
30 – 9 – 15

D/7440

3rd Division

30th Bde R.F.A.

Oct '15

Vol XII

Army Form C. 2118

WAR DIARY
or
INTELLIGENCE SUMMARY.
(Erase heading not required.)

Instructions regarding War Diaries and Intelligence Summaries are contained in F. S. Regs., Part II. and the Staff Manual respectively. Title pages will be prepared in manuscript.

Hour, Date, Place	Summary of Events and Information	Remarks and references to Appendices
YPRES. 1.10.15.	No firing	
2.10.15	No firing	
3.10.15.	129 fired 16 lyddite 8 Shrapnel on Trenches 129a for Registration. Enemy retaliated on our trench opposite. 130th Bty fired 27 lyddite at trench mortar J13C51-52 on request of Infantry Brigade.	
4-10-15.	130th fired 30 lyddite for registration at J13C 3.9 + 2.0 130th Bty heavily shelled. Dug-outs damaged. Enemy balloon up all the time, and went down on cessation of firing	
5.10.15.	130th Bty fired 24 Shrapnel at about J13C9.2 at trench mortar on Infantry request.	

WAR DIARY
or
INTELLIGENCE SUMMARY.

(Erase heading not required.)

Army Form C. 2118.

Instructions regarding War Diaries and Intelligence Summaries are contained in F.S. Regs., Part II. and the Staff Manual respectively. Title pages will be prepared in manuscript.

Hour, Date, Place	Summary of Events and Information	Remarks and references to Appendices
YPRES 6/10/15	130th Bty fired 16 Lyddite at T19 a 7.3	Retaliation
7/10/15	129th Bty fired 40 Lyddite at front edge of SHREWSBURY FOREST I 30 b/d	Infantry request
8/10/15	130th Bty fired 12 Lyddite at trench opposite B 9	Retaliation, 2 Lieut.
9/10/15	130th & 129th Bn shooting	
10/10/15	130th Bty fired 14 Lyddite Trenches opposite C.	Retaliation. 9th Iny Bde request.
11/10/15	130th Bty fired 10 Lyddite at Trenches maVa at 13 c.4.4.	Retaliation. Request of Infantry
12/10/15	2/Lt Montague admitted to hospital.	

WAR DIARY
or
INTELLIGENCE SUMMARY.

(Erase heading not required.)

Army Form C. 2118.

Instructions regarding War Diaries and Intelligence Summaries are contained in F.S. Regs., Part II. and the Staff Manual respectively. Title pages will be prepared in manuscript.

Hour, Date, Place	Summary of Events and Information	Remarks and references to Appendices
YPRES 12.10.15	130th Bty fired 114 Lyddite at Crater situation B4 also at B7 on Enfly Regiment	
13.10.15	129th Bty fired 68 Lyddite at J.15.a.5.0 By order 130th Bty fired 14 Lyddite at B4 + J.15.a.2.2. Registration. Arrival of 2nd Lt Jacob + Slope.	Posted to 129th Bty Instruction of Lieut freshly joined officers
14.10.15	No firing	
15.10.15	129th Bty fired 18 Lyddite at J.19.c.4.8. Enemy put 10 rounds in railway square YPRES from division	Retaliation
16.10.15	HILL 60 6th Siege at 3p.m fired 10 Lyddite at J.13.a.	
17.10.15	130 Bty at 12.50p.m fired 40 Lyddite at J.13.a.5.0 + I.15.d.9.5 - I.18.d.9.7 + 6.9 + I.12.d.4.1 6th Siege fired 80 Lyddite at J.18.a.2.4 - I.12.d.6.2 6th Siege fired 26 Lyddite at I.18.b.0.9 - I.12.d.4.1 130th Bty at 2.5 p.m 10 Lyddite J.13.d.2.5 - I.12.d.6.2	Retaliation + Testing " overhauled Gun
18.10.15	129th Bty at 11.5.0 20 Lyddite at I.30.c.6 - J.30.d.1.7	Retaliation

Army Form C. 2118.

WAR DIARY
or
INTELLIGENCE SUMMARY.
(Erase heading not required.)

Instructions regarding War Diaries and Intelligence Summaries are contained in F.S. Regs., Part II. and the Staff Manual respectively. Title pages will be prepared in manuscript.

Hour, Date, Place	Summary of Events and Information	Remarks and references to Appendices
YPRES 17.10.15	130th Bty fired 10 Lyddite at 2.5pm at I.18.b.0.9 & I.12.d.4.1	Retaliation
	6th Siege 25 Lyddite at 2.5pm at J.19.a.6.5 — J.15.c.5.6 and I.18.b.2.5 — I.12.c.8.2	"
18.10.15	129th Bty at 11.50 am fired 20 Lyddite at I.30.c.5.5 — I.30.d.1.7	Registration
19.10.15	130th Bty fired 6 Lyddite at J.13.a.4.5	
20.10.15	No firing	
21.10.15	No firing	
22.10.15	No firing	
23.10.15	C/81 & B/81 commenced relief of 129 & 130 Btys	
24.10.15	Relief completed and 30th Bde marched during night 24—25 Oct to rest Billets to W.	
25	STEENVOORDE. Brigade in rest	
26	Brigade in rest	

Forms/C. 2118/10

Army Form C. 2118.

WAR DIARY
or
INTELLIGENCE SUMMARY.
(Erase heading not required.)

Hour, Date, Place	Summary of Events and Information	Remarks and references to Appendices
STEENVOORDE 27.10.15	Party of NCOs and men dispatched for special inspection by His Majesty the King at RENNINGHELST. Brigade still at rest.	
28.10.15	Brigade at rest. Signalling class begun. General overhaul of equipment.	
29.10.15	Still resting.	
30.10.15	Still resting.	
31.10.15	Brigade conference on duties of F.O.O. in present phase of TRENCH WARFARE.	

Shuttamt /Col
Comg. 30th Bde RFA.

30ª Base R.I.A.

Nov.
vol XIII

12/
7730

Army Form C. 2118.

WAR DIARY
or
INTELLIGENCE SUMMARY.
(Erase heading not required.)

Hour, Date, Place	Summary of Events and Information	Remarks and references to Appendices
STEENVOORDE 1/11/15	Discussion by $DA & Infantry Re duties of F.O.O's.	
2/11/15	Brigade still resting.	
3/11/15	Brigade still resting.	
4/11/15	Brigade still resting. Arrival of 2nd Lt Snape.	Posted to 150 Bty
5/11/15	Brigade still resting	
6/11/15	Brigade still resting. Arrival of Lt MARSH.	Posted to AMM.COL.
7/11/15	Brigade still resting.	
8/11/15	Demonstration of use of tube helmets in gas attack, at WINNEZEELE.	
9/11/15	Lecture to HQ staff on previous day's demonstration. Gas explained to be harmless if helmet properly fits on. Tube helmets put on & worn by Bde staff during exercise for 20 minutes.	

Army Form C. 2118.

WAR DIARY
or
INTELLIGENCE SUMMARY.
(Erase heading not required.)

Instructions regarding War Diaries and Intelligence Summaries are contained in F.S. Regs., Part II. and the Staff Manual respectively. Title pages will be prepared in manuscript.

Hour, Date, Place		Summary of Events and Information	Remarks and references to Appendices
STEENVOORDE	10/11/15	Orders received that 30th Bde will be inspected to-morrow by General Sir Herbert Plumer commanding II Army.	
	11/11/15	Inspection and address by General Sir Herbert Plumer	
	12/11/15	Orders received that 30th Bde is to parade in column of route for review by Army Commander.	
	13/11/15	Parade cancelled.	
	14/11/15	Orders for inspection on Monday 15th inst.	
	15/11/15	Brigade inspected by General Sir Herbert Plumer.	
	16/11/15	Brigade resting	
	17/11/15	"	
	18/11/15	"	

(9 29 6) W 4141—463 100,000 9/14 H W V Forms/C. 2118/10

WAR DIARY
or
INTELLIGENCE SUMMARY.
(Erase heading not required.)

Army Form C. 2118.

Hour, Date, Place	Summary of Events and Information	Remarks and references to Appendices
STEENVOORDE 19/11/15	Orders received that 3rd DA will march on Nov 24 + 25 to relieve 24th DA. Lt MARSH on leave for	
20/11/15	8 days. Battery to march	
21/11/15	Capt BEERBOHM sick 9/24 TRH.H. & Co & AMM: COL	
22/11/15	Orders received that standing and into one	
	gun now required. B.de employed in pulling down previous three weeks work.	
23/11/15	Ref: any 7pm move. Arrival of 9/24 & AUSTIN	Postin to Amm: Col:
24/11/15	Advance parties from 129 + 130 Bdes leave.	
25/11/15	HQ, 129th + 130th Btys. (less 2 Sections) and AMM.COL: Marched to new positions & billets in RENINGHELST area.	
	129th Bty relieves A/109 Bty. 130th Bty relieves D/109.	
	129th Bty grouped under Maj. Yan: DECHESNE (Belgian Arty)	
	130th Bty grouped under H.2nd Bde.	
26/11/15	30th Bde HQ + AMM COL in billets of 106 Bde AMM.COL:	

WAR DIARY
or
INTELLIGENCE SUMMARY.

(Erase heading not required.)

Army Form C. 2118.

Instructions regarding War Diaries and Intelligence Summaries are contained in F. S. Regs., Part II. and the Staff Manual respectively. Title pages will be prepared in manuscript.

Hour, Date, Place	Summary of Events and Information	Remarks and references to Appendices
27/11/15	1/Col. LAMONT went of leave for eight days.	
28/11/15	2/MARSH returned from leave & is O.C. AMM. COL:	
29/11/15	HQ + AMM.COL: working on improvement of billets.	
30/11/15	Work on roads + standings continued.	

John Lamont Lt Col
Comg 30th 13th RFA.

30ú. Bda. R.I.A.

A / XIV / 138

3.

3rd D.

Army Form C. 2118.

WAR DIARY
or
INTELLIGENCE SUMMARY.
(Erase heading not required.)

Instructions regarding War Diaries and Intelligence Summaries are contained in F. S. Regs., Part II. and the Staff Manual respectively. Title pages will be prepared in manuscript.

Hour, Date, Place	Summary of Events and Information	Remarks and references to Appendices
REMMGHELST for Dec 1st 1915	130 Bty in position near STAUB as DRIKEBUSCH. 129 Bty now BELOEL CHAU Arm: Col: + HQ at REMMGHELST.	
2nd	129 fired 14L opposite Trench 34. Retaliation few Trench Mortars	
3rd	129 fired 8L opposite Trench 29.	
4th	30L in confusion about at engine on Canal bank	
5th	No shooting	
6th	7L opposite Trench 32. One round lost in dug out e.g.	
7th	18L " 55. 20L counter battery work	
8th	8L attempted aeroplane cooperation, failure wireless unreliable wireless 100 from. 20L into HOLLEBEKE retaliation for German shooting at BELGIQUE CHAU.	
9 + 10th	Nothing to report	
11th	5 am 18L "retaliate F. 18L opposite March 33 at S.S.O.12L HOLLEBEKE	
12th	18L counter battery work at 8 a.m. Lt MORRISON rejoined 130 Bty	
13th	129 Bty 20L opposite Trench 15.55.34. Arrival of 2/Lt AUSTIN. OC 130 Bty caught in ARSY HOUSE (0.8 D 8 K.8) + PICCADILLY FARM (0 SW 24.b)	
14th	129 Bty 20L counter battery shoot. 130 Bty.	
15th	129 " 20L at HOLLEBEKE	
13th	9L few minutes of 2/Lt AUSTIN 10L retaliate M. 130 # Bty	
	Lt WHITRIDGE caught bow on 012 - 11 - 010 7.6.	

Army Form C. 2118.

WAR DIARY
or
INTELLIGENCE SUMMARY.
(Erase heading not required.)

Instructions regarding War Diaries and Intelligence Summaries are contained in F.S. Regs., Part II. and the Staff Manual respectively. Title pages will be prepared in manuscript.

Hour, Date, Place	Summary of Events and Information	Remarks and references to Appendices
RENINGHELST Dec 17th 1915	Lt. SHAPE of 130th Bty fired 80 rounds on O.3.c.7.5. 129 Bty SOS on continuing about opposite Trench 30.	
18th	130th Bty OP strengthened.	
19th	Gas attack on 6th Corps. Both Bty stood to until gas helmets and goggles on. 129 Bty fired 130 L. 130th Bty fired 64 L on Canvas	
20th	O.5.R.2.6. O.9.d.2.5. O.11.d.O.8.	
21st	130 Bty 22 L at MOUND.	
22nd	Lt. OSGOOD ranged on O.2.07.6. 18.9 Bty 15 L 108 on Canal Bridge N. HOLLEBEKE. 9.41am combined shoot	
23rd	129's retaliation S.O. Shoot: apparent a post trenches. 129 Bty 15 L at HOLLEBEKE 130 Bty 16 L at MOUND.	
24th 25th	Peace if not goodwill.	
26th	129th Bty recommenced was firing 50 L at HOLLEBEKE and on center battery about 130 Bty fired SOL on O.5.d.9.9 O.2.c.8.0.	
27th	129 Bty 20 L counter battery shoot. 130 Bty 15 L on BUSHARD Rd.	
28th	129 Bty 16 L at trench mortar + working party.	

WAR DIARY or INTELLIGENCE SUMMARY.

(Erase heading not required.)

Army Form C. 2118.

Hour, Date, Place	Summary of Events and Information	Remarks and references to Appendices
RENINGHELST Dec. 29th 1915	129 Bty. SOL N 37 E4.01. 150 Bty fired on O 2 d 9.2.	
30th	129 Bty. 166 counter battery shoot. Lt. Col. LAMONT left assisted general Laurentsen, on being appointed to RHA with 2nd Cavalry Corps.	
31st	129 Bty. 60L opposite trench 35. The weather during the month was generally cloudy & depressing, with some heavy falls. The Bde had so casualties from enemy fire, except one man of the Amm. Col. who was wounded on PROPERINGE station by a shell splinter on returning from leave. A class for young officers was opened on Dec 13th and attended by 2/Lts R.W.WHEELER, R.E.W.BUCHAN, O.D.BARNETT, + W.D.LOUDON. (3rd DAC) ('O' Bty) (A2 BAC) 2/Lt BARNETT was recalled to Bty on Dec 21st. 2/Lt WHEELER went sick on Dec 31st. His theory that his ailment was **not** amplified by the formal of a saddle did receive general credence.	Lieut Comp O.C. 30th Brigade RFA

Forms/C. 2118/10

3rd Divisional Artillery.

30TH BRIGADE R. F. A.

J A N U A R Y 1 9 1 6.

BDE broken up May 1916

Army Form C. 2118.

No. 6
30th Bde RFA

WAR DIARY
or
INTELLIGENCE SUMMARY.
(Erase heading not required.)

Instructions regarding War Diaries and Intelligence Summaries are contained in F.S. Regs., Part II. and the Staff Manual respectively. Title pages will be prepared in manuscript.

Hour, Date, Place	Summary of Events and Information	Remarks and references to Appendices
FONQUEVILLERS 1/6/16	4th AT, Lt. G.S. MAFFRAVES returned on departure to G.R. 11th en route to Army Depot.	A quiet + uneventful month
2nd	Rain + snow + grey dawn. Fair + [frost?] snow falling	with one actual casualty from hostile fire, F.O.O.S
3rd	129 HB [new General Bty.] 130 RFA ~ O9A7·7 + O9 D9·8·Gnm Range 70° Dist of new laced maps. 129 HB 40L at [new Bd fronts] with [fine?] appet 130th [Bty.] Rounds ~ O5C10·0	+ telephones however had many narrow escapes in trenches.
5th	2/Lt-DAWSON attached to 129th Bty. for introduction G-FLORRY with 130 Bty. 130 [fired] 46 ~ O9a7·5 + O9d9·8	AMM: very limited. Weather mild but wet + windy
6th	130 [fired] 46 ~ O2C9·1	
7th	129 [fired] HE in orchard about 150 R&L or where	
8th	outside "C"	
9th	Horace B O.K attacked 124 from DURHAM HOW. BDE. 4 & L by 4·0 ~ latitude "C" + destruction of MOUND. 12·7 [fired] 162, DHB retaliate H. 20 rounds or every Bty 130 & [firing]	

Army Form C. 2118.

WAR DIARY
or
INTELLIGENCE SUMMARY.
(Erase heading not required.)

Instructions regarding War Diaries and Intelligence Summaries are contained in F.S. Regs., Part II. and the Staff Manual respectively. Title pages will be prepared in manuscript.

1915 Date, Place	Summary of Events and Information	Remarks and references to Appendices
JAN. REMINGHELST		
11th	Sgt. BROMAE. D.W. of 130 killed by premature. Sol by 15th Bty. in connection with Siege operation by 2nd Bde.	
12th	129 fired 20 rounds searching for enemy Bty. 130 fired 12 rounds retaliate "D"	
	Orders to fire only in retaliation. 130 fired 30's behind BOIS QUARANTE.	
13th	Lt. R.C. SMITH. attached 130 Bty with 8 or 9 for instruction.	
14th	SCOTTISH WOOD shelled. G2 H GG of 130 slightly hit.	
15th	129 fired 6L + 2 Shrapnel registering new put zone. 130 fired 22L PUSHMANS RD.	
16th 17th	NIL	
18th	130th N.L at M.P. enfilement at O30c7.6	
19th	130th 18L on trenches opposite O9c 3.8.	
20,21st	2/Lt. SUTHERLAND joined 134th Bty.	
22nd	GERMANS exploded mine at BLUFF. 129 fired 65L at S.E.corner of BLUFF. 130th 34L on O30 7.5 + retaliate "B".	

Forms/C. 2118/10

WAR DIARY
or
INTELLIGENCE SUMMARY.
(Erase heading not required.)

Army Form C. 2118.

Instructions regarding War Diaries and Intelligence Summaries are contained in F. S. Regs., Part II. and the Staff Manual respectively. Title pages will be prepared in manuscript.

Hour, Date, Place 1915	Summary of Events and Information	Remarks and references to Appendices
JAN 23rd RENINGHELST	Various officers called at Bde HQ attended by 2/Lts H. L. BROMET 6 tyBy, Pw. LEIGH PEMBERTON 108 tyBy, E.E. GRIFFITH 45 By. E.E. SMADE 110 By.	
24th	NIL	
25th	DICKEBUSH retrenchment hit at dusk. 130 fired 10 rounds retaliation on O 9 a 6.4	
26th	129 tyB 18 L retaliated H. Lt WHITRIDGE taken over Bty position from acceptance.	
27th	109 tyB 10L in direction of N SUTHERLAND. 12 rounds by 130 ~ O 36 c.1 - O 9 6.0.6	
27th	129B one indirect round came from HILL 60 — YPRES-COMINES Count. 30 rounds by 130 ns 0366.1	
27th 3rd	129 tyBy. 21 rounds by 130 on 06 d 9.8 / 015 26.7.	

Turner Leakelet
O.C. 30th Brigade R.F.A.

3rd Divisional Artillery.

30th Brigade R. F. A.

No diary for:-

    FEBRUARY 1916

    MARCH   1916

    APRIL   1916

    MAY   1916.

www.ingramcontent.com/pod-product-compliance
Lightning Source LLC
Chambersburg PA
CBHW080804010526
44113CB00013B/2320